Career Moves

Libbie Rifkin

Career Moves

Olson, Creeley, Zukofsky, Berrigan, and the American Avant-Garde

The University of Wisconsin Press

The University of Wisconsin Press
2537 Daniels Street
Madison, Wisconsin 53718

3 Henrietta Street
London WC2E 8LU, England

5   4   3   2   1

Printed in the United States of America

Library of Congress Cataloging-in-Publication Data
Rifkin, Libbie.
    Career moves: Olson, Creeley, Zukofsky, Berrigan, and the American avant-garde /
    Libbie Rifkin.
    pp.   cm.
    Includes bibliographical references and index.
    ISBN 0-299-16840-9 (cloth: alk. paper).
    ISBN 0-299-16844-1 (paper: alk. paper).
    1. American poetry—20th century—History and criticism. 2. Avant-garde (Aesthetics)—
United States—History—20th century. 3. Experimental poetry, American—History and criti-
cism. 4. Olson, Charles, 1910–1970—Criticism and interpretation. 5. Creeley, Robert, 1926—
Criticism and interpretation. 6. Zukofsky, Louis, 1904–1978—Criticism and interpretation. 7.
Berrigan, Ted—Criticism and interpretation. 8. Authorship—Collaboration—History—20th
century.
    I. Title.
    PS323.5 .R53   2000
    811'.540911—dc21   99-053743

CONTENTS

ACKNOWLEDGMENTS

This book owes its existence in large part to the support of several institutions and more people than I can adequately thank here. Cornell University's Mellon Fellowship program allowed me to complete the first phase of the project, and summer research and travel funding from the University of Alabama Department of English enabled me to revise the manuscript. At Alabama, Elizabeth Meese, Hank Lazer, Harold Weber, and Michael Martone provided useful feedback as I was revising. Jill Christman, Bruce Smith, and Susan Holbrook sustained me, and by their daily example, enriched my sense of how to write and to live. I would like to thank my special committee at Cornell—Roger Gilbert, Jonathan Monroe, and Debra Fried—for years of reading and advising. The fourth member of that committee, Bob Perelman of the University of Pennsylvania, helped inspire the project, read every word many times, and has been an invaluable mentor and advocate. Warm thanks are due to Barrett Watten, Alan Golding, Ron Silliman, Alice Notley, and, most recently, to Lynn Keller, Cristanne Miller, Mary Margaret Sloan, and Kathleen Frazier, all of whom responded helpfully to various queries, on- and off-line. I'm grateful as well to Cathy Henderson of the Harry Ransom Humanities Research Center; Kathleen Manwaring of the Syracuse University Library, Department of Special Collections; Rodney Phillips of the Berg Collection of the New York Public Library; and Bradley Westbrook of Mandeville Special Collections at the University of California, San Diego for guidance in navigating those institutions. Katherine Seidler, my research assistant at Alabama, put the finishing touches on the book—proofing, editing, and assembling the index. I deeply appreciate her help.

It is with tremendous joy that I thank my family and friends for their years of good humor and loving support. This book is dedicated to my parents and to my husband, Douglas Usher.

Alice Notley's poem "Flowers," from *Mysteries of Small Houses*, copyright Alice Notley, is used by permission of Viking Penguin, a division of Penguin Putnam Inc. Brief excerpts from two unpublished letters: Letter of November 2, 1960 and Letter of May 2, 1962, both to Donald Hutter, housed in Scribner's

Archives, are used by permission of Robert Creeley. Excerpts from "Projective Verse" and "Human Universe," from Charles Olson's, *Selected Writings of Charles Olson,* ed. Robert Creeley, copyright 1958 by Charles Olson, is reprinted by permission of New Directions Publishing Corp. Robert Creeley's poems "The Business," "The Invoice," and *Pieces,* from *Collected Poems of Robert Creeley,* copyright 1983, and excerpts from Charles Olson's *Collected Poems of Charles Olson,* edited by George Butterick, copyright 1987 by the Estate of Charles Olson (previously published poetry) and by University of Connecticut Press (previously unpublished poetry), are used by permission of University of California Press. Earlier versions of Chapter 1 and 4 appeared in *Poetics Today,* and *Contemporary Literature* and are used by permission of the journal's editor, and the University of Wisconsin Press, respectively.

Career Moves

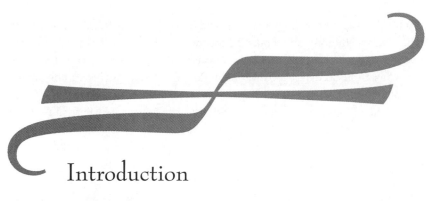

Introduction

Reading the Poetic Career

William Wordsworth may have been the first reception theorist for the avant-garde. In the essay supplementary to the preface of his 1815 collected poems, he pronounced a basic truth about the relation between the production and consumption of innovative literary works: "every Author, as far as he is great and at the same time *original,* has had the task of *creating* the taste by which he is to be enjoyed" (*William Wordsworth* 657, his emphasis). This study examines the ways in which a select group of postwar American poets with ambitions to greatness conceived of and performed the task of taste-making, analyzes the stakes *for poets* of this form of cultural production, and registers its effects on the literary artifacts they produced and as well as the literary history to which they now belong.

Wordsworth's is a model of authorial agency in a double sense; in his formulation, authors bear the burden of and get the credit for what institutional theorists would describe as big business; they do William Morris's job themselves, and they do it both in their poetry and—as we can gather from Wordsworth's own example—in the machinery of prefaces, advertisements, appendices, and supplements that often accompanies innovative work when it makes its debut. In most cases, they don't do it alone. Without Coleridge's assiduous advocacy of Wordsworth's genius in general and the *Lyrical Ballads* in particular, the decisive edition of 1800 might never have found a publisher and might have been lost to Wordsworth's own mismanagement.[1] Modern poets from T. S. Eliot and H.D. to Basil Bunting and Louis Zukofsky owe their careers in part to Ezra Pound's long reach in the arenas of publishing and promotion. In the more populous, more accessible postwar field, Pound's job was divided among many different poet-publishers, poet-impresarios, and poet-critics. Three of the four poets studied here—Charles Olson, Robert Creeley, and Ted Berrigan—were among the most important such figures to follow in Pound's institutional footsteps; a longer list might include LeRoi Jones, Diane Di Prima, Lawrence Ferlinghetti, Jonathan Williams, Anne Waldman, and many others.

It may be objected that "creating the taste by which he is to be enjoyed" refers to nothing so crassly economic as developing a marketing strategy, and that Wordsworth was meditating on such lofty topics as genius, originality, and tradition, not the fallen concerns of audience and reputation. Eliot himself argued in "The Social Function of Poetry" that serious poets should not be too successful in these latter areas: "if a poet gets a large audience very quickly, that is a rather suspicious circumstance: for it leads us to fear that he is not really doing anything new" (11). Even future immortal poets need a contemporary readership, however; someone has to be responsible for the "maintenance of . . . an elite . . . who are independent and somewhat in advance of their time or ready to assimilate novelty more quickly." But Eliot stops short of delegating that task to poets themselves. Instead he conceives vanguardism in passive terms as itself a function of "the development of culture"—a gradual process that takes place primarily in the amorphous zone of language. "Taste," and that other important Wordsworthian concern, pleasure, give way to the poet's "direct duty," which is "to his language, first to preserve, and second to extend and improve" (9).

While more contemporary theorists of reception and even materialist literary historians tend to reverse the order of the Eliotic imperative, they retain a strange asceticism, a focus on the impersonal evolution of discourse as a whole over the interested activity of particular writers and readers. In Hans Robert Jauss's model of aesthetic development, for instance, authors' agency is significantly obscured: "to advance art has to be considered socially formative, to contain future realities within it," he writes (24). But what is "art" here? Is it a given work, the history of a particular genre, or the nexus of networks known as the "artworld"? And what is the "social" of which this art is formative? Important for licensing an interpretive, text-immanent approach to questions of readership otherwise left to sociology, Jaussian reception theory is premised on too narrow a conception of the "aesthetic" and—at least in the more programmatic theoretical formulations—too schematic a map of the literary field to capture the transgeneric textuality of postwar innovators and the micropolitics of cultural production, reception, and transmission in their present-tense historical moment.[2] In "Literary History as a Challenge to Literary Theory," Jauss conceives reception in diachronic terms as "the successive unfolding of the potential for meaning that is embedded in a work and actualized in the stages of its historical reception as it discloses itself to understanding judgment" (30). In his theory a truly artistic (as opposed to popular or "culinary") work projects a reception beyond its contemporary readers' "horizon of expectation," often taking several generations to find an audience capable of fully consuming it. Contending that "the ideal case is a work that evokes an horizon only to destroy it," he values an art that bypasses the contemporary, registering as art only in retrospect and only, we gather, at the hands of readers schooled in both tradition and the history of the work's prior receptions.

Jauss's is a history motored by avant-gardist revolution, but with no time for a living avant-garde. The Jaussian scene of reading, wherein an official reader's "horizon of expectation" finally catches up with the demands of the work, is the end of the line, a canonizing moment that though dialectically dependent on interim processes of cultural circulation, must ultimately forget them.[3] The three players in this game—the receptive reader, the reflective critic, and the productive author—remain distinct, staggered over time, and preferably centralized through a single institution, namely, the academy. While this may be an accurate though schematic model of canonization, it cannot capture the variety of roles avant-garde *poets* play in the less stable, always emergent, synchronically experienced institutional environments in which they conduct their careers. For Jauss along with most of his American peers and descendants, interpretation, judgment, and ultimate canonization are the only game in town. As the principal site where these activities are practiced, the academy is the primary agent of artistic change in the reception theory model. For academic readers charged with the production, maintenance, and transmission of the canon, there are two basic options: to conserve or to revise.

Given the relative clarity of the task, it is astonishing how much self-reflection, even self-flagellation academic critics have engaged in. As Michael Bérubé has usefully documented, critical discussion of "institutionalization" has framed the process as a matter of life or death. Bérubé ventriloquizes the question facing "literary professionals" thus: "is institutional literary study a means to the preservation of culture(s), or does it mark the death-by-assimilation of vibrant, challenging writers, movements, and modes of thought?" (18). Such a dire vision of the stakes of literary consumption is endemic to the language of canons, whose disembodied formalism allows for easy slippages between "death-by-assimilation" and the literal deaths of individual authors on which canonicity is so often premised. For all of its contentiousness, the canon debate is, in a formal sense, closed. The notion that literary value is institutionally determined, tied to a host of social, professional, and fundamentally historical factors, has been a commonplace of canon studies for the last decade. The "contingency of value," as Barbara Herrnstein Smith called it in her important 1988 book by that title, holds great potential as a spur to historical studies of "the social function of literature" for producers as well as consumers. Tethered to the question of the canon, however, calls to historicize have resulted in proliferating critiques of academic hegemony, histories of the English department, and sociological-materialist analyses of the "school."[4] Whether or not these accounts participate in the oversimplification that Smith herself warned against by figuring the academy as an "objectively (in the Marxist sense) conspiratorial force," in their neglect of the whole range of scenes in which texts are exchanged and literary and social value transacted, they contribute to the very narrowing of the field that they are concerned to criticize. The academy, and the English department in particular, begin to take on a kind of talismanic quality by dint of the sheer volume of attention they receive.

In this study, I seek to loosen canonicity's grip on the analysis of reception by reconceiving the stakes of literary exchange in the narrower terms of the poetic career. A focus on career over canon enables an examination of institutions from the interested perspective of particular, historically situated individuals, and it allows for an understanding of the poet's "duty" that includes Eliot's bid to "extend and improve" the language, but is also responsive to local material, ideological, and psychosocial demands. This is not a collection of compressed literary biographies, though it does trace the crossings of life and writing in the work of four poets; rather it is an attempt to capture different instances of what M. M. Bakhtin would call the "social evaluation" of 1950s and 1960s avantgarde poetry: the interlocking set of textual and historical factors that, in his terms, "unites the minute of the epoch and the news of the day with the aim of history" and thus "actualizes the utterance both from the standpoint of its factual presence and the standpoint of its semantic meaning" (121). Poetic careers are both produced by and productive of this larger social texture; struggling to "make it" individually—to generate innovative work and motivate their artistic lives—Louis Zukofsky, Charles Olson, Robert Creeley, and Ted Berrigan helped to construct the physiognomy of their period. This study continues the process of selection and aggregation started by the poets themselves in the form of the intentional production of literary communities. It is by no means an exhaustive survey of "the" postwar avant-garde; it is instead an analysis of the cultural poetics of that particular moment in the history of American poetry, read in and across the "literary facts" of four contemporaries.

"Contemporaneity" is the product of decisions—both individual and collective—to participate in the same set of struggles on the field of culture. It is also a function of the power to make those decisions matter—the accumulation of enough social capital not only to register one's presence in a particular collective consciousness, but to define the rules and norms of that shared space. Women poets were by turns ignored or excluded from Olson, Creeley, Zukofsky, and to a lesser extent Berrigan's sense of the contemporary literary field. These poets were aware of their female counterparts, and often maintained close personal and even poetic relations with them—I'm thinking of Zukofsky and Lorinne Niedecker, and Creeley and Denise Levertov in particular—but when it came to building and sustaining alternative institutions, women poets seem to drop from view. The ease with which women poets were "disappeared" during the processes of community formation is testimony to the selective traditionalism of the avant-garde: when it comes to patriarchy, there's little incentive to break too fully from the past. Freed from the regulatory processes that would begin to render larger-scale institutions at least marginally accountable to some measure of diversity, the institutions these poets developed were at once more capricious and more vehement in their exclusions than their mainstream counterparts. Of perhaps the best known of these institutions, Black Mountain College, Martin Duberman noted in his 1973 history that "the hierarchy could be as rigidly exclusive, as impassible to the uninitiated—and *more* male chauvinist—than anything found on a traditional university campus" (433).

The gendered relations of power in the broader culture weren't merely mirrored in the masculine excesses of this avant-garde, they were refracted through the organizational dynamics of its various subcultures and came out both different and worse. Several recent scholars have begun to suggest that the absence of women—and/or the dismissal of the feminine—was a constitutive feature of postwar innovative poetries.[5] I extend that discussion throughout this book as I analyze the structural function of exclusion per se—which at different moments may be either predicated on or predicate the actual ouster of women—at the core of both authorial identity formation and avant-garde institution building. Clearly, male poets throughout literary history have had an interest in maintaining whatever power the larger culture allots them; in the twentieth century this has worked through the simultaneous devaluing of the feminine and the instrumentalization of women as patrons, muses, and the like. In creating the social conditions for their poetic ascendancy the poets in this study did not, obviously, start from scratch. As white, generally middle-class men choosing to be poets in (with the exception of Zukofsky) the second half of the twentieth century, they started from a specific cultural position of modified dominance. But as "revolutionaries"—and I'll be elaborating my sense of that term in the next chapter—they chose social trajectories whose indeterminacy denied complacency and enforced vigilance in idiosyncratic ways.

While there is a presettled quality to the gender limits of their "social evaluation," for these poets—avowedly straight representatives of an increasingly gay poetic community—questions of sexuality are much more persistent and vexed. As Eve Kosofsky Sedgwick has shown, these two phenomena are constitutively linked. In her groundbreaking work *Between Men* (1985), Sedgwick argues that "the status of women, and the whole question of the arrangements between genders, is deeply and inescapably inscribed in the structure even of the relationships that seem to exclude women—even in male homosocial/ homosexual relations" (25). Sedgwick names her subject "male homosocial desire" in order to posit a continuum between the male social relations around which patriarchal systems of power are structured and the sexual relations between men which they generally prohibit (2–5). She claims that "in any male-dominated society there is a special relationship between male homosocial (including homosexual) desire and the structures for maintaining and transmitting patriarchal power," going on to suggest that "for historical reasons, this special relationship may take the form of ideological homophobia, ideological homosexuality, or some highly conflicted but intensively structured combination of the two" (25).

It is this recognition of historical and cross-cultural variability in Sedgwick's theory that makes it resonate with the evolving, internally divisive institutions under study here.[6] In spite of the fact that several of its scenes were gay-identified—the Jack Spicer–Robert Duncan circle, for instance, or the first generation of the New York School—it is virtually impossible to generalize about the status of homosexuality within the postwar avant-garde. Undercodified as a rule, avant-garde institutions were especially mercurial on this issue, and their founders and participants paid a price for this structural indeterminacy. Queerness plays different roles in the career strategies and self-conceptions of each of the poets under study here, but for all of them it works as an iodine, highlighting the areas where their poetic identities and their relationships to the field of their contemporaries are most contingent. Whereas for Zukofsky homoerotic imagery functions semiotically, marking the fault lines of poetic language, the resistance of reference, biography, and the body to the poet's efforts at "clear music" and social control, for Berrigan, gayness is a named feature of the literary landscape, required for true belonging in the circles that he covets. Embodied in Frank O'Hara, gayness signals Berrigan's only partial approximation of his ideal, and, more generally, his dependence on his over-crowded social network for the completion of his poetic self. Olson and Cree-ley's collaborative intimacy was a formative moment in their poethood, a strate-gic response to the forces of isolation. But their homosociality—manifest on the physicalized surfaces of their correspondence and resonant in the more performative moments of their projective poetics—also accords with their most exclusive and domineering tendencies; it marks the limits of composition by field as a truly "open" model of community.

For avant-garde–identified poets working under various lengths of modern-ism's shadow, to be contemporary was also to share a historical sense. These poets had to "make it new" *after* the generation that had challenged lineage with collage and literariness with "direct treatment of the thing." Postwar poets watched modernism's breach become an institution. A sense of belatedness unites all four poets; separated by as much as thirty years in age, they are members of the same generation by dint of common literary parentage. The strength of filial obligation varied amongst them. Conceptions of generation, influence, and their futuristic third, posterity, were especially decisive in the self-fashionings of Zukofsky and Berrigan, poets who bookend the period un-der study; whereas Olson and Creeley, bound by their more-than-daily corre-spondence during the early years of their careers, developed a shared myth of synchronicity, a full-on investment in the present. I argue that their collabora-tion was *institutive;* it introduced two new agents onto the literary field, and it also changed the options for other emerging poets.

In Pierre Bourdieu's terms, this collaboration between Olson and Creeley, made public through *Origin* magazine and the *Black Mountain Review* and ob-jectified in their poetry and critical writing, was a "position-taking" that *took,* and thereby altered the "space of possibles" (*Field* 30–32). In his model—elab-orated for American literary scholars in such translated collections as *The Field of Cultural Production* (1993) and *The Rules of Art* (1996)—cultural institution formation is seen as a species of "position-taking," homologous to strategic be-havior across the fields of economic and political power, yet embroiled in the art world's distinctive system of values. In Bourdieu's cultural field, behavior is broadly economic: it is always aimed at maximizing the accumulation of capi-tal, but the nature of that capital varies depending on where the agent is posi-tioned in the field. There are any number of fields in a given social order, and though the kinds of agents and the "lines of force" that develop within them

can differ tremendously, they are all related by a "logic of homology," an underlying structural similarity that ensures, for instance, an alignment between producers within the cultural field and their audience within the generalized field
of power. Bourdieu splits the field of cultural production into two major sub-
fields, "large-scale" and "restricted" production, corresponding to the relative
valuation of economic or "symbolic" capital within them. In other words, large-
scale production—such as trade press publishing—is closely tied to fluctua-
tions of the commercial market, while in the field of restricted production (the
one in which avant-garde poets generally move) what matters is consecration
by one's peers, a less tangible quantity than money, though one that remains
at least partially determined, via the "logic of homology," by deeply economic
distributions of power and privilege (*Rules* 142–46).

While his analysis of artistic production as social strategy provides a basic
framework for understanding poetic careers that are both shaped by and shape
the "field of restricted production," Bourdieu's economic coordinates can't quite
map the postwar avant-garde's contentious psychosocial terrain. Throughout
this book, I keep the field as a whole in view, but I focus my analysis on individual actors, attempting to articulate career at the intersection of individual ambition and collective production. Chapter 1's account of the Berkeley Poetry
Conference of 1965 is an analysis of a particularly congested moment at this
intersection. Reading Olson's closing address to the extended avant-garde community gathered for this watershed event, I show how it is simultaneously productive and reproductive—steeped in the sedimented history of his own cultural practice, situated within an institution he helped to form, yet compelled
to new acts of emergence. I begin with the Berkeley Conference—at the end,
so to speak—in part because Olson, Creeley, and Berrigan were all in attendance, in part because the event sets the retrospective terms through which the
breakthroughs of the 1950s and 1960s become legible, and in part because it
foreshadows social dynamics still operative in current avant-garde formations.
My objective is to complicate theories of the avant-garde that conceive innovative practice in purely negative or oppositional terms. I argue instead that, at
least in ambition, the postwar avant-garde was an accretive rather than a destructive movement, committed to the possibility of "permanent revolution."
Chapter 2 returns to the originary moment of Olson and Creeley's collaboration
in order to trace the development of their distinctive poetic stance out of their
complex relationship to each other, to the concept of professionalism, and to
different professions—from cultural anthropology to publishing. Their "company of love"—the cottage poetry industry that developed out of their correspondence—combined an amateur commitment to openness and immediacy

with decisive assertions of limits on their community. I examine the implications of their collaborative practice for their individual careers as well as for the "social evaluation" at large.

Louis Zukofsky and Ted Berrigan were, in very different ways, beneficiaries of Olson and Creeley's institutive activities. To say this about Zukofsky, whose poetic career began with the *Exile* publication of "Poem Beginning 'The'" in 1928, when Creeley was only two years old, is to countenance an obvious anachronism. As I argue in Chapter 3, however, such a reversal is absolutely consonant with Zukofsky's own understanding of literary temporality. Claiming that a poet's work must be "durable" as "one thing from itself never turning," and conceiving influence as "impersonal friendship . . . removed from yet out of time," Zukofsky envisioned a cryogenic poethood, carefully packaged for a more ideal future, which he found—to a limited extent—in the attentions of Creeley et al. (*Bottom* 13; *Prepositions* 25). *"A," Bottom: On Shakespeare*, his mythification of his family, and his relationship with the archive at the University of Texas are all readable in part as strategic attempts by a perpetually underread poet to predict and contain a more hospitable "space of possibles." Berrigan's career strategy was similar, though significantly compressed. As if he knew that he would be "gone in a minute," as he put it, he packed his debut book, *The Sonnets,* full not only of the names and lines of the poets who emerged with Olson and Creeley, but also of his own proleptically complete oeuvre. Like Zukofsky, he established an early relationship with a university archive. These poets were among the first of their contemporaries to forge ties to the large-scale institution through this particular branch. In both of their cases, self-archiving functions as a particularly forward-looking effort to "create the taste by which [they are] to be enjoyed" that also has strategic relevance within their present-tense careers and homologues in their poetics.

Maintaining a complex and not always symbiotic relationship with English departments, archives work a wedge into the notion of the university as monolith. Describing it in these terms, I do not mean to launch "the archive" back into the conceptual ether where it has lived for contemporary critics since Michel Foucault's theorization of it in *The Archeology of Knowledge* (1972). Foucault defines "the archive" as "the law of what can be said," going on to emphasize that "the archive is not that which . . . safeguards the event of the statement, and preserves, for future memories, its status as an escapee; it is that which, at the very root of the statement-event, and in that which embodies it, defines at the outset *the system of is enunciability*" (129, emphasis his). Whereas Foucault conceives "the archive" as a set of constraints embedded in discourse, in my account, archives (literally buildings and the financial and social transactions through which the material traces of poets' careers come to be located in them) don't constrain writerly agency; rather they are extensions and even instruments of it. At once acts and repositories, institutive and conservative, private and public, productive and reproductive, archives epitomize this study's sense of literary history as a crowded and profoundly interested field, subject to the self-fashioning intentions of a wide variety of actors. Zukofsky grasped the challenge of writing (and living) this kind of history—its idiosyncrasy, its partiality—in his provocatively contradictory formulation of "an objective," the statement of purpose for his "poem of a life":

> An objective—nature as creator—desire
>   for what is objectively perfect
> Inextricably the direction of historic and contemporary particulars.
>
> ("A"-6 24)

> History: the records of taste and economy of a civilization.
> Particular: Every fall season, every spring, he needs a new coat
>   He loses his job—
> Poetry? it has something to do with his writing of poetry.
>
> ("A"-6 26)

1

Charles Olson's "Queer University"

Institutionalizing Postwar Avant-Gardes

OLSON: No, I wanna talk. I mean, you wanna listen to . . . a poet? I mean,
you know, like, a poet, when he's alive, whether he talks or reads you his
poems is the same thing. (SLAPS TABLE)
VOICE: RIGHT!
OLSON: Dig that! (APPLAUSE). And when he—and when he—and when he
is made of three parts, his life, his mouth and his poem, then, by god, the
earth belongs to us. And like—and what I think has happened is that
that's—wow, gee, hmm, one doesn't like to claim things, but god, isn't it
exciting? I mean, at least I'm—I mean, I can, I feel like a kid. I'm in the
presence of an event, which I don't believe, myself.

Berkeley Reading

On July 23, 1965, Charles Olson took the stage of Wheeler Hall to give the
final reading at the Berkeley Poetry Conference. It had been a heady two weeks;
avant-garde, or as it might have been said then, "anti-Establishment" poets
gathered to top their experience at a similar conference that had taken place in
Vancouver two years before. In convening again, they were witnessing themselves as an amalgamated movement already both staunchly supported and
sharply criticized. *The New American Poetry, 1945–1960* (1960), *The New Poets
of England and America* (1957), and the rush of critical responses that those two
anthologies continued to generate had given many of the poets in attendance
an early taste of literary history.[1] Poets identified with the New York, San Francisco, and Black Mountain "schools," not to mention the Beats, knew what it felt
like to be canon fodder. In debates everywhere from the scholarly quarterlies to
Time magazine, these poets were positioned as the wild Other of the academic
poetry establishment and—having worked that terrain throughout the 1950s—
on the verge of becoming a species of "tenured radicals" themselves. By 1965,

over a decade's worth of formally innovative, academically marginalized, and yet increasingly public cultural activity had sedimented into a group identity. The poets at the conference recognized themselves in the uncanny role of permanent revolutionaries.[2] At Berkeley, they staged this sociohistoric positioning as an event.

It was a difficult speech act to bring off. Olson's performance—considered by some to be a tour de force, while others walked out—embodied the contradictory dynamics at work at the conference and the tensions within the community at large.[3] Billed as a "reading," identified by the poet himself as "talk," and later derided as a "filibuster," it has been viewed both as a brilliant enactment of the open-form poetics that Olson is credited with founding, and as a drunken ramble. Marginal even within a narrow avant-gardist margin, it thus points up divergent communities of reception; Olson was a central figure within the constellation of poets gathered at Berkeley, but the nature of that centrality—and even the nature of their community—was various and vexed amongst them. Rather than seeking to resolve the ambiguity surrounding the literary value for his talk, I treat its resistance as a spur to understanding the ways in which social value—and indeed social identity—get generated and reproduced in this particular segment of the cultural field.

The Theory of the Avant-Garde and Practice

While the relationship of modernism to the rise of the New Criticism and the "academicization" of poetry has been documented, the institutional history of postwar poetic avant-garde formations has evaded scholarly attention.[4] This is partially attributable to the fact that Peter Bürger's *Theory of the Avant-Garde* has controlled the terms of the discussion since its publication in English in 1984. In that now-canonical text, Bürger argued that the historical avant-garde forced the bourgeois "institution of art" into a stage of self-reflection; he claimed that it revealed the functional role of aesthetic autonomy in reproducing social hierarchies without, however, reintegrating art into the life-praxis of culture. This avant-garde—and for Bürger it was the only one—thus failed in its historically determined mission (49). To the extent that a movement such as surrealism had any effect, Bürger claimed, it was to render art more vulnerable to the recuperative forces of the culture industry, to pave the way for the precommodified ironies of pop and other neo-avant-gardes.

Bürger's argument has affected thinking about contemporary innovative poetry in a number of ways. His emphasis on institutions is a welcome addition to theories of reception: it adds a layer of materiality to Jauss's model of literary evolution, promises to broaden the tight hermeneutics of Wolfgang Iser's elaborations of the reading process, and helps to rationalize the empirical observations of reader-response studies.[5] But Bürger's own use of the term institution is more limiting; for him, it worked as a sociological wedge only in one brief moment of self-reflection. By his account, *the* institution of art became visible through the agency of the avant-garde sometime around 1915. After that historical moment, he argues, the terms lose their materiality: "institution" and "avant-garde" remain frozen forever in a bloodless battle, opponents in theory only. In the aftermath of his work, scholars of innovative art movements have taken the two terms to be mutually exclusive. For Bürger, the failure of the historical avant-garde is to blame for what he claims is the now purely gestural, ineffectual nature of cultural revolution. For scholars, practitioners, and enthusiasts, the persistence of his theory itself proves a formidable obstacle.

With the exception of Bürger, history has never been a problem for the theory of the avant-garde, which prefers to work on the level of the concept. As Paul Mann has argued in *The Theory-Death of the Avant-Garde* (1991), a book that darkly promises to be the "last word" on the subject, traditional scholarship of the avant-garde has had two preoccupations that are in fact intertwined: definition and death. As self-proclaimed exception, the avant-garde both lives and dies by definition: "The avant-garde consistently defines itself both in terms of and against definitions imposed upon it" (9). Mann's text weaves a fugue on this basic dialectical theme: "the avant-garde is first of all the instrument of attack on tradition, but an attack mandated by tradition itself" (11); "the avant-garde is not a victim of recuperation but its agent, its proper technology" (92); and finally "criticism is not an adversary force but rather a means by which culture discovers its contradictions so that it can accommodate them to itself" (118). Once "recuperation" is revealed to be the "syntax of cultural discourse, its elementary propositional form," the only answers for art with pretensions to resistance are anonymity, silence, exile, and cunning.

Without the benefit of Mann's linguistic turn, most avant-garde scholarship has come to a similar conclusion, largely because it attempts to deduce sociology, aesthetics, and politics from logical problems within the concept. Hans Magnus Enzensberger's classic "Aporias of the Avant-Garde" (1962) consolidates this tradition's typical moves. Enzensberger traces the military roots of the term "avant-garde," breaking it down into its component parts and pushing each to its aporetic limit. The first aporia emerges when the avant-garde moves from the synchrony of the battlefield to the diachrony of historical progress. Confronting the enemy up ahead, the "en avant of the avant-garde would, as it were, realize the future in the present, anticipate the course of history"(23). In

spite of tremendous advances in prognostication by the "consciousness industry," this is, of course, impossible. And yet the whole system depends on this
impossibility; the avant-garde is the engine of advancement for the main body
of artistic works, but the scene of its reception is, by definition, always just out
of reach. The avant-garde's value, in fact its very identity, can be determined
only by the future generations for whom it is already passé. Put most suc-
cinctly: "The avant of the avant-garde contains its own contradiction: it can be
marked out only a posteriori" (28). The social contradictions derive from the
temporal one, in Enzensberger's analysis. In the military milieu, the "guard" is
a collective, united by discipline and proud of its distinction from the majority.
Transferred to the artistic realm and from a spatial to a temporal plane, the
avant-garde's militant energies turn backward, and the elite corps attacks the
majority it is supposed to be leading. Without an obvious enemy, Enzensberger
suggests, avant-gardes in the arts are constrained to embody the "anti," to live
the ideals of "freedom" and "revolution" in a doctrinaire, and ultimately self-
destructive, capacity.

Following these models, an institutional analysis of postwar poetic avant-
gardes would appear both oxymoronic and anachronistic. Once we realize that
the theory of the avant-garde universalizes one moment in European modernism, and that aesthetic autonomy is just one of many problematics that innovative art addresses, we can see that poetic avant-gardes continue to emerge in
the second half of this century, and that their breakthroughs as well as their
failures have complex and continuing effects.[6] Recognizing the "perpetual institutionality" (Mann 63) of avant-gardist practice need not then amount to an
acceptance of de facto complicity. Rather, it can serve as the foundation of rigorously local inquiries into different kinds of artistic marginalities, the uses to
which they are put, and the various centers that they both emerge from and
oppose. Contemporary avant-garde poets have, as Ron Silliman puts it, "grown
out of the same historical conditions that raised the question of theory itself
within the academy," a genealogy they share, I'd argue, with their postwar forebears. These poets are poised to "offer a specific reading of theory" and thereby,
in some sense, "reverse the parasitical relationship between poetry and its critique." This reversibility raises "the question of institutionality per se as a con-
stituent element within theoretical, as well as aesthetic, discourse." Silliman
suggests that "one conclusion that necessarily follows is that *each theoretical
approach should radically reformulate its conception of a proposed canon*"("Poets"
124, emphasis his). Theory-death, multiplied, could thus offer an infinite
number of new leases on life.

Bourdieu's theory of the cultural field comes much closer to capturing this sense of possibility than the theories of the avant-garde. Describing the various semi-autonomous cultures of competition out of which art is produced, Bourdieu achieves a kind of panoptic perspective, capable of articulating the "refractive" relations between even the most isolated of struggles. But he does not exempt himself from the dynamic he describes. By locating the battle over the rules and norms of each segment of the cultural field at their various cores, Bourdieu not only offers the possibility for some degree of generalization, but also builds into his theory an understanding of the way theory distorts its object. Unlike the hypostatizing gaze of "closed" theories of the avant-garde, then, he retains a certain dynamism of perspective:

> The semantic flux of notions like writer or artist is both the product and the condition of struggles aiming to impose the definition. In this way, it belongs to the very reality which it is concerned to interpret. To decide on paper and in more or less arbitrary fashion debates which are not decided in reality, such as the question of whether this or that pretender to the title of writer (etc.) belongs to the population of writers, is to forget that the field of cultural production is the site of struggles which, through the imposition of the dominant definition of the writer, aim to delimit the population of those who possess the right to participate in the struggle over the definition of the writer. (*Rules* 224)

Institutions of the avant-garde are persistently inchoate, and to the extent that they reach codification, it is in the form of what Bourdieu calls "anti-institutional institutions," paradoxical sociotextual universes—like the term "avant-garde" for example—in which freedom from institutions is inscribed in those institutions (*Rules* 258). Bourdieu thus models a relation of theory to practice that seems extremely useful for analyzing the work of poets who were engaged in both. However, his map of the cultural field—drawn, as it is, according to rigidly economic coordinates—cannot be truly responsive to the "flux" that he finds within it.

"His Life, His Mouth, and His Poem": Articulating Institutions

Working as editors, publishers, librarians, and promoters, as well as teachers and critics, the constellation of anti-Establishment figures who came to be known as the "New American" poets reconceived the social role of the poet as what Bourdieu would call a "double personage," a figure who operates on the border between the narrowly aesthetic dimension of artistic labor and the more broadly economic processes of its publication and valuation (*Rules* 167–73, 227–29). This "institutional strategy" was a defining feature of both their poetic and their self-making practices.[7] The publication record of Olson's Berkeley talk encapsulates one component of this strategy: transcribed twice with the help of the poet and various members of his audience—once with extensive annotations and indexing—it was published three times by small presses, ending up most decisively in *Muthologos*, Olson's collected lectures. However unstable it may be aesthetically, this text's continuous circulation among Olson initiates has come to signify "being there," a badge of honor whose peculiar value derives, in part, from Olson's own promotion of "muthologos"— "running at the mouth" granted transtemporal significance. At one point in the talk, he claimed, "writing is publishing. I am now publishing . . . tonight . . . because I'm talking writing" (*Berkeley* 15). While the transcripts' meticulous registration of Olson's every verbal stumble gives this claim to vatic singularity a certain retrospective truth, his stand for "his life, his mouth, and his poem" was very much a collective production.

At Berkeley, Olson shared the privilege of top billing with at least three other poets: Allen Ginsberg, Robert Duncan, and, in a more limited capacity, Jack Spicer, all of whom drew large audiences. Conference organizers, led by Richard Baker at the University of California Extension, anticipated and enforced this hierarchy of renown; readings by these poets were heavily advertised and scheduled during the evenings in large venues, while younger, more regionally identified poets such as New Yorkers Ron Padgett and Ted Berrigan, and Bay Area poets George Stanley, Howard Dull, and Joanne Kyger, were grouped together for significantly smaller, word-of-mouth events.

Indeed, the geography of the avant-garde, the relationship between communal identity and a sense of region or locale, was changing in 1965, and it was one of the many markers of difference between and amongst the poets at Berkeley. The San Francisco poetry scene was itself divided on the issue. As Michael Davidson has shown, poets based in the Bay Area inherited a unique "spirit of place," saturated with utopian myths of the West and nurturing of a typically San Franciscan combination of antinomianism and sectarianism. This led to the formation of a variety of subcommunities or "circles": the "Berkeley Renaissance" group—Duncan, Spicer, and Robin Blaser—built an exclusive gay brotherhood out of their shared interests in medieval art and occultism, while Kenneth Rexroth, William Everson, Gary Snyder, and, in some senses, Jack Kerouac carried on the western regionalist tradition that had been developing amongst California writers since the frontier communities of the mid-nineteenth century (*San Francisco* 7–16, 28–29). Allen Ginsberg's 1955 reading of *Howl* had been a founding moment for the gallery and coffeehouse movement known as the San Francisco Renaissance, but, like many of his Beat peers, he'd always been a bicoastal poet, and by 1965 he was an international one, having been crowned "Kraj Majales" (King of the May) by thousands of Prague students just before the Berkeley conference. Ginsberg's avant-gardism (and his celebrity) was becoming increasingly political, linked to liberation movements on a world scale.

Olson was also on the international circuit, though hardly a paparazzi target like Ginsberg; he traveled to Berkeley from the Spoleto Festival in Italy where he'd read with Ezra Pound, John Weiners, Barbara Guest, and John Ashbery, as well as Pablo Neruda, Salvatore Quasimodo, and André Frenaud, among others. Dominated by Americans, the event marked the end of international modernism and signaled a new plateau in U.S. cultural and economic globalism; since the early 1950s, Olson's travels had always been conducted at the intersection of these two currents, whereas his collaborator Robert Creeley's were modeled more on the former.[8] Ashbery had been living in Europe on and off since the early 1950s. In July of 1965 O'Hara joined him there on business for the Museum of Modern Art, under whose auspices he was curating two large traveling exhibits, "Modern Sculpture, U.S.A." and "Recent Landscapes of Nine Americans," which opened at the Spoleto Festival. Both poets remained overseas during the events at Berkeley. At least for the more established of its members, the New York School was a coterie without national borders, its cosmopolitanism sustained by a network of globe-trotting insiders. They were notably absent from the conference, represented instead by "second-generation" poets Berrigan and Padgett, whose klatch had a more ghettoized, downtown air.

These different geographic orientations spawned distinctive relations of reception and styles of performance. Davidson contends that the performative impulse in San Francisco poetry—"the way the poem enacts in its own realm forces . . . that structure the natural world"—emerges from the romantic "spirit of place" that I mentioned above (*San Francisco* 20). Spontaneity, as in Kerouac's "spontaneous bop prosody," negative capability, as in Spicer's theory of "dictation," and Ginsberg's Whitmanian oracularity are all poetic versions of the participatory ideal for which San Francisco provided a setting at once urban and sublime. The camp wit of New York poets, on the other hand, was bred out of the double world of uptown patrons and the cruisy gay underground more or less gracefully mingling in the close quarters of the cocktail party and the gallery opening. Poetically closer to his San Francisco peers—indeed his "breath

line" was the acknowledged influence on most oral poetries of the period—
Olson was primarily a pedagogue, more comfortable in the classroom, however
open, than the café. While he also valued participation, it was of the scholarly,
exegetical variety, and he was at his best in what Robert von Hallberg has called
the "georgian" orders of isolated communities like Black Mountain and
Gloucester (*Charles Olson* 33). At Berkeley, however, he seemed compelled
to do as the West Coast poets did, goading Ginsberg at the intermission to
acknowledge his performance as "improvisatory, spontaneous poetry." He
was clearly out of his element, conceding later that "I never read in a coffee
house in my life. I never spent an hour in jail. You know, I'm—I'm the White
Man . . . the ultimate paleface" (*Berkeley* 51).

However alienated he may have been from his younger, hipper, more urban
contemporaries, Olson was moved to speak for them—literally to contain their
various modes of address and performance within his own. He had to construct
a verbal net that could rein in the community's dispersion. A wary disciplinar-
ian, Olson set himself an even more difficult task: he had to "discover" the
"initial" organization at its root.[9] *The Maximus Poems* idealize a similar organic
dynamic, in which the poet "would be an historian as Herodotus was, looking /
for oneself for the evidence of / what is said" (87), delving into the diverse facts
of Gloucester history and emerging with a form that is, as he prescribes in
"Projective Verse," "never more than an extension of content" (*SW* 24). In
"Causal Mythology," the lecture Olson delivered at Berkeley three days before
the reading, he figured this process as both a personal journey into "the dark-
ness of one's own initiation" and a recipe for social and political organization:

> I think we live so totally in an acculturated time that the reason why
> we're all here that care and write is to put an end to that whole thing.
> Put an end to nation, put an end to culture, put an end to divisions of
> all sorts. And to do this you have to put establishment out of business.
> It's just a structure of establishment. And my own reason for being, like
> I said, on the left side and being so hung up on form is that I feel that
> today, as much as action, the invention, not the invention, but the discov-
> ery of formal structural means is as legitimate as—is for me the form of
> action. The radical of action lies in finding out how organized things are
> genuine, are initial. (*Muthologos* 95)

"Put establishment out of business" was becoming a familiar battle cry, but
Olson is not content here to embody the "anti." The goal is radical (read "genuine," "initial") organization, not anarchy, and the action called for is the measured, backward movement of recognition, not revolution.

This careful archeology hardly anticipates Olson's breakout performance three days later, however. Indeed the incoherences of the talk reveal the problems that arise when his open-form poetics are transposed into the social realm.[10] Recasting Olson's method in terms derived from Bakhtinian formalism, Barrett Watten has argued that Olson works by using an "in-time romance of the self" as the basic structure or "axis of combination" on which to order "divided subject matter" (*Total Syntax* 123–25). At the Berkeley reading, the speaker's insistence that "we could talk forever" proffers his own logorrhea as the armature on which the "we," the "future society," might hang. However, Watten also suggests that the "imagistic stand" of the hero-poet is itself an outcome of the form's obsessive inclusiveness: "Olson's refusal of closure gives the affect of presence," he writes (125). In other words, the coherence of the speaking subject gets bound to the unity of his audience in a highly unstable chiasmus. The absence of a common code, or, in Bakhtinian terms, the lack of a uniform social evaluation, keeps the utterance from achieving "finalized structuredness" (Bakhtin 183). Boundaries, of both genre and ego, remain disturbingly open, awaiting the retrospective certainty only literary history can provide.

And the disjunctions at Berkeley were temporal as well as spatial. Although they stood at different points in their individual careers, the poets' collective destiny nevertheless hung in the balance. Olson sought to compensate for this problem rhetorically by wavering between a present-tense, highly embodied mode and something more scholarly, a kind of annotated bibliography of his published work. Robert Duncan's introduction—"as I think all of you, or almost all of you, must know, the man I am introducing is visibly a large man," who "has had to occupy an area in history big enough for some spirit size"— shared this doubleness. Relying on an intimate sense of person, but also tapping the avant-garde canon for the poetical notion of "size" that Olson had elaborated in "Projective Verse," Duncan did the poet the ambivalent honor of describing him in his own words.

A brief sketch of the institutional history of Olson's most influential essay might be useful here. Published initially in *Poetry New York* in 1950, "Projective Verse" became known within the avant-garde community through *Origin*, the little magazine that Olson and Creeley helped Cid Corman to found and edit. In 1951, William Carlos Williams republished a substantial section of the essay in his *Autobiography*, and by 1960 its call for "composition by field" to counter the "closed-verse" of the New Criticism-sanctioned poetic mainstream was generally considered the mantra of the "raw" poets. Donald Allen's placement of Olson at the beginning of *The New American Poetry* and of "Projective Verse" at the beginning of its poetics section lent theoretical cachet and the patina of unity to the otherwise errant energies of the work collected along with it. The practicality of its injunctions to the would-be-poet to "USE USE USE the process at all points," "the HEAD, by way of the EAR, to the SYLLABLE / the HEART, by way of the BREATH, to the LINE" (SW 17), etc. is open to question, but "Projective Verse's" effectiveness as a touchstone for oppositional poets is without dispute.

Citing this seminal essay in his introduction of Olson at Berkeley, Duncan set the terms for the performance that followed. Would Olson "sprawl" and thus "find little to sing but himself," or would he stay "contained within his nature as he is a participant in the larger force," and thereby achieve "projective size"(SW 25)? Fifteen years after "Projective Verse's" first publication, at the event that marked the efflorescence of the poetic movement it was widely credited with spawning, Olson became a test case for the possibility of "getting rid of the lyrical interference of the individual as ego, the subject and his soul." He was painfully aware of this framing, and recognized the stakes to be social as well as poetic. The talk is punctuated with apologies for his bluster:

> If I'm bold tonight, I told Allen Ginsberg, it's simply because I've discovered . . . in the presence of . . . the poets, and, like, ourselves, on having lived, how to be modest—I mean, to be modest, to realize that Charlie Olson, shit, he made it. Hm! I mean, he's gotta still—he's gotta still do it if he can, or he's nothing. (*Berkeley* 22)

The shift from first to third person here ventriloquizes the skepticism of a hypothetical spectator, one who will ostensibly outlive him. Facing poets who were members of his "generation" in name only, Olson—who was ten to fifteen years older than the other established poets in attendance—registers the gap in age as a premonition of his own posterity. Having achieved a certain degree of canonicity, the poet has himself to live up to as well as the onus of "representativeness," and less room in which to do it.

Olson accepted the titles of "boss poet" and "daddy" with all of the irony and excess such bohemian honorifics seemed to require. Drinking, fumbling with the microphone, carrying on extended conversations with selected audience members like Duncan and Ginsberg, and jeering at others who walked out during the proceedings, Olson put on a performance that was, he said, "oral, private, public." Abandoning the recognizable strictures of the "reading," Olson eschewed as well the academic proprieties of "the talk," calling himself instead "a talker" and "a story-teller." Throughout the proceedings, this genre trouble gets linked to anxieties about vocational identity, though—in a typically Olsonian turn—these appear more often as excessive bravado than outward insecurity. At one point during the evening Olson suggested that the gathered poets resembled a group of senators in a convention hall, saying "I wouldn't mind proving tonight that I belong where I have been, in Madison Square Garden" (*Berkeley* 16), and later, "I really could run the nation if I didn't prefer to talk" (35). He claimed that poets were "the only political leaders" (21); he labeled the conference a "queer university," and called himself "a professor of posture" (36). He opened with two short poems and read from *The Maximus Poems,* but he interrupted himself so many times, and loaded each poem so heavily with commentary and anecdote, that the effect was closer to citation than reading. At one point, he addressed the crowd, "I mean, you want me to be a poet?" claiming instead to be "a result of having listened" (12) to the poets who'd read earlier in the week, and later venturing, "tonight . . . I think I've entered their company" (23).

It would be relatively simple to understand Olson's behavior as a kind of reverse anxiety of influence. Biographer Tom Clark favors this reading, describing Olson as a "lonely, aging and insecure man" desperately trying to "maintain his dominance" (324). I've been suggesting, however, that such an individualizing, psychologizing account doesn't do justice to the multilateral space of avant-gardist identity formation. Without a fuller sense of the institutional moment, individual idiosyncrasies are impossible to isolate. For in spite of all its exploded, hysterical bluster, Olson's performance wasn't entirely off the map. Rather, it was predicated on the accumulation of a certain amount of social capital, both individual and collective. In *The Academic Postmodern and the Rule of Literature,* David Simpson situates the turn toward anecdote, conversation, and other personal modes characteristic of contemporary academic discourse within the "broad history of modernity." He diagnoses the current tendency as a symptom of "empowerment," and argues that "at the very point where we accede to the power we so desperately desire, we become critically anxious about the implications of employing it" (52). Simpson claims that the "conversational ideal" recalls a "bourgeois culture of preprofessional freedom," which— at least since the eighteenth century—hasn't actually existed, except as the defining ideal of the literary profession. "It has always been literature and criticism that have . . . positioned themselves as alternatives to . . . the whole culture of specialization and divided labor by which modernization has been achieved," he writes (76). And these have always been relatively exclusive alternatives. Simpson analogizes the conversational ideal of, for instance, contemporary neopragmatism to eighteenth and ninteenth century belletristic genres, suggesting that conversation "presupposes having enough education to have something to say that is worth hearing . . . and it assumes that one does not have any awkward convictions that might put an end to talk" (48). Anecdote performs a similar bourgeois function of providing a "sense of difference in sameness." These forms depend on the fiction of "the common reader": a reception free of the professional constrictions of other disciplines, but clearly privileged in its access to a special set of rhetorical codes and forms of knowledge.

A kind of bohemian table talk, the free-ranging rhetoric and disciplinary dilettantism that Olson displayed at Berkeley can thus be read as participating in the dialectic of disciplinarity "by which modernization has been achieved." Olson's projective poet is on a continuum with the old-style man of letters, an interdisciplinary pioneer whose poaching license has a long literary history. Positioned at the opposite end of the literary field, he is nevertheless a precursor to Simpson's "academic postmodern"; the specific rhetorics differ, but the conjunction of "empowerment" and institutionally buttressed amateurism is very much the same.

Olson had been establishing this double positioning since the early '50s. Due in part to his organizing efforts—which helped to generate such landmark institutions as *Origin* magazine, the final incarnation of Black Mountain College, and the *Black Mountain Review,* which in its last issue in 1957 brought East Coast innovators together with the San Francisco Renaissance—by 1965 an entire community of avant-garde-identified poets had caught up with him. At Berkeley, Olson could assume an audience already familiar with his rhythms of rupture and excess, prepared to shelve his talk alongside their growing collection of Olsoniana. As Ralph Maud's extensive annotation and indexing suggest, the talk manifested no shortage of book learning—referencing Hesiod, Herodotus, Alfred North Whitehead, and Herman Melville, amongst other Olson favorites—but it also depended on and reproduced a less objective kind of literacy: the assimilation of a structure of value in which orality and spontaneity meet textuality and history in order to form a more "authentic," because less objectifiable, literary object. Specific referents might have been lost on the intended recipients of this kind of cultural product—though many had "gone to school" with Olson and Pound before him and were thus well versed in their stable of greats—but the "process of the thing" was a text to be read, the stuff of collective recognition. Take the following exchange:

> OLSON: Drunk? I'm really drunk! Huh . . . Like Omar Khayyam: that son of a bitch is—really should be added to the masters.
> GINSBERG: Anacreon.   OLSON: Huh?
> GINSBERG: Anacreon.
> OLSON: Well, gee, you know, that's what Ed said he'd say if he introduced

me, was that goddam Pindar. I mean, I put Pindar down . . . I plan to
read that "Letter 23" in honor of Robin Blaser. I will for those of you who
will stay . . . Or is Anacreon—I mean, you know—but he and Pindar . . . I don't know, maybe I don't even know Anacreon. I don't think I
do. I'm confusing two poets, ain't I? Huh? Am I, Robin? Tell me; show
the people how—how unknowledgeable I am, how ignorant . . . Because
I do—I mean, look, I sound so goddam intellectual and so knowing and
so literate . . .
VOICE: You're the boss poet here, daddy. (*Berkeley* 26–27)

That Olson didn't, at this moment in his performance, sound particularly
intellectual or literate and yet could still earn the honor of "boss poet" is precisely the point. Literary history—in this case, the history of poetic carous-
ers—is at stake here, but more the spirit than the letter. Being entertaining
while drunk is at least as important as remembering the lushes of the ancient
world, and the capacity to do both at once (or try) allows one to be "added to
the masters." Recent literary production, namely Letter 23 of *The Maximus
Poems* (1960) and Ed Sanders's Catalogue #1 (1964), gets added into the mix,
weighted equally with the classical canon. But what seems most crucial for this
particular moment to work is a dynamic of one-upsmanship and competition—the typically subterranean workings of tradition and the individual talent rendered in the present-tense, colloquialized form of literary politics, or
simply friendship. Inter- and intragenerational angst operates on the surface of
this discourse; oedipal dynamics are played as farce. Let me cite one more
particularly laden exchange, which took place approximately halfway through
the evening:

OLSON: . . . Isn't it wonderful? People cannot wait for poetry. (SLAPS TABLE)
Ha, ha! The activity has to be produced in a time schedule. I mean, you—
you remember how we write these things? The same way I'm try—I'm
behaving. I'm—I mean, I'm a Professor of Posture, and I'm proving it.
(LAUGHTER)
DUNCAN: Charles, can you give us time to go pee? . . . Five minutes
OLSON: You're—you're—I mean, "Teacher!" (LAUGHTER. APPLAUSE.
TROUBLE WITH MICROPHONE CORD.) That's called "recall." Ha! I mean,
I'm—I'm either going to lose my position or I won't, that's all. (36)

Clark makes much of the fact that Duncan didn't return to the hall after the
intermission, claiming that he "walked out in protest" at Olson's excesses (324).

Here, however, he appears fully immersed in the tenor of the proceedings, gamely styling himself as ephebe to Olson's elder, simultaneously pointing up the institutionally overdetermined distribution of power and—by interrupting the speaker with such an undignified request—signaling his own comfortable position within it. It clearly takes more than the public mention of "pee" or an uncontrolled oratory to "lose [one's] position"; however, here, as throughout the talk, a certain amount of insecurity underlies the banter. Between Olson and Duncan—and between Olson and a large portion of the Berkeley audience for that matter—sexuality is both a source and a symptom of this insecurity. By 1965, the scales have shifted to such an extent that the professedly straight poet is put on an awkward defensive. At the intermission following Duncan's request, for instance, Lew Welch asked Olson if he'd like to go "pee" too. "Nah, shit, pee? I never pee," Olson replied. "That's one of the only—the reason why I'm not a queen is I don't have to pee to prove that I'm a man . . . Go pee, Allen. We got over that tonight" (36).

But "homosexual panic"—as Eve Kosofsky Sedgwick has named the "fear of one's own homosexuality" produced in men as they accede to the simultaneously homosocial and homophobic conditions of masculine entitlement (*Epistemology* 186)—is *not,* I'd argue, the primary source of discomfort here. Rather Olson's is a state of "authorial panic," if such a condition could be diagnosed. Having opened up his monologic positioning in order to create space for articulating his community, Olson finds that his ego defenses are down. Barrett Watten has recently characterized authorship as "a social construction in defense of the narcissistic self" ("Secret History"). Doffing this armor while still desiring vatic-heroic poethood, Olson is caught in a fundamentally self-destructive position. In a synchronic field of acknowledged peers where rules of hierarchy and power are played as farce, there is little to prevent the trauma of, as Watten has put it, "the unstable relation of a narcissistic ego in its form of undoing in another" (32). In this context the sexual (or more specifically, urinary) quips can be read as a post facto attempt to mark territory; an attempt rendered especially feeble by the absence not only of women, but of the stabilizing alterity that they would represent. By the end of intermission a rapprochement has apparently occurred, but in this "queer university" there's a sense that the rules might change at any moment, and openness—of professional etiquette, social mores, and, most important, ego boundaries—is purchased at the cost of a perpetual crisis.

Permanent Revolution and the Construction of the Contemporary

> No one is ahead of his time, it is only that the particular variety of
> creating his time is the one that his contemporaries who also are creating
> their own time refuse to accept . . . And it is very much too bad, it is
> so very much more exciting and satisfactory for everybody if one can
> have contemporaries, if all one's contemporaries could be one's
> contemporaries.
>
> Gertrude Stein, "Composition as Explanation"

The discussion of "the margin" in literary scholarship—in which the theory of
the avant-garde participates—has generally focused on two questions: whether
or not it exists, and whether it can offer a critical, liberatory perspective on the
functioning of the center. I hope that the preceding analysis of the contradictory forces at work both within Olson's talk, and between it, its intended audience, and the institutions and interests productive of their contemporary moment, has begun to suggest that these are not the most useful questions to ask.
They aren't useful to the extent that they posit a single binary structuring the
entirety of cultural conflict and then allow the dismantling of that binary to do
away with all possibilities for resistance. There's a debilitating stasis implicit in
the notion of the "standpoint" that develops out of this line of questioning: in
the unstable, diversified field of cultural production in which these poets operated, new "centers" keep cropping up. No point remains peripheral long
enough to plot a unified plan for revolution, nor—more important—is revolution always seen as the most attractive or viable option.

Strategies of marginality—by which I predominantly mean such decentering practices as the insider rhetorics of anecdote and conversation, the
Rimbaudian drunken ramble, or Olsonian "composition by field"—are often
deployed by agents who already enjoy a certain amount of institutionalized
authority, and they tend to want to retain it. The acknowledgment of this fact
need not be read, however, as a cynical pronouncement on the "stabilization"
or cooptation of all radical projects by the voracious forces of the system—be it
capitalism, discourse, the academy, or any one of a host of monoliths. However
institutionally savvy, self-aware, and canonically secure Olson may have been,
he was still compelled to put on a performance that was originary in its ambitions and embarrassing in its excesses. This suggests both that he felt his authority to be transient, and that revolutionary impulses can coexist with the
more "conservative" project of shoring up one's position via the creation of new
institutions, new relations of production and reception.

In "The Author as Producer" (1934), Walter Benjamin proposed a shift in the terms of the debate over revolutionary art: "Rather than ask, 'What is the attitude of a work to the relations of production of its time? Does it accept them, is it reactionary—or does it aim at overthrowing them, is it revolutionary?' . . . I should like to ask, 'What is its position *in* them?'" (222, emphasis mine). This reframing of the question seems to me to be absolutely necessary if scholarship of the avant-garde is to rise above, or, perhaps more accurately, get underneath the disembodied concepts in which it has been content to traffic. Benjamin's question is the beginning of a polemic whose end is to define the role of the writer in the proletarian revolution. His vision is thus more single-mindedly political than that of the poets at Berkeley, but his prescription nevertheless describes their practice quite presciently. Of the author "who has reflected deeply on the conditions of present-day production," he writes:

> his work will never merely be work on products but always, at the same time, on the means of production. In other words, his products must have, over and above their character as works, an organizing function, and in no way must their organizational usefulness be confined to their value as propaganda . . . What matters, therefore, is the exemplary character of production, which is able first to induce other producers to produce, and second to put an improved apparatus at their disposal. And this apparatus is better the more consumers it is able to turn into producers—that is, readers or spectators into collaborators. (223)

Benjamin cites Brecht's notion of the "functional transformation" of the means of production, as well as his epic theater, as embodiments of this revolutionary ideal.

Though they were motivated as much by tactical dramas of life in the literary field as by visions of large-scale revolution, the self-institutionalizing practices of the "New American" poets extend this avant-garde tradition—along with all of its interested, embattled implications—into the second half of the century. In "Aesthetic Tendency and the Politics of Poetry: A Manifesto," a self-proclaimed statement of the "first principles" of language writing, this "institutional strategy" reaches explicit articulation:

> What seems so troubling about our tendency, is that its social constitution is not hidden behind the kinds of neutral evaluations of poetic competence that are reflected in the practice as 'craft' . . . Aesthetic tendency—the politics of intention—as opposed to aesthetic arbitration, offers an entirely different way of seeing the poem as produced and received. (Silliman et al. 271)

What seems so troubling about language poets' academic "recuperation" is that it has been precisely "intentional" on their part, a moment in the ongoing social negotiations of their avant-gardism, not the end.

I've been tracing the structure of the postwar avant-garde's "aesthetic tendency" out of the concentrated moment at Berkeley: a poetic collective subsisting in the unstable temporal zone between impulse and institution, and a poet pressed to articulate that collective in all of its complex contemporaneity. Courting megalomania in the name of social cohesion, Olson put on a performance whose psychological stakes were impossibly high. There were few models for his brand of egotistical sublimity. In "Advance-Guard Writing, 1900–1950," a 1951 *Kenyon Review* essay that both Olson and Frank O'Hara read and praised,[11] Paul Goodman proposed an understanding of the advance-guard as "a species of art differentiated by a certain social relation," characterized not by "a direct attack on inhibiting forces" but by a complex process of introjecting and "disgorging" the social and aesthetic norms of its audience (359). Against the prevailing trope of the "alienated" artist, Goodman argued that advance-guard production is a "response to an inner irk" that "takes the side of what it attacks and suffers the conflict through" (361). "If we are to use the concept of 'alienation,'" Goodman wrote, we must not mean "rival warring camps," but rather "self-estrangement," the artist's integration and critical reproduction of a culture alienated from itself. Sketching a brief history of avant-gardist development from naturalism's working through of "offensive subject matter," to the historical avant-garde's "revolution of the word," Goodman claimed that in a postwar climate of "shell-shock," the "present-day advance guard is the physical re-establishment of community":

> This is to solve the crisis of alienation in the simple way: the persons are estranged from themselves, from one another, and from their artist; he takes the initiative precisely by putting his arms around them and drawing them together. In literary terms this means: *to write for them about them personally* . . . But such personal writing about the audience itself can occur only in a small community of acquaintances, where everybody knows everybody and understands what is at stake; in our estranged society, it is objected, just such intimate community is lacking. Of course it is lacking! The point is that the advance-guard action helps create such community, starting with the artist's primary friends. The community comes to exist by having *its* culture; the artist makes this culture. (375–76)

This scenario obviously resonates with the coterie poetics of the New York School, as well as with the larger scene at Berkeley and the peer politics of language writing. As we've seen, avant-gardist community formation is a highly conflictual and unstable process; the self-destructive pathos of a performance like Olson's puts utopian ideals at risk. Goodman suggests an explanation for the troubling psychosocial territory into which the Berkeley talk travels, one that captures the crisis at the literal crossing of the psychological and the social:

> The advance-garde artist, unwilling to accept the introject as his own . . . begins to wail and reach out—to the audience for a new possibility. He becomes a cry-baby and then an unwanted lover . . . The art of the artist is to invent ways needfully to throw himself on the mercy of the audience. (372)

Avant-garde community formation embraces conflict at its core. Made to face its own sense of self-estrangement, the audience responds by trying to wipe it out. Not with outrage, but with embarrassment, the denuding blush of identification.

Bourdieu would understand the confrontation between "poet" and "community" at Berkeley in more differentiated, starkly competitive terms as a showdown between those outsiders who have an interest in pushing history forward and the lone insider who wants to live on. Having distinguished the fields of restricted and large-scale production, and the different kinds of capital on which they run, he elaborates what he takes to be the prevailing opposition both within and between them, namely, the opposition between two "modes of aging" (*Rules* 146). This distinction can be understood in economic terms as the difference between short and long production cycles, between the palpitations of the best-seller market and the more languorous evolution of the classic. But Bourdieu's sense of the economics of temporality *within* the cultural field is both more nuanced and more foundational. "The privilege accorded to 'youth,' and to the associated values of change and originality, cannot be completely understood through the relationship between 'artists' and 'bourgeois' alone," he writes. "It also expresses the specific law of change in the field of production, that is, the dialectic of distinction—whereby institutions, schools, works, and artists which have 'left their mark' are destined to fall into the past . . . to see themselves thrown outside history or to 'pass into history'" (156).

The field of restricted production, the quadrant of culture most isolated from narrowly monetary motivations, is thus in Bourdieu's analysis a space of "permanent revolution": a world defined by time, motored by the perpetual, transpersonal destruction of the old by the new. The uncomfortable—though necessary—conjunction of determinism and voluntarism active throughout his work is never more embattled than it is here, in his installation of the avant-garde as the inexorable engine of cultural history. Bourdieu addresses this conflict, but doesn't resolve it:

The aging of authors, works or schools is something quite different from a mechanical sliding into the past. It is engendered in the fight between those who have already left their mark and are trying to endure, and those who cannot make their own marks in their turn without consigning to the past those who have an interest in stopping time. (*Rules* 157)

Because the position takings define themselves, to a large extent, negatively, in relation to others, they often remain almost empty, reduced to a stance of defiance, rejection, rupture. The 'youngest' writers structurally . . . reject what their most consecrated precursors are and do . . . and the youngest also affect to spurn any mark of social aging, starting with the signs of consecration . . . For their part, the consecrated authors see in the voluntarist and forced character of certain of the intentions to outmode them the indisputable signs of a 'gigantic and hollow pretension,' as Zola put it. (240)

Olson's ecstatic ambition disrupts the bureaucratic inevitability of these passages. Bourdieu is describing—but in his magisterial expansiveness, not really registering—an ambivalent process, clogged with melancholy and motored by "progress" in equal parts. In his system, "permanent revolution" means nothing more than continuous recycling, whereas within the cultural field that I've located at Berkeley, the term captures the simultaneous crisis of individual and collective identity: the perpetual, mutual construction of authorship. It is in the interests of time—his system needs a futuristic drive in order to avoid hardening into straight structuralism—that Bourdieu keeps the motor running. But this means he has to ignore the varied saliences of a moment, such as the one with which I began, in which the poet embodies the possibility of changing the system:

OLSON: And when he—and when he—and when he is made of three parts, his life, his mouth, and his poem, then, by god, the earth belongs to us . . . by god, isn't it exciting?

2

"The Company of Love"

The Collaborated Careers of Charles Olson
and Robert Creeley

In the summer of 1996, the National Poetry Foundation sponsored a conference entitled "American Poetry in the Fifties" at the University of Maine. Attended mostly by academics, the conference nevertheless sustained an outsider air: a strong sense of partisanship and internal cohesion. In the 1970s and 1980s the National Poetry Foundation had established itself as one of the primary institutional organs promoting the "other tradition," and the Black Mountain wing in particular.[1] The conference was a celebration of the other fifties, a reclaiming of the decade of conformity for the "raw" poets. At a panel on Olson and Duncan, I presented a paper in which I discussed Olson's early poetic career in the context of postwar "professionalization." Ed Dorn—Olson's student at Black Mountain College and an elder statesman at the conference—began the response period with a cool dismissal of the term "professional," suggesting that it was an entirely inaccurate characterization of the way Olson would have conceived of his social positioning. Olson was a "bohemian intellectual," he said, "*dentists* were 'professionals.'"

As Dorn's remark suggests, in the segment of the contemporary poetic field which owes its existence in part to Olson and Creeley's 1950s collaboration, "professional" is a charged term. On it is staked a set of gender and (to a lesser extent) class distinctions that have been crucial to avant-gardist identity formation for the better part of this century. Dorn's dentist, for instance, repudiates a particular version of compromised masculinity: more akin to technicians than men of science, dentists make good livings and are suspiciously easy to bring home to Mother. Likewise, the professional poet—practitioner of conventional techniques, product of accredited training programs—functions as a constitutive outside for both academic theorists, who thereby manage to evade charges of professionalism themselves and forge alliances with the marginal, and avant-garde poets, who may be employed in the academy but not in the "commoditized" field of creative writing.[2] In the slippery avant-garde equation of aesthetic experiment with cultural outlawry more generally, the professional poet threatens to soften bohemian edginess with complacent breezes from the suburbs.

Forging his avant-garde poetic career in a climate of inchoate anxiety over masculine authority and cultural centrality, Olson's own stances around the issue of professionalism were nevertheless more complex than Dorn's somewhat nostalgic shorthand can fathom. Even an occasional, relatively minor poem like "Letter for Melville 1951," a verse polemic written "to be read AWAY FROM the Melville Society's 'One Hundredth Birthday Party' for MOBY DICK at Williams College," reveals Olson working through an array of identifications and disavowals as he stakes out a place on the literary field. Addressed to a nameless friend whom we now know to be Eleanor Metcalf, Melville's granddaughter,[3] the poem is both "for Melville"—that is, advocating on the dead author's behalf—and, even more forcefully, *for Olson,* a Melville scholar who left behind his academic career after finishing his Ph.D. course work at Harvard. Several years later, after receiving a Guggenheim Fellowship and working in the Roosevelt administration, he wrote and published *Call Me Ishmael,* the collaged study of *Moby Dick* that he hoped would "actually *arrest the West*" but which was instead summarily dismissed by his scholarly contemporaries (Clark 120–21). In "Letter for Melville," Olson spews his contempt for "these creatures," asking Metcalf to "carry my damnations" to the "bunch of commercial travelers from the several colleges" who will spend the weekend "scratch[ing] each other's backs with a dead man's hand" (*CPCO* 233).

Pitted against the figure of Melville, whom he imagines at sea "July / above the Sigsbee deep . . . a muscular man knowing / that knowledge / is only what makes a ship shape," Olson's parody of conference cocktail party chatter is merciless, and remarkably dead-on: "ask one to tell you," he advises Metcalf mockingly,

> . . . that no matter how difficult it is
> to work in an apartment in a bedroom in a very big city
> because the kids are bothersome and have to be locked out, and the wife

is only too good, yet, he did republish enough of this other man
to now have a different professional title, a better salary
and though he wishes he were at Harvard or a Whale,
he is, isn't he, if he is quite accurate, much more liked
by his president?

(*CPCO* 237)

Rejecting the enterprise of academic professionals as feeble self-promotion, and, more dangerously, self-serving plunder of authentic artistic products, Olson exalts poetry as "such labor / which knows no weekend" and suggests that, in practicing it, he enjoys a privileged union with Melville not unlike Metcalf's, who "ha[s] the blood of him." His loathing for bloodless technocrats does not translate into a full-scale rejection of professionalism itself, however. Olson knows that simply celebrating Melville as a heroic sailor-poet makes the writer fair game for a critic who would figure him as a romantic wild child–"a risky but creative mingling . . . of the fortunate and the injurious"(240)—in order to keep him in scholarly captivity. Olson calls this sort of scholarly zoo keeper a "clear neuter" and imagines him arguing that "Herman Melville / was no professional, could not accomplish / such mentality and so, as amateur . . . / was anguished all his life in struggle" (239), in order to claim the writer as his sole analytic domain. As the cultural field is currently constructed, Olson recognizes, representation has become the professional's specialty, but the poet must not cede that ground without a fight. Here as throughout Olson's work, negotiations over writerly agency and value fall out along sexualized lines: the "muscular" poet risks emasculation at the hands of the "neuter" critic unless he is willing to trade a bit of his bohemian machismo for a measure of professional authority and self-determination.

Written in the summer of 1951 upon returning to Black Mountain College, taking on the rectorship of the struggling experimental institution, and launching his poetic career with the publication of the inaugural *Origin* magazine devoted to his work, Olson's salvo against the academic establishment was fired from a bastion of alternative literary culture that—in the next fifteen years— he would do much to secure. Indeed the poem's boldly oppositional postures endeared him to the Black Mountain students—among them, Dorn himself— who published it as a pamphlet on the college's press, at their own expense (Clark 207). That "Letter for Melville" countenances a qualified acceptance of professionalism (Melville was not *not* a professional, just a different kind) in an effort to strengthen the cultural hand of the writer, is testimony to Olson's awareness and negotiation of the complex forces structuring the "stance" of the outsider-poet. Countering the false clarity of academic judgment, he offers an alternative professional identity: a vitalist crossing of sailor, writer, "brave man," and proudly amateur scholar whose credentialing process is more idiosyncratically selective than any Ph.D. exam. "It is not the point / either of the book of the plume which lies / cut on this brave man's grave / —on all of us— / but that where they cross is motion," Olson concludes. Understanding this strategic self-positioning, not cynically as calculation and complicity, but analytically as a primary component of Olson and Creeley's "field" poetics, is the goal of this chapter. Two very different poetic personae emerge in *The Maximus Poems* and *For Love*—volumes whose publication marked the end of their collaborative decade—but on the question of what it meant socially to be an avant-garde poet, and what it took "professionally" to succeed as one, Olson and Creeley formed a united front. Together, they established a powerful and, in some respects, deeply flawed precedent. Examining the shared origins of their poethood—in particular, their production of "projective" institutions whose values of immediacy and spontaneity were grounded in exclusion—is a first step toward building a constructive critique of their legacy.

"Both a Poet and an Historian": Reading Professions

I begin my account of Olson and Creeley's career collaboration by juxtaposing two seemingly tangential scenarios of literary position taking—scholarly conferences, forty-five years apart, one attended by me, the other the subject of Olson's satirical poem—not only to introduce terms that will be central to the discussion (tradition, opposition, institution, profession) but to reveal the role that these concepts play in the ongoing process of producing literary history, a process in which poets as well as critics have an active stake. In the context of poetic careers, oppositions such as professional versus amateur, mainstream versus avant-garde, technical versus organic, closed versus open—binaries deployed by literary historians for heuristic purposes—become sites of intentional activity, socially charged choices that poets make and remake. Collaborating on career, Olson and Creeley rendered such choices dialogic, legible. I've tried to capture something of the current scene of reception because I will be discussing ways in which they anticipate such a scene in letters, essays, publication ventures, as well as poems. My purpose is not to prove that these two poets were peculiarly preoccupied with reputation, or that they were especially prescient. Instead I articulate the social and poetic contours of the contemporaneity that developed between them because I want to suggest that in conceiving and institutionalizing a distinctive reading formation, Olson and Creeley had a hand in their own posterities. Without a ready-made reception, they had to invent themselves as readers as well as writers; their poetic self-fashioning was the enactment—and ultimately the production—of an audience.

As "Letter for Melville's" baldly competitive satire suggests, poems are often made to bear the burden of this enterprise, and they don't always do it gracefully. While Creeley's lyric minimalism helped to make *For Love* (1960) one of the decade's best-selling books of poetry, for Olson career concerns rendered genre a vexed issue and vice versa.[4] Slated to follow the *Cantos* into epic greatness, *Maximus* can read more like a hope chest of letters, citations, and other ephemera than a tale of the tribe. An extended portion of the long poem's first volume is given over to an angry lecture on the politics of little magazine publishing, prompted by a friend's unsatisfactory contribution to that field. Olson devotes most of a hinge poem early in the series to a loving physical description of his second collection of poems, *In Cold Hell, In Thicket,* published by Creeley's Divers Press in Mallorca, Spain. The material considered suitable for poetry is both personal, though not lyric, and oddly instrumental, institutional in the most mundane, material sense.

This anti-aesthetic may have slowed Olson's large-scale acceptance as an important poet, but it also helped to open his closets and dresser drawers for both publication and scholarly perusal.[5] Since his death in 1970, a small group of committed scholars have brought out a tremendous amount of primary material, including at current count sixteen volumes of correspondence, four volumes of lectures—most of which were originally delivered extemporaneously—and two volumes of interviews. The multi-volume *Curriculum of the Soul* pamphlet series—to which poets Robin Blaser, Alice Notley, and John Wieners have contributed—took its impetus from a note scribbled by the poet to one of his students at the University of Buffalo. *Charles Olson's Reading: A Biography* (1996), by Ralph Maud, arranges the chronology of the poet's life around lists of the books he read, or at least owned, and the four thousand entries in George Butterick's *Guide to the Maximus Poems of Charles Olson* reproduce large portions of the poet's often idiosyncratic source materials, each scholarly endeavor bolstered by a commitment to "treat Olson on his own terms." The interdisciplinarity, or simply eclecticism, of Olson studies is justified by the poet's own theorization of his poetic/scholarly practice. "The trouble is," Olson wrote in a 1951 letter to Creeley, "it is very difficult to be both a poet, and an historian" (*SW* 130). Olson's is a career, a poetics, and a critical industry structured around the difficult "both . . . and."

One way to resolve this difficulty, if the *Curriculum of the Soul* series is any indication, is to establish the communal conditions by which your autodidacticism can be reproduced, to surround yourself with a group of like-minded individuals trained in the idiosyncratic discipline that you practice. Since modernism's polemical break with nineteenth century paradigms of poethood, "the professions" have provided a model for such a tactical community, particularly useful for poets positioned outside of large-scale institutions.[6] In his early essay "I Gather the Limbs of Osiris" (1912), Pound argues for specialized poetic training as a social necessity. "Technique" is the only common virtue in a decentralized society, he claims, arguing that no matter the occupation, "the man who really does the thing well, if he be pleased afterwards to talk about it, gets always his auditor's attention; he gets his audience the moment he says something so intimate that it proves him the expert" (*Selected Prose* 33).[7] In a post-epic age, poets striving for universality must join the brotherhood of those who hone their craft: "every man who does his own job really well has a latent respect for every other man who does his own job really well." Instrumental to the extent that it "gets his audience," technique is nevertheless offered as the basis of an ethics of recognition and restraint, an antidote to the excesses of the "disagreeable young person expressing its haedinus egotism" (34).

Pound's identification of the poet with the working man is somewhat disingenuous; harkening back to preindustrial modes of artisanship and patronage, he finds a place for poetry within a cohesive culture while sidestepping the feminized, "separate sphere" solution of romantic and postromantic aesthetics. It is no accident, for instance, that the poet who eschews technique as "antipathetic to 'poetry'" (conceived as the lush lyricism of the Victorians) is likened to "your fourteen-year-old daughter . . . [who], never having taken a music lesson in her life, hears Busoni play Chopin, and on the spur of the moment, thinking to produce similar effect, hires a hall and produces what she thinks sounds somewhat the same" (*Selected Prose* 31). Pound defines his expertise against this girlish effusion: "If technique is thus the protection of the public," he writes, "it is no less a protection of the artist himself during the most crucial period of his development" (34). The rhetoric of professionalism is here deployed to place the poet squarely within culture, albeit a much narrower version of it, by precise definition of his boundaries. Without indulging false populism, the hard-working poet can be one of the guys.

Maximus' Epic Exclusions

Most commentators agree that Olson's poetic career began in 1945, when he withdrew from Washington political circles with plans to write a long poem called, simply, *West*.[8] In conceiving of a massive verse epic spanning the history of the Western world but rooted geographically and emotionally in the American West, Olson was clearly coming into poethood under the sign of Pound (and to a lesser degree Williams), a continuity which he freely admitted, and for which he has been branded derivative by at least one influential critic (Perloff 285–306). Of course from Olson's perspective, the issues are more complicated: like his orientation toward academic professionals, Olson's relationship to his modernist predecessors can be conceived as either fiercely ambivalent or strategic, depending on whether one analyzes influence from a psychopoetic or a sociocultural perspective. Early Olson writings, such as the following 1945 note about Pound, provide fodder for both approaches. Addressing himself, Olson writes:

> Maybe Pound discloses to you a method you spontaneously reached for in all this talking and writing . . . But should you not best him? Is his form not inevitable enough to be used as your own? Let yourself be derivative for a bit. This is a good and natural act. Write as the father to be the father. (Butterick, *Guide* xxvi)

These were private musings. In an angry 1953 letter to *Origin* editor Cid Corman, Olson notoriously called Williams and Pound "inferior predecessors," though the letter's animus is mostly directed at Corman, with whom Olson had many bitter editorial disagreements. And then there is the biting doggerel of "A Lustrum for You, E. P.," also written in 1945, though withheld from publication until the posthumous *Collected Poems*:

> You wanted to be historic, Yorick.
> Mug the mike with your ABCs
> you even made Sligo Willie sneeze:
> revolutionary simpleton.
> Ezra Pound, American.
>
> Sing out, sing hate.
> There is a wind, mister
> where the smell, o anti-semite
> in the nose is as
> vomit, poet.
>
> (*CPCO* 38)

Admire the poetic skill, hate the politics: Olson was among the first Poundi-ans to utter this now-familiar mantra of ambivalence. But he was also working through his poetic ties to the master in more measured and intellectually com-plicated ways. In a much-cited March 8, 1951 letter to Creeley, Olson—now thinking toward *Maximus*—confronts Pound on the all-important question of "correct methodology," an obsession, not incidentally, that draws on Pound's own early concern with "technique." In Olson's assessment, Pound strayed from the values of careful craftsmanship and restraint that he had stressed in "I Gather the Limbs of Osiris," and instead "[drove] through [his material] so sharply by the beak of his ego" that he can never "speak . . . in [his] slash at the State or the Economy, basically, for anyone but [him]sel[f]" (*SW* 82). The gentler Williams "HAS an emotional system which is capable of extensions & comprehensions the ego-system . . . is not," Olson allows, but he succumbs to "localism" and thus "completely licks himself, lets time roll him under as Ez does not." Both poets' methods are out of sync with the current reality, however: "Ez's toucan" doesn't work "after 1917," Olson argues, because since then "not only did Yurrup (West, Cento, Renaissance) go, but such blueberry America as Bill presents . . . also WENT" (84). In phonetic slang ("Yurrup") borrowed di-rectly from Pound, Olson declares the older poets' "society as we have had it" obsolete, and argues that an "ALTERNATIVE TO THE EGO-POSITION" is nothing less than a historical imperative (83).

As in "Projective Verse," which I will be discussing in some depth, these capitalized proclamations should be taken first as performatives, meant to goad the poet himself into action and to clear some space on the field in which to act. Manifesto-like, Olson's distinguishing act presents an ideal case, a position easier declared in prose than worked out in poetry. Thus far, his poetic efforts had relied heavily on the first person, as in the 1945 breakthrough poem "The K," which includes the poet's promise "to mount / the run again and swell / to be tumescent I" (*CPCO* 14). "The Kingfishers" (1949) journeys into the rubble of "The Four Quartets" and *The Pisan Cantos* in order to emerge with a quietly triumphant assertion of the self's sufficiency: "I have interested myself / in what was slain in the sun . . . I hunt among stones" (93). The "I" here is layered, an allusion to Rimbaud's "si j'ai du goût, ce n'est guères / que pour la terre et les pierres" cited earlier the poem, but the Olsonian ego's drive to break free of the fathers remains the motive force of the poem.

Pressed to find an alternative to the "ego as beak," *The Maximus Poems* begins more unevenly; it eschews the verticalities of literary tradition in favor of a more horizontally social environment. Written in response to his friend Vincent Ferrini's news that he was starting a little magazine in Gloucester, the first poem in the series, "I, Maximus of Gloucester, to You," emerges confident of an audience, however small. From its inception, Olson's long poem is as concerned with the second person as it is with the first. This recognition of the other doesn't diffuse the self's insistence, nor is anything like parity achieved; however, the addressee does function as a limit on Maximus' exuberances. Even when he's transgressing the bounds of polite intersubjectivity, this poet knows he's not alone. The poem opens:

> Off-shore, by islands hidden in the blood
> jewels & miracles, I, Maximus
> a metal hot from boiling water, tell you
> what is a lance, who obeys the figures of
> the present dance.
>
> (*Maximus* 5)

The opening clause sets the poem in ambiguous grammatical terrain: both prepositional and appositional, it simultaneously positions the speaker and modifies him. From the outset, Maximus is defined by where he stands, and spatially if not rhetorically, this is indeterminate territory. "Off-shore, by islands hidden in the blood" mingles geography with physiology; as the poem progresses, Maximus' gigantism enables these two registers to coexist with an almost grotesque literality.[9] "Islands" are both "in the blood"—clotlike—and a figure, in Letter 3, for the alienated citizens of Gloucester to whom Maximus directs himself: "Isolated person in Gloucester, Massachusetts, I, Maximus, address you / you islands / of men and girls" (*Maximus* 16). Here again, the ambiguity of the first clause's reference works to blur the distinction between the "I" and the "you," who thus become joined, paradoxically, in their isolation. Written just as the scope of the long poem was beginning to become apparent, Letter 3 ends on these lines; the activity of "address"—postal pun intended— becomes *The Maximus Poems'* primary theme.[10]

Olson scholarship tends to highlight the more mythopoetic elements of the poem's opening. In his *Guide*, Butterick gives credence to Olson's claim that the hero of the poem is "in truth" Maximus of Tyre, and that his position offshore is "indeed an enormous expropriation of the other side of the Atlantic, the other side all the way back to man's first leaving the massive land continent of Asia for Cyprus, the 1st 'island' in that aspect of Westward movement" (*Guide* 10). I'm arguing, however, that Maximus' positioning is social and rhetorical before it is historical or mythological; "I . . . tell you" is spat out with a projectile force whose direction and immediacy appear an effort to compensate for the murkiness of the poem's oceanic origins.[11] The ensuing images of "lance," "mast," "bow-sprit," and "swordsman" objectify the gender allegiances of this act of individuation in the phallic accouterments of fishing. For Olson, fishing is one of the few honest jobs left in an alienated mass economy. In Letter 6, recalling his own clumsy, "face-flat" excursion on the *Doris M. Hawes,* he celebrates "the brilliant Portuguese owners / . . . [who] pour the money back / into engines, into their ships," and proclaims that "professional" fishermen "are but extensions of their own careers" (*Maximus* 32), an echo of "Projective Verse's" "form is never more than an extension of content," and for Olson, high praise. Engaged in "the world's businesses" as well as nature's, fishermen offer a kind of vocational halfway house for the poet seeking meaningful masculine employment. Olson admires the special kind of "polis" that develops on a ship, a workingman's community not unlike the fellowship of craftsmen that Pound revered. For fishermen, and for the poet Olson hopes to become, "there are no hierarchies, no infinite, no such many as mass, there are only / eyes in all heads, / to be looked out of" (*Maximus* 33).

But this benignly ecological ideal is premised on exclusion, the foundational conviction that "so few / have the polis / in their eyes." Robert von Hallberg has argued that Maximus is best understood as a commanding rhetorician, but the rhetorical model isn't entirely accurate, suggesting the open air and civility of the agora (*Charles Olson* 29–51). Despite its classical concern for "polis," *The Maximus Poems* is composed of letters, and it retains the sense of privacy, license, and intrigue implicit in the epistolary mode. While the long poem might draw on the classical and Renaissance tradition of the exhortatory letter, its occasionally violent merger of public and private remains fundamentally resistant to generic decorum. Letters 5–9, which carry out an extended argument against Ferrini's little magazine, *Four Winds,* reveal a certain brutality in Olson's position-taking practices, a willingness to exceed the limits of social and literary etiquette in the name of asserting limits on his poetic cohort. Not particularly consistent in its substance, Olson's attack on his friend's work is best understood as a rejection of the insufficiently determinate difference that Ferrini himself—whom Olson refers to in his first letter to Creeley as "that Twin of mine"—appears to represent. Olson excoriates Ferrini's populism, his "habit of / 'the people,'" arguing that "that sentimentality / has no place, least of all Gloucester" (*Maximus* 26), but he also accuses the editor of backroom antics:

> . . . a literary magazine is not,
> for example,
> politics
> >   (even a man's own personal politics—
> >   what sticks out in this issue is verse
> from at least four other editors
> of literary magazines

> do you think such scratch-me-back
> gets by our eyes, the few of us there are
> who read?
>
> (*Maximus* 28)

Letter 5's conclusion is especially damning:

> It's no use.
> There is no place we can meet.
> You have left Gloucester.
> You are not there, you are anywhere
> where there are little magazines
> will publish you.
>
> (*Maximus* 29)

Such personalized vitriol is unrepeated throughout the rest of *The Maximus Poems,* which reserves its criticism for representatives of the "pejorocracy"— "corporations, newspapers, slick magazines, movie houses . . . these entertainers, sellers"—or such public figures as the president of Harvard University. Letters 6 and 7 temper the negativity of Letter 5 with admiring portraits of local fishermen, the painter Marsden Hartley (who spent summers in Gloucester), the poet's father, Pound ("the whole man / wagging, the swag / of Pound"), and "that carpenter" William Stevens, one of the founding citizens of Gloucester (Butterick, *Guide* 50). Olson maintains that Stevens "was the first to make things, / not just live off nature," and celebrates the other men for following a similarly organic "practice of the self / that matter, / that wood" (*Maximus* 35). Against Ferrini's disembodied literariness, Olson wields Hartley's hands as fetish: "each finger so thick and independent of the other . . . they were so much . . . their own lives' acts" (*Maximus* 34). The pathos and heroism of these hands derive in part from their "refusing woman's flesh"; Hartley's homosexuality is figured as uncorrupted phallic wholeness. Repudiating the neutered Ferrini (and the disconcerting equivalence to himself that the Gloucester poet represents) gives Olson access to this sanctified physicality. The specifically sexual politics of this practice are difficult to disentangle. Eve Kosofsky Sedgwick has argued that the "special relationship between male homosocial (including homosexual) desire and the structures for maintaining and transmitting patriarchal power . . may take the form of ideological homophobia, ideological homosexuality, or some highly conflicted but intensively structured combination of the two."[12] Olson's "polis" of "few" appears to be a wilder version of the final alternative.

The Maximus Poems "ALTERNATIVE TO THE EGO-POSITION" is thus by no means radical egalitarianism. In the modest moments for which the poem strives, representativeness and cultural centrality matter less to the poet than the understanding gaze of one good man, figured most prominently as Creeley. "Maximus, to himself," one of the most lyrical sections of the first volume, finds the poet "with the sea / stretching out / from [his] feet," contemplating his belated discovery of the poetic vocation and comparing his "distances" to the "sharpness (the *achiote*)" that he admires in those "who do the world's / businesses / And who do nature's / as I have no sense / I have done either" (*Maximus* 56). "One man," Creeley, is credited with giving this lonely, Fisher King–like figure "the world." The dedication page of *The Maximus Poems* reads:

> for ROBERT CREELEY
> —the Figure of Outward
>
> *All my life I've heard*
> *one makes many.*

Ferrini was the unnamed addressee of the first Maximus poem, his little magazine its instigation. Rejecting the long poem's first reader—and the contemporary Gloucester that he would embody—Olson signals a willingness to alienate a "mass" audience. "Limits / are what any of us / are inside of," he tells Ferrini in Letter 5, just prior to launching into a vigorous tongue-lashing of his friend. For Olson, "limits" are no less urgent for being idiosyncratically determined; his was a strictly *unconventional* model of literary exchange. Meditating on the dedication in a notebook entry dated May 1969, he wrote:

> the Figure of Outward means way out way out
> *there:* the
> "World," I'm sure, otherwise
> why *was* the pt. then to . . . write to Creeley
> daily? to make that whole thing
> double, to
> objectify the existence of an
> "Outward"? . . .
> And so to *forward* a
> motion I
> make him.
>
> (Butterick, *Guide* 3)

In August of 1950, in notes toward a never-written series called BIGMANS III, Olson had proposed a character who would disclose "the root principle, that the PERSON accomplishes the SINGLE by way of the FACT that experience is always DOUBLE" (Butterick, *Guide* xxxiii). A few months into his correspondence with Creeley, Olson was pursuing the ontological implications of collaborative practice. Figuring themselves as complementary halves of a "single human figure," the two poets could decenter the "ego as beak," save each other from solipsism, and yet avoid the disruptive intrusion of true outsiders.

"What's On between Us Is a Methodology": The Correspondence and Its Institutions

Edited and annotated by George Butterick and published by Black Sparrow Press, the first two years of Olson and Creeley's correspondence alone fill nine volumes.[13] In the most heated periods of their relationship, the poets wrote several letters to each other a day, and, on average, the correspondence was certainly a daily business for both, as regular a job as either of them had during this time. In the spring of 1950, Creeley was a twenty-three-year-old Harvard dropout living in New Hampshire with his wife, Ann, on her small trust fund, raising pigeons and chickens, and attempting to start a little magazine called the *Lititz Review.* Up to this point, his only publication experience had been his editorship of the Harvard experimental magazine the *Wake.* That an untried writer and literary entrepreneur living far afield of a major literary center could feel authorized to solicit work from Pound, Williams, Wallace Stevens, and Marianne Moore suggests just how open the literary field actually was.

The response was just encouraging enough. Of the four, Stevens and Moore politely cited overcommitment and begged off until future issues, and Pound, mostly through his wife, sent extremely partisan but consistent editorial advice. However, Williams, still laboring in relative obscurity, warmed to the strength of Creeley's editorial convictions. He also pressed Olson to send the would-be editor some material. Creeley's rejection of the poems on the grounds that Olson seemed to be "looking for a language" sparked a correspondence that would span over a thousand pages and spin off two influential little magazines. Olson and Creeley's alliance would prove to be a key axis of power in the poetry wars of the next decade and following.

The letters proved tremendously productive for both Olson and Creeley. The revised versions of "Projective Verse" and "Human Universe," as well as most of the stories Creeley would collect in *Gold Diggers* and poems that would form the first section of *For Love,* all took shape in this epistolary workshop. The letters take on a range of subjects: the *Lititz Review, Origin* magazine and publishing politics more generally, commentary on individual texts, theories of literary form, and personal life. Though there are moments when the charge of intimate connection is palpable—they call it having each other "under hand"—central events in Olson and Creeley's emotional lives (e.g., the various roles played by women, from their wives to intellectual compatriots such as Olson's other letter partner, Frances Bolderoff) are absent from these pages.[14] Reading and reworking each other's texts, they share a union on the page; they did not meet in person until March 1954 when—on Olson's urging—Creeley briefly joined the faculty at Black Mountain College. Creeley regularly invited Olson to visit New Hampshire, and Olson—bunkered in his Washington, D.C., apartment while his wife, Connie, worked as an office manager to support them—regularly declined, prompting Creeley to ask, "who is around these days . . . that can come over, thru for me" (*CC* 1:117). For Creeley, Olson's writing develops the status of a physical thing, and in his more alienated moments, a fetish: "Jesus / O / I ask nothing, absolutely, nothing from you but that you stay within reach: letters—let build this thing" (*CC* 2:39).

Olson shares a sense of the relationship's importance, though his interventions are less urgent and more frankly strategic. Referring to Creeley's most recent rejection—by the *Hopkins Review*—as well as the tepid attentions of quasi-sympathetic little magazine editors such as Richard Wirtz Emerson of *Golden Goose* and Robert Payne of the *Montevallo Review,* he writes, "how many years do we put up with'em? WE don't. Let's you and I, by God, write for eachother! I swear—what we have to do is quick, intimidate 'EM. And then go right ahead sans regard, sans anything but, make use of 'em" (*CC* 2:43). "Look, between us, we can euchre," he continues,

> A PACT: A FACT: between us . . . And none of the cheap stuff, no 1916 costume machiavel, "you, E, the cardinal, I the king," you the right, I the left, none of that, just keep our heads above, and in order that, each day, the work get done.(*CC* 2:43)

This dense, typically stenographic passage reveals just how overdetermined, even cloyingly self-conscious, the literary correspondence can be. Even as the poets provide each other with much-needed companionship, they are attempting to carve out a new position within a tradition of which they are all too aware. "A PACT" alludes to Pound's early poem by that name, which begins, "I make a pact with you, Walt Whitman— / I have detested you long enough" (*Personae* 89). Upstaging Pound's "pact" with his "fact," Olson lays claim to the materiality missing from Pound's "costume machiavel" and thus links his relationship with Creeley more immediately to Whitman's own insistent physicality than Pound's lettristic model of literary tradition could manage. The passage also seems to anticipate "I, Mencius, Pupil of the Master . . . " (1954), in which Olson transforms such lines from "A Pact" as "It was you that broke the new wood / Now it is time for carving. / We have one sap and one root— / Let there be commerce between us" into "o Whitman, / let us keep our trade with you when / the Distributor / who couldn't go beyond wood, / apparently, / has gone out of business" (*CPCO* 319). With Pound reduced to a mere "distributor," Olson (and select members of his generation) can "trade" directly with Whitman. Pound's "commerce" comes to appear formal and, despite the organicism of "one sap and one root," mildly stale.[15]

References to Whitman pepper the correspondence, often routed through Pound, and often marking the two poets' efforts to conceive the peculiarity of their literary intimacy. In a June 22, 1950 letter, one of three he wrote to Creeley on that day, Olson contemplates his debt to Pound and Pound's to Whitman: "And where, the single intelligence, to put his hand to it? / hunch again (beside, of course, his / native energy, / WHITMAN, WHITMAN, WHITMAN" (*CC* 1:140). It seems fruitful to acknowledge as well the debt Olson and Creeley's sociopoetics pays to Whitmanian homoerotism. The correspondence bears many of the attributes that Wayne Koestenbaum has identified with homoerotic collaboration: the simultaneous dismissal of women and, via a metaphorics of generation and fertility, appropriation of the feminine; the demarcation (however fluctuating) of active and passive roles; and the eroticization of the text as the conduit of intercourse between men (1–15). This last is particularly apparent in the correspondence and in the various "field" documents that emerge from it, in which the book-as-body trope of "Whoever You Are Holding Me Now in Hand" gains the added physical advantage of typography. On rare occasions, exchange works through the mediation of a female third term. Take, for instance, Olson's sated close to the letter in which he announces "A PACT: A FACT: between us": "ain't it beautiful what a kicken around . . . language can take? / ain't she lovely, / our old whore? / god damn / good" (*CC* 2:46).

While it would be possible to accumulate numerous examples of sexualized, sometimes frankly misogynistic rhetoric in Olson and Creeley's writings, this is not the most productive approach to understanding the reading formation that developed out of them. Gender and sexual anxieties are entangled in their self-fashioning rhetoric, but they do not undergird it. Clearly the quest to find an alternative to the "ego as beak" is launched from a secure home base, preferably one in which Penelope not only waits patiently but also pays the rent. I'm suggesting, however, that the spasmodic power surges in Olson and

Creeley's work derive primarily from their only partial assimilation of professional norms and behaviors, their unstable merger of "openness" and vehement selectivity. Along with "technique" and "expertise," theirs is a "company," less rationally, "of love," as Creeley puts it in the title poem of *For Love*. Problems arise when this folie à deux is made to engage other people, male or female, gay or straight.

Nine years later, Frank O'Hara would send up the absurdity of founding a "movement which will undoubtedly have lots of adherents" on the realization that "I could use the telephone instead of writing the poem," in "Personism: A Manifesto" (O'Hara, *Selected* xiv). Without the benefit of a decade's hindsight or the escape valve of camp, Olson and Creeley's hothouse collaboration not only takes seriously the possibility of "put[ing] the poem squarely between the poet and the person Lucky Pierre style," it attempts to found an oppositional poetic on this method, using it as a means of "making a way" in a literary field dominated by formalist disinterest. It is important, then, to register the charge that less overtly sexual language is made to bear in its passage between them, the relative (dis)satisfactions of their jointly conceived myth of linguistic immediacy as it becomes the basis of their friendship, their poetics, and their place in literary history. When Olson writes, in the June 22 letter, "what's on between us is also a METHODOLOGY / (you pull out, i pull out) . . . This is a LIVE WAY," the salient verbal moment is the slippery deictic "this," which both refers to "a METHODOLOGY" and, ideally, embodies it (*CC* 1:141). It may also refer to their friendship, the piece of paper that is "under hand" for both of them, and/or the Pound-Williams tradition of speech-centered poetics that they are aggressively entering.[16]

Throughout the 1950s, this methodology bore both poetic and institutional fruit. "Maximus to Gloucester, Letter 27," one of the best-known Maximus poems, can be best understood as emerging directly out of the correspondence's intense environment of linguistic intercourse. Written in 1954, but withheld from publication until the 1968 printing of *Maximus IV, V, VI*, the poem documents the experience of "generation"—a coming-into-poethood in the tradition of the *Prelude* and "Out of the Cradle Endlessly Rocking"—as present-tense revelation. Beginning with a spot of timelike "first memory" of Gloucester, Letter 27 proceeds, with cryptic excitement, to explain itself:

> This, is no bare incoming
> of novel abstract form, this
> is no welter or the forms
> of those events, this,

Greeks, is the stopping
of the battle
. . .
There is no strict personal order
for my inheritance.
. . .
      An American
is a complex of occasions,
themselves a geometry
of spatial nature.

    I have this sense,
that I am one
with my skin

    Plus this—plus this:
that forever the geography
which leans in
on me I compell
backwards I compell Gloucester
to yield, to
change
      Polis
is this

        (*Maximus* 184–85)

As Butterick's *Guide* reveals, several lines of this poem are lifted, with only slight variation, from *Adventures of Ideas* by Alfred North Whitehead, whose posthumanist "cosmology"—long known to Williams and the Objectivists—Olson had recently discovered. [17] Butterick also cites Olson's December 8, 1954 letter to Creeley, in which Olson announces the writing of "two—count em— 2 Maximuses" and notes, "I see I stole a line from you, even though it was not intended, and what I was searching for was the simplest, to say how we do have this sense of unity with our body" (*Guide* 262). The irony of this inadvertent ventriloquizing at the moment the poet feels moved to declare his personal "unity" is obvious, though not particularly shocking. Eliot's pronouncement that "immature poets imitate; mature poets steal" is already a truism in the poetic world Olson and Creeley are entering. (*Selected Essays* 182) One might argue, as Barrett Watten has, that Olson's primary mode is allegorical, an encounter of word with word, rather than of word with *world*. But one needn't take such a demystifying tack as Watten's "what appears to be an absolute of reference . . . is in fact highly tendentious, an argument with and transformation of a prior text" (*Total Syntax* 155) to grasp the referential density of the repeated "this". Olson's iteration is as much an effort at founding a "polis" of the page as it is a self-aware phenomenological exercise and—via Whitehead—an engagement with modernist metaphysics. In Letter 27 at least, textuality doesn't register as resistant; the incorporation of Whitehead and Creeley's written words is as seamless as Olson's characteristically halting rhythms will allow. There is nothing conspicuous, beyond, perhaps, the ecstatic tone that often accompanies Olson's discovery of relevant material, to mark phrases like "a complex of occasions" or "bare incoming / of novel abstract form," or indeed, "I have this sense, / that I am one / with my skin" as foreign. This blithe indifference to conventions of intellectual and literary property is fully appropriate within the correspondence's integrated relations of production and reception, Olson and Creeley's collaborative commitment to write, literally "for [in place of] eachother."[18] In this context, the poet needn't subscribe to a naive belief in the co-presence of sign and referent to write the multivalent "this" with sincerity. The legibility of that word depends, rather, on a radically limited circle of reference; it works for a readership so close to the poet that they can follow his pointed finger. The password to Olson's "polis"—his ideal community—is literally "this"; full access is granted to those who can read the deictic gesture in both performative and constative terms.

Creeley's "form is never more than extension of content" also emerges from the correspondence's overdetermined (and underpopulated) environment. Cited prominently by Olson as the second principle in "Projective Verse," Creeley's remark quickly became that essay's most-quoted soundbite. Read in its context in the letters, however, this classically avant-gardist battle cry appears as part of a strategic assessment of the literary profession and Creeley's place in it. The June 5, 1950 letter, which I'll read up to the famous formulation, begins with a citation from a memo sent him by the *Kenyon Review* and then moves to a discussion of objectivity and formalism. A refusal to send an advance check for Creeley's story "The Unsuccessful Husband," the memo is one in a series of partial rejections that would culminate in John Crowe Ransom's decision not to publish the story because it lacked plot. The ensuing theoretical discussion is thus informed by a clear sense of establishment literary values. After quoting the memo, Creeley writes:

Well, subjectivity, etc. For my money / never was: else. I.e., take it, or not (little matter): that concurrent with the 'deliberatism' of 'science':

came the supposition: that a 'cool head' needed an explicit tag. A disastrous split, nonetheless; and opposition on this head altogether useless & a waste of precious time. No such thing as 'objectivity' for the man who wants to do a good job. (*CC* 1:77)

Hermetic even by Creeley standards, this passage counters the journal's coolly conventional prose with a virtual Morse code of harshly clipped expletives. Whether Olson himself understood such writing remains an open question; his response to this letter, in which he praises Creeley's "cadence" but chides him for relying too heavily on "etc.," suggests a mutual recognition that style is an ongoing experiment. "Juxtaposition," as Olson goes on to note, is Creeley's main compositional strategy; here it enables him to skewer the false neutrality of the *Kenyon Review*'s selection criteria at the same time as he mounts a critique of formalism's philosophical premises. In the essay version of this letter, published as "Note on the Objective" the following summer, he makes the connection between objectivity and the professional self-interests of mainstream literary culture more explicit: "objectivity has become the apparent trademark of the careful mind" (*Quick Graph* 18–19).

In arguing that there is "no such thing as 'objectivity' for the man who wants to do a good job," Creeley echoes Eliot's famous contention that no verse is free for the man who wants to do a good job, itself reminiscent of Pound's paean to artisanal expertise in "I Gather the Limbs of Osiris." As in that essay, the stakes of Creeley's professional self-definition are social as well as aesthetic. In place of the instrumental use of form currently winning the favor of "the intelligence that had touted Auden as being a technical wonder," he offers Olson's injunction that "man must create himself—instrument," arguing further that it is the "possible variations on the center/creation: that make up the plot of art"(*CC* 1:78). The commodification of mind is thus replaced with a kind of intellectual Ludditism. Creeley names his "center" the "Single Intelligence" and claims that "I see no need for MORE than ONE head: if its a good one. Or better: I cannot see that such a head should feel that OTHERS were essential." In the context of Creeley's recent disappointment, the poetics of self-reliance espoused here seems at least partially defensive. Without the distraction of "possible audiences," the Single Intelligence has no choice but to create itself out of its own "essence": "form is never more than an *extension* of content." (79). The unpublished poet living quietly in New Hampshire can found a poetics on isolation.

Olson's response on June 8 makes plain the immediate and literary historical value of Creeley's formulation. Inspired by the line "form is never more than an extension of content" to comment on Creeley's poetry, Olson takes on the hyperbolic tones of a book jacket blurb, stating, "this man can truly return us to the antient anglo-saxon heart" (*CC* 1:86). Olson cites Creeley's sentence twice in his letter, once in all capital letters and once dated for posterity: "sd. R. Cr. . . . June 1950" (94). Stepping into his role as publicist and impresario for the pair, Olson capitalizes "FORM IS NEVER MORE THAN AN EXTENSION OF CONTENT," and thus suggests that it can be capitalized *upon,* both as a wedge into the current field of literature and a wager on the future. In the compressed world of the correspondence, the two poets can iterate one another into literary history with all of the efficiency the postal service can muster.

"Projective Verse," or as it was then called, "PROjective Verse vs. the NONprojective," is audible throughout this entire exchange. Accepted for publication by *Poetry New York* just prior to the poets' first contact, the essay evolved through several drafts during the first months of the correspondence. The final version, which emerges in fragments in the letters following Creeley's formulation, appeared in the October 1950 issue of the magazine surrounded by distinctly "nonprojective" poetry, including a special feature on "New British Poets."[19] Despite its inauspicious debut, the essay enjoyed a totemic status from the outset, due in part to Olson and Creeley's vigorous circulation of its precepts, both between themselves and, with the publication of *Origin* magazine, within an accumulating community of peers. In a letter to Ferrini, featured near the beginning of the special first issue of *Origin,* Olson mentions the "PV piece" so frequently that the letter concludes with an editor's note explaining that "PV refers to the significant essay in POETRY (NY), Number 3, 1950, by Olson, where he discusses what he calls PROJECTIVE VERSE" (Creeley, "Notes" 6). In "Notes for a New Prose," published in the second issue of *Origin,* Creeley also cites from the essay, ending his opening remarks on the line, "Form is the extension of content. This was the first rule" (95). Virtually unknown yet apparently significant enough to merit such oblique, past-tense references within a year of its publication, "Projective Verse" functioned as an organizational touchstone. With it, the "company of love" went public.

With the exception of a few powerfully concise imperatives, the essay itself is abstract and theoretical, an unwieldy amalgam of "new physics," wild celebrations of organic form, and quasi–New Critical notions of the well-wrought poetic artifact.[20] The first of its two parts features a technical manual for the production of open verse which proposes to get inside the "machinery, now, 1950, of how projective verse is made," and culminates with the formula: "The HEAD, by way of the EAR, to the SYLLABLE / the HEART, by way of the BREATH, to the LINE" (Olson, *SW* 17, 19). The way to get the "speech-force of language" back into poetry is formulaic, or as Olson calls it half jokingly, "dogmatic." Organic form hinges on exhortation. Promoting his technique, Olson assumes the role of the efficiency expert, stopwatch ticking as he oversees the "management of daily reality as of the daily work," urging anyone who would "set up as a poet" to "get on with it, keep moving, keep in, speed . . . USE USE USE the process at all points" (17). There's a certain Fordism in these injunctions, compromised only by their desperate tone. Projective effectiveness entails a retooling of work habits: "contemporary workers go lazy RIGHT HERE WHERE THE LINE IS BORN," and this will not do, for "*any* slackness takes off attention, that crucial thing, from the job in hand, from the push of the line under hand at the moment, under the reader's eye, in his moment" (19, 20). Technical manager morphs into birth coach/midwife; the rhetoric of "labor" culminates in a parthenogenic vision of delivery—the birth of the line from the "job in hand." This birth has to be carefully monitored, lest a "whole flock of rhetorical devices"—the lush "descriptive functions" that Pound so vigorously banished from poetry—be allowed to "sap the going energy of the content towards its form." Unabashed in its simultaneous plunder and ousting of feminized possibilities for poetic becoming, "Projective Verse's" masturbatory fantasy of simultaneous production and reception is highly precarious—"spontaneous" and yet demanding specialized care.[21]

The projective poet attempts to span two competing terrains of masculine authority—the organic ("the necessity . . . to be as wood is") and the technical. This position of precarious doubleness persists into the second half of the essay. When Olson proposes to "suggest a few ideas about what stance towards reality brings such verse into being, what that stance does, both to the poet and the reader," he sets up a system of poetic production in which poem and poet seem to have equal agency, each conditioned by a "stance" which is itself responsive to changes in the material of poetry. Arguing for "getting rid of the . . . 'subject' and his soul," Olson claims that "man is himself an object" and "the more likely to recognize himself as such the greater his advantages" (*SW* 24). The projective poet is at once an object amongst others, a "participant in the larger force," and self-reflecting witness to his object status. The boundaries of the field of "larger force" are at once open, waiting to be "enter[ed]" by the poet, and constrained by the "content and context" under hand. This double positioning produces a compromised sense of the poet's agency in the projective act:

The objects which occur at every given moment of composition (of recognition, we can call it) are, can be, must be treated exactly as they do
occur therein and not by any ideas or preconceptions from outside the
poem, must be handled as a series of objects in a field in such a way that
a series of tensions (which they also are) are made to **hold,** and to hold
exactly inside the content and context of the poem which has forced
itself, through the poet and them, into being. (20)

The parenthetical remarks interspersed throughout this passage contribute
to its spoken quality, but they also point up a certain semantic ambivalence. In
proposing the synonymy of "composition" and "recognition," Olson introduces
a waver into the text for which he then has to compensate with a series of
increasingly urgent imperatives. For "recognition" suggests a kind of leveling
mutuality that threatens to upset entirely the poet's "hold" over his material.
Objects may "occur" of their own free will, but for the poem to achieve any
aesthetic success, to become a "high energy-construct," they can't simply be,
but "must be treated." In the interplay of relations that make up "recognition,"
the objects at once "are" a "series of objects in a field" and "must be handled"
as if they were. "Tensions" are at once organic to the objects themselves and
dependent on the holding power of their container. The poet is at once "inside"
the "content and context of the poem" along with the objects, and the medium
(if not the origin) of its production.

But the slippage between subject and object, inside and outside, produces
the greatest difficulty for Olson in theorizing the projective poem's reception.
The problem arises from the fact that at some point the poet releases the poem
from "under hand" and is replaced as the vehicle for transmission of energy by
language. At once an object amongst others and the container of the other
objects' tensions, written language is a highly permeable medium, threatening,
"at all points," to discharge the poem's energies, to spill its seed in an unpredictable gush of dissemination. The distancing mechanisms of "manuscript, press,
the removal of verse from its producer and its reproducer" exacerbate a problem already endemic to the medium itself. Olson poses the question of reception early in "Projective Verse" as the first of the "simplicities" of composition
by field, but it remains open throughout the essay. Under the heading of "kinet-
ics," Olson writes:

A poem is energy transferred from where the poet got it . . . by way of
the poem itself to, all the way over to, the reader. Okay. Then the poem
itself must, at all points, be a high energy-construct and, at all points, an
energy-discharge. So: how is the poet to accomplish same energy, how is

he, what is the process by which the poet gets in, at all points energy at least the equivalent of the energy which propelled him in the first place, yet an energy which is peculiar to verse alone and which will be, obviously, also different from the energy which the reader, because he is a third term, will take away? (*SW* 16)

Far from the "first thought, best thought" ideology it would become in its "Beat" manifestations, Olson's prescription for "get[ting] in" here turns on a tortured logic of equivalence that threatens to break down over both the qualitative difference of its terms and the temporal gaps that separate its discrete moments. "Open form" does not give way to gleeful antiformalist abandon; rather it demands a highly technical, craftsmanly engagement on the part of the poet. If his role in creating and maintaining the boundaries of the "construct" is called into question in the latter part of the essay, here the poet takes center stage; he is responsible for setting the chain of equivalence into motion. The curious, textbooklike formulation, "accomplish same energy" bespeaks the difficulty of enacting this role. Moving from "same" to "at least the equivalent" to "different," the halting, extended question loses ground, inching by increments away from the immediacy of reception that it proposes. The rest of the essay can be read as an extended attempt to regain this ground by arguing for the embodied quality of poetic language and by reclaiming the typewriter for its capacity to mime the pacing of breath. But whatever it accomplishes toward getting the "speech-force" of language back into verse is done by effacing the machinery of equivalence, and by dropping the reader, as a "third term," out of the equation entirely. "Projective Verse's" circuitry of poetic exchange calls up two paradigms of male avant-garde poethood—the vatic wild man and the scientistic experimentalist—and demands that they form an unstable alliance for the sake of the poem as "high energy-construct."

Origin magazine and the *Black Mountain Review* sought to institutionalize this model of reception, to test the potential of "Projective Verse" as a technology of *community*. Each was a publishing endeavor committed—at least in principle—to literary goals beyond promoting either pure innovation or neglected writers, driven as much by poetic theory as by professional imperative. As I suggested in my context analysis of "Form is never more than an extension of content," the politics of little magazine publication was never far afield of Olson and Creeley's poetics laboratory. From the beginning of the correspondence, "the process by which a poet gets in" targeted the boundaries of the poetry scene as well as the poem. When the *Lititz Review* was still a live prospect,

Olson proposed his vision of it in a letter to Creeley: "'the job: *systematic disor-ganization*': which goes for a MAG and for a MAP and for MAK-a pome: com-position in field is such" (*CC* 1:51, italics mine).[22] When Cid Corman, an aspir-ing poet and host of the Boston public radio show "This Is Poetry," got financial backing from a wealthy listener to edit a little magazine that he planned to call either THE SPRING & THE SOURCE or *re SOURCE,* he stated his intentions to Olson in similar terms: "I'm trying to organize the issue on the principle that the mag ought to be read from cover to cover as a single effect (like a novel) not as an anthology" (G. Evans 1:79).

Lititz Review soon collapsed along with Creeley's friend Jacob Leed's printing press, and *Origin's* editorship became collective, though not necessarily conge-nial. Letters reveal Corman struggling to retain final decision-making authority in the face of the Olson/Creeley putsch. As in the first volume of *The Maximus Poems, Origin's* community—as Olson put it, "the company you cause me to keep" (G. Evans 1:180)—appears contingent on repudiation, though in the case of *Origin,* the conflict remains behind the scenes. Perhaps the most vehe-ment of the initial disputes arose over Corman's rejection of Olson's proposal that the first issue be "a movement, a composing fr. the shifting correspondence of two writers, poems and stories coming up in the progress of that correspon-dence." Such a movement "could almost be anonymous," Olson maintains, ar-guing that he wasn't trying to "arrogate . . . control" away from Corman; rather, "i am thinking of your readership and what such an intimate, moving, upshoot-ing thing as this would be for them, in the pages of, a MAG, coming, new, to their hands" (1:58–59). When Corman, apparently feeling besieged by such a joining of forces, returns, "NO assurances . . . Editing my headache. All judg-ments mine . . . Will give you whatever seems due you—as contributor . . . deal is to get the best we can: . . . Along the PROJECTIVE trail" (1:60), Olson's rejoinder—shot back immediately upon receipt of Corman's letter—is telling. Among other sources, his irritation seems to stem from Corman's unacknowl-edged use (even capitalization) of his term of art:

> You are a great fool, Corman . . . You do not know the difference between any of us just as writers who will use you and your mag to get things published and quite another will & drive, of some such writers who, recognizing the deep use a magazine can be to all who read, would be willing to go along with you in a project to put a magazine out which would be of that kind of USE. (1:62)

Personal sensitivities aside, what's at stake in this repartee is the difficulty of composing a little magazine "in the open"—without an explicit, externally determined hierarchy or division of labor ("no hierarchies . . . only eyes in all heads"), in the absence, that is, of any pretense to objectivity. Such openness courts instrumentalism, Olson argues, a criticism whose relevance to his own treatment of Ferrini and Corman I've been suggesting.

Tensions over editing philosophy are only faintly legible in the magazine itself, which—in its important 1951–57 first series—is organized around a featured writer or pair of writers, whose work spans roughly two-thirds of a given sixty-page issue. In the absence of editorial comment beyond the requisite notes on subscription and submission, the featured writer is given full reign over the "scene." Consciously or not, several of Corman's compositional decisions operate at cross-purposes, however. In the first four issues, which feature Olson, Creeley, William Bronk and Samuel French Morse, and "New Foreign Poetry," respectively, the collaged organization, the table of contents grouped by author rather than page order, and the absence of bylines on individual pieces all militate against the dominance of the featured poet even as they bank on the assumption that the various writers' work will be recognizable as their own. In a typically "projective" irony, the lack of editorial cues forces the reader to engage in a compensatory process of identification; for outside readers, the magazine's "single effect" gets lost in a series of reflexive returns to the table of contents. As if in response to this problem, issue 6 reverts to a more conventional compositional strategy, grouping the work of featured writers Williams and Duncan on consecutive pages at the beginning and end of the magazine. Here and throughout the rest of the first series' twenty-issue run, all work is identified by both author and page order in the table of contents and, in the body, by the authors' names. Oddly enough, this turn to a more user-friendly format coincided with Corman's reduction of the magazine's print run from 1,000 to 500 copies, 125 of which were subscriptions (Golding, *Outlaw* 201). *Origin's* was a readership of insiders, by necessity as much as choice. As Olson described the state of the "literary mart" in *Maximus*, Letter 16: "what do we have / but our wares? / And who to market them to, things being / how they are, but our friends? / It has come to barter, it's got so / primitive" (76).

Issues of anonymity and name value, and questions about the role of the editor as either public tastemaker or (in Olson's terms) "the agent of a collective" (G. Evans 1:138), were also pushed to the fore during the *Black Mountain Review's* 1954–57 lifespan. As rector of Black Mountain College, Olson proposed the magazine as a means of boosting low student enrollment and delegated the task to Creeley, who could edit it from his Divers Press headquarters in Mallorca.[23] Positioned, according to Olson, to "compete with Kenyon, Partisan, NMQ [New Mexico Quarterly] . . . that sort of thing" (G. Evans 2:103),

BMR was a more traditional-looking magazine than *Origin,* with a conventional masthead and contents page, identification of editor, contributing editors and contributors, critical essays, and an expansive "Books and Comment" section. Creeley was, by all appearances, a conservative editor. During the planning stages of the *Lititz Review,* he had sought the advice of Pound, who gave him "a kind of *rule book* for the editing of a magazine"(Creeley, "On *BMR*" 250). Among other principles, Pound suggested that the editor gather a nucleus of at least four writers who could be counted on to drive the content of the magazine, and then open up the rest to variety, "so that any idiot thinks he has a chance of getting in" (Creeley, "On *BMR*" 252). Creeley adhered to this advice in editing *BMR:* each issue has at least three contributing editors whose work fills approximately half of the magazine's pages. Selectivity won out over variety, however, and Creeley himself often had to fill pages using false initials and pseudonyms.

The *Black Mountain Review* was a coterie publication, drawing its contributors from Creeley's expatriate community, Black Mountain students past and present, and scattered *Origin* regulars. Though Olson had initially planned a circulation of 2,500, Creeley printed approximately 600 copies per run, of which, according to his estimates, only 200 were ever distributed ("On *BMR*" 261). Less a conscious application of "projective" compositional principles than was *Origin, BMR's* content, its form, and its positioning within the literary field often seem at odds with one another—sometimes to the point of parody. Issue 3, for instance, contains an essay entitled "Eliot and the Sense of History," which proposes to "consider seriously whether or not . . . [Eliot's] juxtaposing of scenes or quotations from the present and the past . . . is properly used," and suggests that "it is time that our Eliot criticism turned somewhat from explication to evaluation" (Kemp 38). The essay's strictly nonprojective approach to its material gives the impression that an inside joke is afoot, with an unnamed contributor to *Kenyon* or one of the other quarterlies as its most likely target. However, the shot is indirect, and, with such a small circulation, it appears certain that it would never hit its mark.

Robert Duncan's "Letters for Denise Levertov: An A Muse Ment," which appears in the same issue, also has a parodic edge, though the object of mockery is less clear. The poem reads like a winking roast of Black Mountain insiders. Lines such as: "in / spired / the aspirate / the aspirant almost / without breath," and "A great effort, straining, breaking up / all the melodic line (the lyr / ick strain?)," appear to refer to the Olsonian breathline, while Creeley's signature stutter is audible in "Better to stumb- / ll to it you cld have / knockd me over with a feather weight of words" (Duncan 19). The entire *Origin–Black Mountain*

play for the modernist inheritance comes under friendly fire in: "a flavor stink-
ing coffee / (how to brew another cup / in that Marianne Moore—/ E.P.—
Williams—H.D.—Stein— / Zukofsky—Stevens—Perse— / surrealist-dada
staind) / pot by yrs. R.D." (Duncan 21). That both Olson and Levertov inter-
preted Duncan's poem as an attack on their styles reveals how infelicitous *BMR*'s
coterie orientation could be.[24] If "to be published in the *Kenyon Review* was too
much like being 'tapped' for a fraternity," as Creeley later commented ("On
BMR" 255), the *Origin-BMR* alternative—literary institutions built on the unstable communal ground that Language writers would later call "the politics of
intention"—was like an SDS meeting without *Robert's Rules*. The little magazines' experiments in community were significantly less explosive than Black
Mountain College itself, however, where creative differences were compounded
by extreme poverty and rural isolation.[25] Olson and Creeley's "polis"—expanded, publicized, granted a small operating budget— appeared to function
most ideally on the epistolary page where it began.

"In the Field, Away from People": Ethnography, Amateurism, Ethics

Edited by Creeley and published in 1954 by his Divers Press, *The Mayan Letters*
brings together a selection of Olson's letters written during his six months in
the Yucatan. The gesture of gathering and publishing the letters only two years
after their active exchange suggests not only that their writing was a self-
consciously literary act, but that the life they record was also composed, at
least in part, under the glare of literary history. Like the hieroglyphs which
decorate the cover, Olson's "Mayan letters" are offered as "act[s] of the instant":
concrete, embodied images of lived moments. In excising his own portion of
the correspondence, Creeley worked to efface the letters' communicative function, pushing them instead toward monument and artifact. In his preface to
the Divers Press edition, Creeley writes that in receiving Olson's letters from
Mexico, he "was witness to one of the most incisive experiences ever recorded."
With a reflexive modesty typical of Creeley's most public literary pronounce-
ments, he goes on to demur, "obviously it is very simple to call it that, that is,
what then happened, and what Olson made of his surroundings and himself"
(Olson, *Mayan Letters* 5).

In the correspondence leading up to *The Mayan Letters,* the problem of place
arises, like Creeley's famous pronouncement about poetic form, as both an is-

sue of financial need and a poetic rite of passage. In the case of the trip to Mexico, money was the compelling motive. For Creeley especially, isolation, delays in the production of *Origin,* and the slim prospects for an income (he was not optimistic about winning the Guggenheim for which he had laboriously applied) were becoming unbearable. Without "degree . . . or access," the expatriate option comes to represent his main hope for both material and creative survival, as well as his only opportunity to assume a certain responsibility in providing for his family.

Olson is also ready to move, and also blames his lack of productivity on his location. When he hears about an inexpensive fare to Lerma, Mexico, and a house rentable at fifteen dollars a month, Olson prepares for departure. However, Connie is resistant to the trip, and, lacking the economic leverage to contest her, Olson reluctantly concedes, passing the information on to Creeley. Excited by the offer, Creeley immediately casts the prospect of travel in literary-historical terms, attempting to position himself among, or potentially ahead of, his expatriate modernist predecessors. In a long letter dated December 7, he muses on the travels of Pound and D. H. Lawrence, who lived in Mexico himself. Bracketing the basic issue of affordable housing for his family, Creeley takes the opportunity to argue for the superiority of Lawrence, who was able to "blend there, move there, without displacing a single THING," over Pound and Williams, who "sitting on ground, trees abt., start to hack clear a circle" (*CC* 4:73). This language will reemerge in Olson's "ego as beak" letter, written a few months later from Mexico.

In the midst of these literary musings, Olson's announcement of his departure for the Yucatan comes as a kind of sudden reality. The Mexican sojourn begins and ends with finances as its central concern. Going to Mexico for cheap rent, Olson comes back with a history of culture, a revised methodology, and an expanded sense of his role as poet/scholar/"single human figure." For Olson, the Yucatan is a "field," or more accurately, an intersection of several different fields, in which he works to immerse himself. On the one hand, it's a kind of terra incognita, its physical objects emanating the force of a history apparently just waiting to be discovered. Devoid of human confusions, this fantastic Yucatan is an ideal playground for the projective poet. On first arriving there, Olson writes, "I've been happier by an act of circumvention, the last three days. I have been in the field, away from people, working around stones in the sun, putting my hands into the dust and fragments and pieces of those Maya who used to live here" (*CC* 5:24).

The other field, whose forces both attract and repel Olson, is the competitive world of professional anthropology and archeology, a "human universe" whose (mostly financially driven) laws threaten to circumscribe his "ranging." In a letter to Corman, Olson begins what will be an ongoing process of constituting himself with and against those he perceives to be the players in this particular game of cultural capital. Remarking on the urgency of learning the Mayan language, Olson speaks of his desire to become "what they call around here a 'Mayista' (in distinction fr 'archeologista')," taking on the still-alien language to figure himself as an insider from within. Olson's capacity as an "aestheticist" to master the "living language" of contemporary Mayans will, he hopes, allow him "in . . . to those passages of man" to which "these professionals . . . these fat & supported characters" have no access (*CC* 5:25). Like the "commercial travelers from the several colleges" in "Letter for Melville 1951," the competition is here figured as financially empowered and yet ultimately "neuter" in the face of the poet's projective capacity to "get in."

But access—in the form of accreditation and the finances necessary to perform his research—doesn't come easily to Olson either; in fact the effort to gain it becomes his main occupation in the Yucatan. In order to make his mark on the field of Mayan studies, which he proposes to do initially by proving that the Mayans were a fishing people and that their contemporary language bears the traces of their ancient past, Olson has to compete for precedence against an entrenched team of professionals funded by the Carnegie Endowment, the Mexican government, and major American museums. The urgency of the struggle forces a keen awareness of self-interest on Olson's part. How can he, as a poet, justify investing time and money in a battle not even on his own terrain? Stepping outside of the domestic literary field, Olson relinquishes one set of institutional guidelines for determining what sorts of investments are relevant to his particular occupation and takes up another—is he looking for "returns in verse" or "a jeep, a job and immediate publication of results"? (*CC* 5:73). In the context of this struggle to define his own domain, the discovery of the ancient glyphs becomes instrumental, "the pay-off, the inside stuff" (73). Imagining an issue of *Origin* devoted to illustrations of his findings that would "sock any reader," Olson immediately secures the permission of a local artist to use his work; scholarly discovery and copyright go hand in hand.

Part of what makes the glyphs so accessible to Olson is that he has poetic precedent for their value. In "discovering" and arguing for the broad cultural import of an ancient nonalphabetic language, Olson is clearly working in the modernist tradition; with the glyphs, he is no longer competing on local turf with Mayan experts but on the international poetic stage with Pound and Fenellosa. Not surprisingly, then, when Olson suggests that *Origin* publish the drawings, he does so with the expressed intent to edge out material on the

Cantos which Corman has recently received. The glyphs are "much more available" than Chinese ideograms, Olson argues, because coming from "this geography" they are "ours" (*CC* 5:91), and because they are "both ideographic and phonetic," imbued with the originary force of spoken language lost to the disembodied logics of the modern West. Of course in executing this linguistic coup, Olson has to further a misreading; in order to assert the superiority of the glyph, Olson has to follow Fenellosa and ignore the phonetic, conventional character of the ideogram.

The argument for the presentational value of the glyphs, the claim that they are language as "the act of the instant," is at the core of "Human Universe" (*SW* 54). This argument is easy to make and impossible to prove because Olson, as he freely admits, does not have command over the contemporary, spoken, Mayan language. In a self-constituting turn typical of his Mayan experience, Olson reclaims his linguistic and cultural ignorance as aesthetic strength. "No one has seen the glyphs as what they are," he claims. "They have all been so blinded by not knowing their 'meanings' that they have missed the real point, that, in themselves as *images,* they tell, tell, tell!"(*CC* 5:91).[26] Olson thus establishes for himself the double position that he will continue to occupy throughout *The Mayan Letters* and into *Maximus*. He is at once a scholar-poet learned enough in obscure, extrapoetic disciplines to outpace his dilettante modernist fathers and a wunderkind in the professional world of social science, equipped with the kind of amateur intuition that allows him to experience the scholarly object in its "authenticity," rather than through the blinders of expert culture.

But in the competitive field of research grants and government subsidies, Olson's defiant amateurism—while gaining him a private sense of superiority—is an economic liability. In order to play the game with any kind of results, Olson must establish a new discipline in which he can be an expert. Since the glyphs are "verse," as Olson argues in "Human Universe," they present the perfect opportunity for consolidating the field of "culture-morphology."[27] An amalgam of ethnography, anthropology, archeology, linguistics, and literary criticism, Olson's culture morphology is radically, and unpredictably, interdisciplinary. "Only a poet," he argues, "now can be said to possess the tools to practice culture-morphology at its best" (*CC* 5:88). Only a few, very special, poets: among his colleagues in this virtually personal field, Olson most openly admires Robert Barlow, a poet and anthropologist who worked among the Mayans and who committed suicide a few weeks before Olson arrived in Mexico. Memorialized in letters to both Creeley and Corman, Barlow emerges as an important role model in the *Maximus Poems,* where he is figured as "the / Androgyne who hates / the simulacrum / Time Magazine / takes for male" (127). The letter to Corman reveals that Olson meant this image to suggest "the combination . . . of documentarian & the selectivity of the creative taste and mind" that he sees as "prime to creative work" (G. Evans 1:95). However, the fact that Barlow's suicide was rumored to be a response to threatened blackmail over his homosexual activities shifts the sexual register into sharper relief. A strikingly Platonic image for a poet who, in "Human Universe," blamed Greek idealism for the corruption of Western civilization, the figure of the androgyne suggests that in treading disciplinary boundaries, the poet/culture morphologist "goes both ways." Given his violent rejection of Ferrini and other (sexually ambiguous) figures who pose threats to the phallic immediacy of his limited cohort, Olson's admiration for Barlow as androgyne appears especially noteworthy; along with "Projective Verse's" merger of hero-poet and technical expert, and his early poem's compromise with professional Melvilleans, it is an instance of his occasional, strategic use of various modes of doubleness as a means of making a way on the cultural field.

Not all of Olson's acknowledged predecessors in his newly established discipline were such marginal, tragic types, however. He also cites as inspiration Bronislaw Malinowski, perhaps the most influential figure in cultural anthropology in the twentieth century. Malinowski's major work, *Argonauts of the Western Pacific,* published in 1923 and reprinted several times thereafter, ushered the discipline into a new era by pioneering the concept of "field work" and inventing the genre of modern ethnography. Distinguishing his methodology from the "armchair" approach that had characterized anthropological study in the previous century, as well as from amateur cultural observers of the colonial era such as missionaries and travel writers, Malinowski argued for the importance of immersion in the culture under study. He maintained that in order to bring some sense of the "flesh and blood" of native life to ethnographic work, the writer must "put aside camera, notebook and pencil, and join himself in what's going on" (21).

Malinowski's method, advanced with great popular acclaim and institutional support in the thirties and forties by cultural relativists like Ruth Benedict and Margaret Mead, framed anthropological research in terms of a distinctive authorial stance.[28] In the field, Malinowski argued, the ethnographer has to be as much object as subject of his scientific gaze: "the writer is his own chronicler and historian at the same time" (3). Malinowskian cultural anthropology turns on the double positioning that would be objectified in the new professional category of "participant observer": the field-worker needs to be immersed enough to develop "equal" relations within the culture he is studying, but si-

multaneously capable of viewing even his own role in those relations scientifi-
cally.[29] Malinowski conceives of this border problem in terms of the constraints
of professionalism. In the area of establishing the patterns of a given culture
via "statistical documentation," he writes, "scientific field work excels over amateur"; however, the "amateur can bring intimate touches of native life . . . flesh
and blood" (17). From Malinowski on, professional anthropology must contain
amateurism, figured in idealized terms as the transcendence of cultural difference, *within* its disciplinary boundaries.[30] The field is founded on the paradox
of privileging Western scientific ideals in the name of cultural relativism: "The
time when we could tolerate accounts presenting us the native as a distorted,
childish caricature of a human being are gone," Malinowski declares in his introduction. "This picture is false . . . and it has been killed by Science" (11).

The similarities between Malinowski's construction of the stance of the ethnographer and Olson's doubled positioning of the projective poet are striking.
Olson was not a disciple of the Polish anthropologist, but—as is the case with
so much of his scholarship—he had read and internalized at least a representative fragment of Malinowski's work. A few months before departing for Mexico,
Olson quotes an extended passage from Malinowski on the role of myth in
primitive societies in a letter to Creeley. Rather than "explanation put forward
to satisfy scientific curiosity," Malinowski claims that myth is "the re-arising of
primordial reality in narrative form . . . through which the present life . . . fate
and work of mankind are governed" (*CC* 3:135). For Olson, Malinowki's rejection of the "desire to explain" in favor of an argument for mythic language
as the "continuance" of an original reality is "the poet's answer." Summoning
Malinowski against "ENEMIES" whom he views as obsessed by "scientific curiosity," Olson begins to construct the argument for the presence of primordial
reality in contemporary Mayan life and language before the trip to Mexico becomes a possibility. A temporary adoption of the professional discourse and
disposition of cultural anthropology enables Olson to better oppose the formalist literary establishment.

Whether or not Olson's Mayan research was directly prompted by his admiration for Malinowski, his formulation of the experience in "Human Universe"
not only echoes the rhetorical positioning of the cultural relativist ethnographer, but contends with similar problems of observation and disruption, translation and projection. Written initially as part of a failed grant proposal to the
Viking Fund, an anthropological foundation, it also registers the impact of the
economic exigencies of that field. I read "Human Universe" as an attempt to
answer the question of transmission that "Projective Verse" leaves open:

> what is the process by which the poet gets in, at all points energy at least
> the equivalent of the energy which propelled him in the first place, yet
> an energy . . . which will be, obviously, also different from the energy
> which the reader . . . will take away? (SW 16)

Despite the fact that, in the Yucatan, he spends most of his time distinguishing
himself from the other agents on the Mayan field, Olson casts the move from
Washington to Mexico as a move to efface difference—professional, cultural,
racial. Moving from Washington to Mexico, Olson attempts to leave behind
the burdensome apparatus of science, philosophy, and poetics that "Projective
Verse" failed to fully assimilate. The shift can be traced within "Human Universe" itself. The essay begins with a long excursus on the alienating effects of
symbol and comparison, breaks, and then begins again in a more personal
register: "I have been living for some time amongst a people who are more or
less directly the descendants of a culture and a civilization which was a contrary
of that which we have known" (SW 56). Next to the relatively heady, academic
language of the opening, the rhetoric of ethnography comes to signify the amateur in the most valued sense of the term—open, immediate, "common." Olson
cites his capacity to fit into the Mayan culture, "the admission these people
give me," as proof of the possibility of a continuous transfer of energy, unbroken
by the alienating differences between object, image, and action in which the
language worker traffics. The Mayan flesh, which "they wear . . . with that difference which the understanding that it is common leads to" (57), holds the
answer to "Projective Verse's" hysterical questioning; it allows Olson to evade
the difficult translation between inside and outside that the earlier essay
struggled with in poetic terms. "The admission these people give me and one
another is direct, and the individual who peers out from that flesh is precisely
himself, is a curious wandering animal like me," marvels the poet, having
found projective paradise. Unable to speak their language, Olson projects his
poetic paradigm onto the silent Mayans, and, in the name of valuing their open
disposition toward nature, assimilates it to his struggle with the poetic
establishment.[31]

In the second and third volumes of The Maximus Poems, as well as in public
appearances such as the "reading" at the Berkeley Poetry Conference of 1965
discussed in the previous chapter, Olson's ethnographic border crossing turns
inward. His capacity to bypass a variety of alienating racial, professional, geo-
graphical, and linguistic constructs in favor of direct access to "high energy"
gets resituated within a self that appears open to boundless expansion, not so

much transcending difference as containing and/or schizophrenically embodying it. The self-given license to travel across institutional domains that I've been calling Olson's "amateurism" is both an outsider's privilege in a world bounded by profession and discipline, and, increasingly, a personal crisis. "Cole's Island," a fairly long yet self-contained poem written in 1964 and included in the third volume of *Maximus,* dramatizes the comeuppance that the projective poet comes to fear, and offers intimations of a mortality that seems to be designed exclusively for him (436–37). Significantly more narrative than any of the surrounding poems, "Cole's Island" tells the story of the poet's confrontation with Death, figured, significantly, as "a property owner," a "sort of country / gentleman, going about his own land." The poem begins simply, "I met Death." It then proceeds to amplify and reamplify the situation of their encounter, which takes place while the poet and his son are exploring Cole's Island, a "queer isolated and gated place" off the coast of Cape Ann. Less surprised to see Death in the flesh than to see anyone in a place "more private than almost any place one might imagine," the poet describes the encounter with remarkable calm as "uncomfortable," noting that "my difficulty, / when he did show up, was immediately at least that I was / an intruder." Nothing happens; after a stretched-out moment, Death "went on without anything extraordinary at all," leaving the poet to ponder the implications of the meeting. And he does, with a quiet wonder that could hardly be further from the hectoring "I, Maximus" of the long poem's opening:

> It was his eye perhaps which makes me
> render him as Death? It isn't true, there wasn't anything
> that different about his eye,
>
>   it was not one thing more than that he was Death instantly
> that he came into sight. Or that I was aware there was a person
> here as well as myself. And son.
>
>   We did exchange some glance. That is the fullest possible
> account I can give, of the encounter.
>
> <div align="right">(<i>Maximus</i> 437)</div>

The sudden awareness of another person with whom the self can "exchange some glance" is rendered equivalent, here, to an encounter with death. In both cases, difference is admitted: a boundary is crossed and suddenly rendered starkly visible. The poet is a guilty trespasser.

After "Cole's Island," volume 3 resumes its exploratory ambition, seeking out "an actual earth of value to / construct one, from rhythm to / image" (584), but the journey is at once more mystical and more personal—much of the large-scale history and geography drops out. Somehow chastened, the long poem never fully recovers its missionary zeal. The final line—written just before Olson's death in 1970 and several years after the car-crash death of his second wife, Betty—reveals the poet returning to a sense of limits, this time without the accompanying repudiations. The last page of *Maximus* reads simply:

> my wife my car my color and myself

and thus lays claim to an isolation and an inwardness from which the ambitious position takings of an entire poetic career have been banished (635). But the trappings of a social existence remain. There's an incongruity between the first two terms in this brief catalogue and the last two ("color" here suggesting the poet's progressing illness), and of course "my wife" and "my car," however tragically conjoined in the poet's memory, could use significantly more distinguishing than the white space between them can accomplish. Yoked together by the reiterated possessive, these elemental nouns are meant to consolidate identity, but the catalogue form leaves their success open to question. Read skeptically, this is a consumer's dirge, its emptiness the payback for a life lived on the right side of the gender, race, and class divide. A more generous reading lingers on the loneliness of this most public of poets' final stand. Culminating but not necessarily encompassing, "myself" is a term in a series whose unspoken commonality is loss.

Creeley and "The Business"

From his early short stories to his most recent poetry, Creeley has always claimed the interior as his personal projective territory, and while Olson sought the public stage, he cultivated the persona of the poet-hermit. He did not remain forever on the margins, however. After a decade of activity on the alternative publishing scene, in 1960 Creeley became the first new poet Scribner's — a respected, private, but nonetheless commercial publishing house—had taken on in eight years. Not surprisingly, he made his entree through prose; Michael Rumaker, a former student from Black Mountain College, recommended Creeley for inclusion in Scribner's annual *Short Story* series, and Creeley convinced his editor, Donald Hutter, to consider his poems as well. The company was in the midst of reevaluating its approach to the publishing of poetry. Hutter recognized the quality of the work immediately, and the question soon came down to a commercially feasible book format. Disappointed by the presentation of his work in *Short Story #3,* Creeley lobbied heavily against the mini-anthology model, arguing that groups of writers cannot be "presented" simultaneously. "Either they are given a single face, or else they become anonymous, simply 'new writers,'" he writes, suggesting that it might finally be more profitable for both writer and publisher to offer several smaller publications and "give one writer a fair chance for being read clearly and without distortion—in paperback" (Creeley to Hutter, November 2, 1960, Scribner's Archives). The editing philosophy pioneered on the pages of *Origin* here translates into marketing savvy. His timing was just right. The third "paperback revolution" had hit the publishing industry in the decade following the war, and Scribner's was reaping the benefits with its reprint series, *The Scribner Library.* A collection of Creeley poetry, of the appropriate size and bulk, would be the prototype for a new paperback imprint of first editions.

When Creeley entered the large-scale publishing scene, then, it was with the cachet of a "collected poems." By dint of the compactness of his lyrics combined with developments in publishing technology, he was already a "major" poet. The book impressed literary figures as various as W. S. Merwin and Lawrence Ferlinghetti, who acknowledged somewhat sheepishly that he hadn't liked Creeley's poetry until it came out under the aegis of a major publisher, saying, "my excuse will have to be that the poems, taken all together, have a gestalt I hadn't sensed before" (quoted in Creeley to Hutter, May 2, 1962, Scribner's Archives). The figure that emerges from *For Love*'s 160 pages is that of the awkward lover: ironic, self-effacing, and poised—by virtue of the poems' careful lineation—somewhere between bumbling and graceful self-restraint. These characteristics, along with the poems' epigrammatic finality and riddling quality, brought Creeley numerous imitators in the sixties.

But the figure of the poet finding his solitary way, and of the poem as a place "stumbled into," as Creeley writes in the preface to *For Love,* doesn't fully register the acute sense that we find in the correspondence of the conditions under which poems are produced. In fact, a closer look at the individual poems reveals them to be working out the problematics of immediacy and exchange that the two poets explored in their letters. Two poems written in the mid-fifties, "The Business" and "The Invoice," make this connection most manifest:

THE BUSINESS
To be in love is like going outside to see what kind of day

it is. Do not
mistake me. If you love

her how prove she
loves also, except that it

occurs, a remote chance on
which you stake

yourself? But barter for
the Indian was a means of sustenance.

There are records.

(CPRC 138)

THE INVOICE
I once wrote a letter as follows:
dear Jim, I would like to borrow
200 dollars from you
to see me through.

I also wrote another: dearest M/
please come.
There is no one
here at all.

I got word today,
viz: hey
sport, how are you making it?
And, why don't you get with it.

(CPRC 183)

Both poems' titles name the impossible situation of the lover; love is structured like capitalism, in which value is never fully realized in the present of exchange. In "The Business," being "in love" is a little like being "in plastics." Betting on the economic weather, the speaker must "stake himself" and wait for a return, but he can never be sure if it's his investment that paid off. An intransitive business, love "occurs"; she may love, but not him. Against this impersonal form of exchange, barter figures the fantasy of immediacy and/as value, the possibility of having each other "under hand." The dark joke is, of course, that colonialist barter destroyed "the Indian"—"staked" him, in fact—and "records" are virtually all that remains from that particular transaction.

"The Invoice" takes up a similar problematic, only here the temporal disjunction of exchange—of both love and money—is figured through halting rhythms of the letter-writing mode. Letters can get lost, or crossed, in the mail;

address, in writing, is never completely direct. And again, the exchange threatens not to pay off. In response to his desperate inquiries, the speaker receives not money or love, but "word"—disembodied and not particularly supportive. The poet clearly isn't "making it"—in the professional or the sexual sense—and the implication is that his failure in both realms is mutually reinforcing.

With their overlapping rhetorics, these poems are representative of much of the work in *For Love*. But the last poem in the volume, which shares its title with the book, occupies the tense intersection of money and love, profession and vocation, not just in word but in deed. Written in September 1960 during Creeley's negotiations with Scribner's, "For Love" is what might be called a "book poem." Quite long by early Creeley standards, the two-page poem gathers up the familiar figures of a decade of poetry and of being a poet. Dedicated, as is the whole volume, to Bobbie, Creeley's second wife, "For Love" operates within the romantic fiction that poems and books are written for private consumption at the same time as it works to package the contents of this particular book—whose narrative, the marriage plot, traces an arc between two wives—for broad distribution. The rhetorical position of the poem's speaker is doubled; he is directly addressing both Love and his book, attempting to occupy the fleeting moment of exchange even as he turns back to survey the past of his own work. "Here is tedium, / despair, a painful / sense of isolation and / whimsical if pompous / self-regard" (*CPRC* 257–58), he says midway through the poem, a kind of ironic self-promotion—as a poet and a lover—that we now recognize as distinctively Creeleyesque. The poem closes with a quiet confidence: "Into the company of love / it all returns." I am tempted to read these lines as bespeaking the certainty of professional affirmation, a return on a decade's careful investment, as much as the optimism of a new marriage.

They are also a citation, a near-direct echo of Hart Crane's "The Broken Tower": "And so it was I entered the broken world / To trace the visionary company of love" (Crane, *Complete Poems* 193). Working to package the volume, the nod to Crane here gestures at the first poem in *For Love*. That poem, an elegy called "Hart Crane," closes by citing the line "And so it was I entered the broken world" in its entirety. "Hart Crane" had been Creeley's only contribution to the inaugural issue of *Origin* magazine, where it introduced him in the shadow of his tragic poetic idol, "stuttering, by the edge / of the street" (*CPRC* 109). Nearly a decade later, the last poem in *For Love* signals the distance Creeley has traveled—from "broken[ness]" to "company"—simply by crossing Crane's linebreak. It also incorporates the dead poet's language into its own without attribution or "stuttering."

Another decade—and two volumes of poetry—later, the final poem in

Pieces (1969) also dramatizes the merger of men and the crossing of boundaries, both linear and bodily. Unlike many of the poems in *For Love* which
narrate a failure to connect, in this poem the fantasy of immediacy prevails—
achieved through the mediation of a woman. In it, we read a headier, more
psychedelic version of "A PACT: A FACT." As in so many of the manifestations of
that earlier social compact, the "meeting" here is forged through the instrumen-
talization/rejection of an Other. Since the enjambment of stanzas is so critical
to the poem's sense, I will cite it in its entirety :

> When he and I,
> after drinking and
> talking, approached
> the goddess or woman
>
> become her, and by my
> insistence entered
> her, and in the ease
> and delight of the
>
> meeting I was given that
> sight gave me myself,
> this was the mystery
> I had come to—all
>
> manner of men, a
> throng, and bodies of
> women, writhing, and
> a great though seemingly
>
> silent sound—and when
> I left the room to them,
> I felt, as though hearing
> laughter, my own heart lighten.
>   (*CPRC* 445–46)

The courtly postures of *For Love* have given way to slipperier poetic surfaces;
Pieces is a looser book, both prosodically and socially. Relations between people
are less rigidly defined, and the scene of exchange is significantly more
crowded. *For Love*'s "I/you" diffuses into "he and I" and "her," and finally an
orgiastic "throng." That these others—"he" and "the goddess or woman / become her" in particular—exist for the main purpose of stabilizing and completing the "I" is obvious from the triumphant final stanza, though the very last
lines of *Pieces,* separated by a bullet from this poem, return to uncertainty:

What do you do,
what do you say,
what do you think,
what do you know.
(*CPRC* 446)

As we've seen, this deflating move is Creeleyesque, a signature humility whose very prevalence in his work opens more questions than it resolves. After all, the "I" of the preceding poem has readily availed himself of whatever knowledge the "goddess or woman / become her" has to offer; "enter[ing] / her" is a matter of simple "insistence." In his insightful, if extreme, reading of the poem, Ted Pearson puts the stakes of this act quite bluntly:

> Now if it is a "woman" who is "entered," whatever else that may imply, it does imply that they fuck her. The manner and intent with which they do so remains unspecified, and perhaps irrelevant; but that her agency, desire, and status as a person are also unspecified . . . is not irrelevant, because . . . this nonspecific "female" figure is reduced to her object status, her use value, and very little else. And if her use is not a form of rape, it very well might be . . . This connection between rape and (male self-)knowledge is, of course, one of literature's most durable tropes. (162)

Olson and Creeley forged their collaborated careers and worked to complete their authorial selves through a complex and often indelicate interplay of openness and force, untrammeled by the limits of professional etiquette, impervious—ideally—to boundaries of either body or discipline. Rape figures an extreme to which even their most brutal sociopoetic practices do not go. We've seen, however, that the liberating promise of projective institutions depends on a range of "insistences"; immediacy and a full recognition of others' difference appear to be mutually exclusive.

3

The Legacy of Louis Zukofsky

In his lifetime, Louis Zukofsky had at least two poetic careers—one in the 1930s and another in the 1960s—neither of which brought him the acknowledgment that he and his most ardent admirers felt he deserved.[1] That he had any public reception at all is surprising, more of a credit to the power of literary networks at two particularly organized moments in the twentieth-century American avant-garde than to vigorous self-promotion on the part of the poet. Chronologically and temperamentally, Zukofsky is not the most obvious candidate for inclusion in a study of avant-garde poetic careers in the 1950s and 1960s. Suspicious and even disdainful of both the contemporary literary marketplace and what he felt to be the homogenizing tendency of academic literary history, Zukofsky began his writerly life as a young, multiply ghettoized fellow traveler of modernism: a communist, Jewish, lower-class would-be Poundian. As his career progressed and his attachment to these identity markers waned, Zukofsky continued to style himself as an outsider to the prevailing literary moment, preferring to concentrate on producing a life's work that would be "durable as one thing from 'itself never turning'" rather than to wrangle for power with his contemporaries on the literary field (*Bottom* 13). Since his death in 1978, scholars have granted him his wish, generally reading his "poem of a life," as he called *"A,"* as an organic progression from modernism to postmodernism, untrammeled by idiosyncrasies of social, psychological, or material situation.[2] In this chapter, I read Zukofsky against this grain, contending that the ambitious sociopoetic cross-pollination that I've been associating with the notion of "career" is in fact operative in his work, albeit in complex and sometimes negative ways. To begin to understand his often resistantly difficult poetry, I argue, we have to uncover the jagged social predicament that both the poet and many of his recent critics would smooth over.

Zukofsky's first poetic career began in 1928 with the Pound-sponsored publication of his "Poem Beginning 'The'" in *Exile*, peaked early with his Pound-sponsored editorship of the "Objectivists" issue of *Poetry* magazine in 1931, and ended—for observers of modernism—with Pound's withering afterword to the *Active Anthology*: "a whole school or shoal of young American writers seems to me to have lost contact with language as language . . . in particular Mr Zukofsky's Objectivists seem prone to this error" (253). True to his unpredictable form, Pound dedicated his *Guide to Kulchur* (1938) "to Louis Zukofsky and Basil Bunting strugglers in the desert," but the war soon supplanted literary politicking as his primary preoccupation. Without the erratic, often personally wounding, but always professionally useful attentions of his well-connected "papa," Zukofsky quickly disappeared from the public stage.

During the late 1930s, 1940s, and early 1950s, he completed the first half of *"A."* Though it fits quite neatly into the twentieth-century long poem tradition, *"A"* is still not a familiar work to many readers. Made up of twenty-four formally disparate "movements," it was begun in 1928 as an effort to transfer the "design of the fugue" (*"A"*-6 38) to poetry, and completed—with similar musical intentions but in a very different voice—in 1974. As I mentioned above, Zukofsky called *"A"* "a poem of a life," and over the forty-six years of its composition, the long poem takes in and transmutes the personal, poetic, and social history with which it coincides. As it progresses, however, it becomes more form-conscious, more "personal"—though this becomes a complex idea in Zukofsky—and more difficult to read, a development that takes place, strangely enough, during relatively successful periods in the poet's career. In the lull before those periods, he finished the first twelve movements, married Celia Thaew in 1939, had a son, Paul, in 1943 ("my wife Celia and son Paul have been the only reason for the poet's persistence," he wrote in *Autobiography* [59]), published two collections of shorter poems to limited notice, and began work on his major critical text, *Bottom: On Shakespeare*. He also pursued a collaborative friendship with William Carlos Williams that resulted in his editorship of *The Wedge* (1948). Williams dedicated that book "To L. Z.," and wrote appreciative reviews of the younger poet's first two collections.[3]

Zukofsky's "renaissance" didn't begin in earnest until 1954, however, when Creeley—piqued by Pound and Williams' dedications, as well as by Edward Dahlberg's encouragements—invited him to contribute to the *Black Mountain Review.* Creeley's commitment spurred Cid Corman into launching the second series of *Origin* magazine with special attention to Zukofsky's homophonic translations of Catullus, and ultimately printing a small run of *"A"*-1–12 in 1960. By 1962, Zukofsky had become a regular presence in *Kulchur,* a review of the New York art scene edited and funded by literary socialite Lita Hornick. His currency within New York and Black Mountain circles yielded the first commercial publication of his work: W. W. Norton's 1965 edition of *All: The Collected Shorter Poems, 1923–1958,* a project facilitated by Denise Levertov, who was then the poetry advisor to the press.[4] For a brief moment, he was simultaneously a respected elder and something of a novelty in poetry circles. After Williams' death in 1963, the Brooklyn home that Zukofsky shared with his wife, Celia, temporarily replaced Paterson as the destination of younger poets' pilgrimages, even as he was being invited to read alongside Jerome Rothenberg, Paul Blackburn, and Jackson MacLow on the downtown café circuit. As Ted Berrigan—who sent Zukofsky the first issue of *"C"* magazine—put it: "in the early sixties in New York, the young guys had Louis Zukofsky jammed down their throats" (Ratcliffe and Scalapino 65). Aware and wary of this precarious situation, Zukofsky expressed the sense, in a 1963 letter to Corman, that younger poets were as ready to accept as to forget him, musing over the relative (de)merits of *"A's"* status as required reading (1/17/63).

Rather than a singular trajectory from anonymity to notoriety, Zukofsky's public career takes the form of a stutter: repetition, forgetting, and loss of control flood the poet's experience of the contemporary literary field. Zukofsky's reputation was out of his hands; from his perspective, production and reception operated as two distinct systems, not negotiable by the poet. As the brief reception histories above suggest, this sense of disjunction is partially attributable to the accident of time, compounded by the poet's own intractability. Modernist networks—with Pound at their center—created the conditions for his poetic debut, but just as he was beginning to acquire enough cachet to shape the field in his own image, the institutional structures sustaining his still-fragile public identity collapsed, or at least shifted significantly. Zukofsky was resistant to becoming a "double personage"; during the editing of the "Objectivists" issue of *Poetry,* the primary institutional activity of his early career, he complained to Pound, "I can't be an editor, midwife to boys & girls, a hysterectomer in private and a poet in public all at once. I'm not a universal" (Ahearn, *Pound/ Zukofsky* 64).

But the ability to wear many hats was becoming an increasingly important part of the postwar innovative poet's job description. Zukofsky's commitment to poetic autonomy condemned him to a passive role in the distribution of cultural capital, a position that he did not accept easily. The artful surfaces of the later poetry occasionally split open under the burden of accumulated neglect. Take these lines from *"A"*-18 (1964–66), for instance, which lash out at the crowded 1960s avant-garde scene in which Zukofsky was so readily superseded:

> . . . dim to sum up
> but that one horror dims another, I cannot
> teach-in, sit-in, orgy-for nor will in obscurity malinger
> for those competing to gag they needed me—
> how ineffable such a small flatulence of the
> intelligent and discriminating General Reader sounder than whose
> *Pew* black or white competitively they're the same.
>
> ("A"-18 398)

Or the more contained and melancholic but no less resentful "Voice off" that interrupts his "translation" of Plautus' *Rudens* in *"A"*-21 (1967):

> I was
> being poor
> termed difficult
> tho I attracted a cult
> of leeches
> and they signed *love*
>
> . . .
>
> And tho love starve
> carved mostly bones
> (not *those* young friends
> put to good use)
> if I'm not dead
> a dead mask smiles
> to all old friends
> still young where else

> it says *take care*
> *prosper*
> without my tongue
> only your own
> ("A"-21 500)

Figuring himself as carrion in the mouths of scavenging younger poets, and then as a Dorian Gray-like death mask whose decay keeps his "old friends" young, Zukofsky endures the ravages of "social aging" on his physical body.[5] The final lines' confusion of pronouns and body parts registers the alienating effects of having to share one's cultural space with an ever-changing set of peers. Less an effort to intervene in the contemporary literary field than to guard against its fickleness, Zukofsky's later work retreats into the more controllable domain of home, family, and a language that would purge itself of social exigency by rejecting models of communication and exchange in favor of what Jean Baudrillard has called a "system of objects": an interrelated set of possessions through which the poet seeks to accrue a self-mastering, timeless subjectivity (17). A species of projective institution not unlike Olson and Creeley's "company of love," the collection—a form that Zukofsky's later work could be said to approximate—is withdrawn from the world but never fully distinct from its values; rather, it transposes them into a closed space where they can be recycled ad infinitum. In what follows, I examine this process of transposition and recycling—Zukofsky called it "fuguing," among other things—as it is anticipated in his early work, theorized in *Bottom: On Shakespeare,* and practiced, not only in the second half of "A," but also in the production of the Zukofsky collection at the University of Texas and in his critical reception. Highlighting moments in which "objects" resist integration into the system, I suggest that Zukofsky's strategy for control over temporal and social contingency demands a sacrifice from both the poet and his "implied reader" as embodied, desiring *subjects.*

As I've already mentioned, Zukofsky's posthumous reception has finally succeeded in securing him a place in the avant-garde canon, where he lives on as a progenitor of postmodernism, a consummate experimentalist, and a left-leaning political savior for beleaguered Poundians. From this most recent perspective, Zukofsky's career was always that of a great and major poet, albeit one who was skeptical of the totalizing assumptions on which "greatness" is premised. Owing partly to the fact that a biography has not yet been published, partly to the tendency of the canonization process to substitute the long view for the shuttling movement of a life lived, and partly to his own poetic practices, Zukofsky's life has been emptied of the most vexed features of his writerly experience: namely, his refusal/failure to "have contemporaries" and its relationship to his elected/imposed obscurity.[6]

I seek to understand the origins of this scholarly treatment in Zukofsky's own self-fashioning practices. The slash marks in the paragraph above locate critical undecidability at precisely the place where a confident assertion of poetic agency should go. I leave them in my text because such undecidability—which might take the form of the question, "Did I kill my career or find it already dead?"—is at the core of Zukofsky's self-fashioning project, the aporia around which he develops his sense of time and poetic trajectory. In phrasing the argument this way, I am reinscribing a compromised kind of agency, what I called in the last chapter the "professionalization of a predicament." That is, I am arguing that passivity functions strategically in Zukofsky; it is a way to avoid both credit and blame for the state of his career. If I err on the side of the biographical—reading the penumbra of the poetic career along with the more polished poetic output—it is a compensatory gesture, one that feels both necessary and slightly heretical in the context of a poet whose publicity campaign consisted of the repeated assertion that "the work says all there needs to be said of one's life" (Autobiography, prefatory). My purpose is not to flout his wishes; indeed, I don't think they are so easy to determine. Rather I want to gauge the pressure that his insistence on privacy along with his commitment to mastering new extremes of formal and allusive difficulty brings to bear on the work as well as on the life. These two tendencies combine to produce a contradictory figure of the poet as a disinterested (Olson might say "neuter") experimentalist in whose work we can detect strong, if often obscured, psychosocial investments. The reader, by extension, is required to be part philologist, part voyeur. In the ideal case, the latter identity motivates and then quickly dissolves into the former.

In "The Death of the Author," Roland Barthes defined writing as "that neuter, that composite, that obliquity into which our subject flees, the black and white where all identity is lost, beginning with the very identity of the body that writes" (52). In Zukofsky's work, the subject's flight into "obliquity" is not accomplished without a sacrifice, of both "the body that writes" and the reader who would pursue an identificatory, empathic engagement. Nor does the writerly "neutrality" of his text displace his distinctively male avant-garde poetic positioning. Svetlana Boym argues with respect to "death of the author" discourse that "behind Foucault's erasure of life, the Mallarmean *blanc,* there is an assumed normative middle-class, eventless life and an assumed historical context that makes it possible." "It is not accidental," she continues, "that the first criticism of the Structuralist resistance to biography came from Feminist critics" (24). As I suggested in my discussion of the ethics (implied and socially manifest) of Olson and Creeley's projective poetics, the "open" stances of the postwar avant-garde are tied to a certain ego imperialism; in their work, immediacy depends on the elision (or the use) of others. A similar dynamic is operative in Zukofsky's work, where Celia—whom he calls "my one reader / who types me"—is offered as the model recipient of his hermetic textuality: so fully literate in his references that they cease to be references, and sympathetic to the point of indistinguishability from the poet himself (*"A"*-12 246). Though he made his debut in the modernist literary field promoting a referential poetry in line with the Poundian "direct treatment of the thing," the mode of perception proposed in *Bottom,* a "looking" in which "certain physical eyes disappear; and, in place of eyes, reality shows up abstractly in . . . verbal symbolism as duration" (79), comes much closer to the kind of reading that his work demands and continues to receive in the form of celebrations of its postmodernism. Late *"A"* has been lauded as a participatory text and, in its move from "a teleological poetics of completion to a more open ended poetics of contingency, discovery and *play,*" even a fundamentally democratic one (Hatlen 288). But what are the ground rules of this game? Can everyone play?

"Looking for a Place to / Bury—Ricky": Objectification and Desire in Early *"A"*

"History's best emptied of names' / impertinence met on the ways" (*"A"*-22 511). So begins six thousand years of history, rendered in two sets of eight hundred five-word lines: *"A's"* wildly ambitious conclusion.[7] The history sections of *"A"*-22 and *"A"*-23, the movements that complete Zukofsky's portion of his long poem, do manage to avoid proper names, a fact that the final twenty-six lines of the poem, which begin, "A living calendar, names inwreath'd" (562), seem designed to remedy. Zukofsky had been interested in the relative poetic value of names from the start of *"A,"* a fascination that he frequently trained on his own not-so-melopoeic moniker. In the original version of *"A"*-1–7, published in *An "Objectivists" Anthology* (1932), Zukofsky's name appears five times, always as a signifier of nonpoetic colloquiality, twice in viciously mangled form.

The opening of *"A"*-2, edited in the final version, reveals the poet's dark sense of his own indecorousness:

> The clear music—
> Zoo-zoo-kaw-kaw-of the sky,
> Not mentioning names, says Kay,
> Poetry is not made of such things.
>   (*OA* 118)

At once a stutter and, as Bob Perelman has suggested, a semantically rich objectification of his ethnic and class difference, Zukofsky's name here stands in for all that resists "clear music" (*Trouble* 191–92). It's not surprising that this monstrosity has been almost completely excised from the final version of the long poem, appearing only in the letters Zukofsky received from a marginally literate soldier named Jackie, which are reproduced in all of their orthographic irregularity in *"A"*-12. Celia and Paul—names that bear a higher literary pedigree—enter the text of *"A's"* second half often, and there's no shortage of self-reference on the part of the poet, but it's always artfully transmuted, pushed a step up or down on the poetic chain. Horses, for instance, are a frequent metaphoric substitute, suggesting both transcendent, virile beauty and the sturdy, workaday side of the poet's persona, as in these lines from *"A"*-14 in which Zukofsky takes Shakespeare's joke seriously: "*as true as / truest horse* (capable) / *music touch their / ears, eyes turn'd / modest gaze—* / destroyed if changed / into a man*" (352).

   At the other end of the spectrum, the letter *z* is offered as a minimal marker of identity which nevertheless holds great personal value. The final line of *"A"*-23, "z-sited path are but us," ends the alphabetic, twenty-six line section with a densely packed inscription of the poet's core identity. The 563-page odyssey concludes on Arbutus Street, Paul Zukofsky's Brooklyn address, a destination reachable only by readers close enough to the Zukofsky family to know where they live. With *"A"*-24, the poem symbolically relocates to the conjugal home, or at least a "musical" version of it. Also called the "L. Z. Masque," *"A"*-24 is Celia's composition of fragments from forty years of Louis's writing, set to Handel's "Harpsichord Pieces"—a bizarre and challenging tribute. The long poem finally concludes with a note of thanks to Paul for the loan of his Handel music, initialed by Louis and Celia. Here, names mark the odd mixture of intimacy and formality that characterizes Zukofsky family relations and makes late *"A"* such a strange reading experience. The note is both a formal acknowledgment of an artistic colleague (Paul was by this time a highly respected violinist and conductor) in a work meant for broader consumption, and an internal family communiqué. The initials with which it concludes don't seem entirely appropriate to either genre.

One nonliterary name that appears with startling frequency in the *"Objectivists" Anthology* version of the first six movements, often with discomfort, but without the irony Zukofsky reserved for his own name, is "Ricky." The diminutive also appears many times in the final version of the poem, where *"A"*-3 remains devoted to a spare elegy for the young man whose death is figured as "Sleep / With an open gas range / Beneath for a pillow" (9). Through a series of connections worked out by Barry Ahearn in *Zukofsky's "A": An Introduction* (1982), we know that "Ricky" is Richard Chambers, Zukofsky's friend Whittaker Chambers' younger brother. In *Witness* (1952), Chambers describes his brother's drinking problems and ultimate suicide in September of 1926, the same year that Zukofsky wrote "Poem Beginning 'The,'" which also contains an elegy for the young man whom Zukofsky calls "lion-heart" (Ahearn, *Zukofsky's "A"* 66–71). The "Objectivists" issue of *Poetry* includes an elegiac poem called "October 21st, 1926," written by Chambers and addressed to "brother." Interestingly enough, Zukofsky did not reprint this poem in the *Anthology*. The association with Chambers attaches a certain notoriety to Ricky and explains, perhaps, some of the mystery surrounding the name: Zukofsky's involvement with the Communist Party was brief and skeptical, and he and Celia were quick to disavow his political experiences in later years.[8] Without the benefit of guidebooks, however, it appears that Ricky is meant to be read as one of the many "historic and contemporary particulars"—such as Bach, Henry Ford, Lenin, and someone named Kay—who populate the first six movements of the long poem. Obviously Ricky is in a different category than the first three of those figures, and as the subject of an entire movement he is different from Kay, whom I will discuss later, as well. Just as "lion-heart" links "Poem Beginning 'The'" to *"A,"* much of the transition from the *"Objectivists" Anthology* version of *"A"*1–6 to the final one happens around "Ricky" or motifs associated with him. In the final version, the name comes to carry a poignantly negative charge, both because its bearer has died and because it functions as a kind of monument, marking the places where the process that Zukofsky calls "exclusion" in his preface to the *Anthology,* and "objectification" and "condensation" in other statements of his poetics, has occurred.[9]

Presented in his prose pieces as technical program, this process—through which the poem is made to "convey the totality of perfect rest"—can also be read in elegiac terms as a melancholic negating and revisiting of a loved object. *"A"*-3 is a conventional elegy; tracing the path along which bodily remains achieve transcendence in nature and song, it begins with "your dead mouth singing" while "Automobiles speed / Past the cemetery" and ends with "Lion-heart, my dove, / Pansy over the heart, dicky-bird"—an image of floral perfection, however sentimentalized (9, 11). But the significance of the elegiac isn't limited to this short movement; rather, the elegy for "Ricky" renders as theme the career-long practice of cutting and culling through which Zukofsky sought to transform both his long poem and himself into models of "objective perfection." This is the practice that would culminate in the effort to render six thousand years of history in sixteen hundred five-word lines. In his public capacity as editor, Zukofsky promoted Poundian frugality, citing prominently the older poet's admonition "to use absolutely no word that does not contribute to the presentation," in his preface to the *Anthology* (17). But the practice of excision, begun with Ricky and repeated throughout Zukofsky's career, appears to bear a psychopoetic significance that exceeds its aesthetic goals.

Cutting and collecting are linked melancholic enterprises in Baudrillard's "system of objects." In his terms, collecting aims to "reach an accommodation with the anguish-laden fact of lack, of literal death," by fixing on an object and "integrating it within a series based on the cyclical game of making it absent and then recalling it from out of that absence" (17). Of course the objects collected never fully make up for the loss, thereby compelling the collector to engage in an infinite pursuit. Perpetuity and subjective wholeness are the goals of the process. Baudrillard suggests that "the missing item in the collection is in fact an indispensable and positive part of the whole, in so far as this lack is the basis of the subject's ability to grasp himself in objective terms" (13). Zukofsky's designedly endless poetic project offers ample evidence in support of this idea. Celia's "L. Z. Masque"—itself a collection of L. Z. fragments—may have ended "A," but it did not complete the collection. In 1978, the year of his death, Zukofsky finished *80 Flowers*, and began work on a book of poems to be called *90 Trees*. He had planned to complete *80 Flowers* for his eightieth birthday, and we can guess that *90 Trees* was meant to sustain him to his ninetieth.[10] In typically Zukofskyan mode, the passage of years is here rationalized as the form of a work; time is rendered in benign terms as number and, ultimately, shape.

In the first six movements of "A" and in "Poem Beginning 'The,'" however, time—as memory and desire—dominates. For this reason as well as their many shared motifs, we can read the two texts together as one expanding and contracting poem. A semiparodic take on *The Waste Land*, "'The'" reproduces much of that poem's design: Zukofsky numbers lines—every line, as opposed to every tenth—and there's an opening notes section in which lines are attributed to "T. S. Eliot's *The Waste Land*," "Modern Advertising," and "Myself," among others (*CSP* 8). "'The'" is broken into six titled movements which build to a more earnest version of Eliot's chanted conclusion: Zukofsky's highly idiosyncratic Marxist-utopic translation of the Yiddish poet Yehoash. Zukofsky also borrows Eliot's collage technique, splicing into his poem a variety of textual fragments—from the high canon to modernism to popular music—sometimes whole cloth, sometimes in cheeky paraphrase.

But the relationship of "'The'" to *The Waste Land* is not purely parodic, and the resemblance between Zukofsky's work and Eliot's—which extends into "*A*"-1–6—goes beyond formal mimicry. Like Eliot, especially Eliot prior to Pound's surgical intervention, Zukofsky uses collage to allow a range of errant desire into his text, under cover of "different voices." Bruce Comens, representative of many recent critics who argue that the second half of "*A*" effects a postmodern displacement of the author, claims that "the 'I' of '*A*' 1–6 clearly represents Zukofsky himself," a figure of "external authoritarian control" (154). But while there's a certain youthful consistency to the voices that emerge in the first half of the long poem, they are far more "wily, deceptive, multiple" (Comens' terms) than the formally contorted but ultimately recognizable middle-aged self who presides over the later movements. Again, I look to the roomier *"Objectivists" Anthology* version for a magnification of the difference. Consider, for instance, the "half-human, half-equestrian" "I" of "*A*"-2, grazing in hazy sensuousness:

> I have stepped with haired ankle,
> As with fetlock, to the center leaf,
> I have looked into the mild orbs of the flower,
> My eyes have drowned in the mild orbs;
> Hair falling over ankle, hair falling over forehead,
> What is at my lips, have I kissed the flower,
> It is green yet graciously ferruginous,
> The flower bears the iron-rust lightly,
> The flower is the steel piston at my chest.
>
> (OA 119–20)

There is something of Eliot's "hyacinth girl" in this passage—lush, decadent. This "I" also resembles the figure that emerges in Zukofsky's translation of Yehoash in both versions of "*A*"-4, where the Yiddish poet's feminized "song" is made to confront the "Speech" of rigidly traditional Jewish elders: "To-day I gather all red flowers, / Shed their petals on the paths, / Shimaunu-San, in the dawn, / Red I go to meet him— / Shimaunu-San, my clear star" (*OA* 125). These singing figures are distinct from the jaded young aesthete who opens the second movement of "'The'":

61 This is the aftermath
62 When Peter Out and I discuss the theatre.
63 Evenings, our constitutional.
64 We both strike matches, both in unison,
65   to light one pipe, my own.

(*CSP* 11)

Or the romantic (but also somewhat jaded) poet who steps out of a Carnegie Hall performance of Bach's *Saint Matthew's Passion* in the *"Objectivists"* version of *"A"*-1:

And I,
Upon the feast of that Passover,
The bloods' tide as the music's
A thousand fiddles as beyond effort
Playing—playing
Into fields and forgetting to die,
The streets smoothed over as fields,
Not even the friction of wheels,
Feet of ground:
Music leaving no traces
Not dying, yet leaving no traces.
Nor any conscious effort,
Nor boiling to put pen to paper.
Perhaps a few things to remember.

(*OA* 115–16)

This passage is largely unrevised in the final version of *"A"*-1, except for the removal of the first line and thus the first-person storytelling mode, and the insertion of a space before the final two lines, separating the mechanics of writing more fully from the ethereal, traceless music to which it is consistently and frustratingly compared.

As in the "Death by Water" section of *The Waste Land,* both "'The'" and *"A"*-1–6 contain embedded elegies at their emotional centers. One of the few sections of "'The'" not otherwise attributed in the notes, lines 76–109 make up a large part of the second movement. Following a snappy repartee between "I" and "Peter Out," the lyricism of this interlude seems sudden. Here's a selection:

76 Lion-heart, frate mio, and so on in two
      languages
77 the thing itself a shadow world.
78 Goldenrod

> 79 Of which he is a part,
> 80 Sod
> 81 He hurried over
> 82 Underfoot,
>
>   . . .
>
> 90 Uncanny are the stars,
> 91 His slimness was as evasive
> 92 And his grimness was not yours,

These last two lines echo Eliot's concluding warning, "Consider Phlebas, who was once handsome and tall as you" (*Collected Poems* 65). But Zukofsky's version continues, pushing past "grimness" into more exalted territory:

> 93 Do you walk slowly the halls of the heavens,
> 94 Or saying that you do, lion-hearted not ours,
> 95 Hours, days, months, past from us and gone,
> 96 Lion-heart not looked upon, walk with the
>   stars.
>
>   (*CSP* 11–12)

In a letter to Pound preceding the poem's publication in *Exile,* Zukofsky writes apologetically about the difficult tempo of the second movement, conceding that he was "at the time of writing too pleased, however shyly, with Peter Out and too distraught with Lion heart to notice such drag." He continues, "Fact is I fear not so much the second movement, as for the too precipitous end" (Ahearn, *Pound/Zukofsky* 5).

If anything, *"A"* overcompensates for the precipitousness of "'The'"; released from the strictures of imitation, it is open and ranging. Rather than resolving the conflicts between "sod" and "stars," bodies and writing, or writing and music, it shuttles between the two registers. This ambivalence comes to a head in the lines from *"A"*-6 that Zukofsky used in several early statements of his poetics:

> But when we push up the daisies,
> The melody! The rest is accessory:
>
> My one voice. My other: is
> An objective—rays of the object brought to a focus,
> An objective—nature as creator—desire
>   for what is objectively perfect
> Inextricably the direction of historic and
>
>   contemporary particulars.
>   (*"A"*-6 24)

In the early movements, the poem treats these issues most explicitly in a dialogue between the Zukofsky figure and an interlocutor named Kay. Indeterminately gendered and utterly without personal attribute in the final version, in the *Anthology* Kay is labeled "Anybody, but a particular Anybody," appearing later "naked, / Pyjamas flung through the crook of his elbow" (*OA* 139). The neutering revision seems apt, given the fact that Kay is made to argue for a poetry of "clear music" while the poet champions inclusiveness. But while Kay promotes organic singularity, he/she infuses the poem with a jaunty dialogism, as this passage from "*A*"-5 demonstrates:

> Our voices:
>> "How? without roots?"
>> "I have said *The courses we tide from.*"
>> "They are then a light matter?"
>> "Let it go at that, they are a light matter."
>> "Isn't it more?" "As you say."
>> "Your people?" "All people."
>> "You write a strange speech." "This."
>
> ("*A*"-5 1/–18)

Perelman has suggested that "Zukofsky's registration of social tones seems pedantic" (*Trouble* 210) in this passage, and I would agree. The lines read more like a bad schoolroom exercise in dialogue than the real thing. From the perspective of the later work's private commerce with "my one reader who types me," however, this encounter with a literary peer seems a genuine—if awkward—effort to imagine what it might be like to have one's poem in social circulation.

Kay opens the second movement with a strong objection to the dialogic mode. He/she denies the collaged "*A*"-1 the status of music, calling it instead "snapped old catguts of Johann Sebastian," and argues that "poetry is not made of such things." Always tending toward indirection and ambivalence, the poet's response breaks down into (at least) two distinct registers. Rather than an all-out defense of "*A*"-1, we get a catalogue:

> —Kay, in the sea
> There with you,
> Slugs, cuttlefish,
> Balls of imperialism, wave games, nations,
> Navies and armaments, drilling,
> Old religions—

> Epos:
> One Greek carrying off at least two wives for his
> > > comfort—
> Those epopt caryatids, holding, holding, the
> > > world-cornice.
> > > > (*"A"*-2 6)

The poem-as-sea is figured both as a stagnant pool of detritus and as the origin of a continually evolving world order, suggesting that with respect to worldly matter the poem can act as an undifferentiating container *and* as an organizing narrative. But if the poem evokes either creation myth or evolutionary theory, it does so with a clear sense of irony. The "higher" orders are just an item in the catalogue away from the "lower" ones; "cuttlefish / Balls of imperialism" comically links geopolitics to the acquisitive practices of simple life forms. It is unclear where "old religions" and "epos" fit in this list. Are they the culminating terms in the chain of development, or foundational to it? What sort of epic weight can one bigamous Greek be made to carry? How sturdy are the "caryatids" buttressing the world?

The poem leaves these questions open; for the introduction of the Greeks leads not to classical solemnity but to a strangely raucous interlude:

> (Agamemnon). Very much like the sailors.
> Lust and lust. Ritornelle.
> All! blue trouser seats—each alike a square
> inch—
> > sticking thru portholes,
> Laughter, laced blue over torus,
> Gibes from the low deck:
> "Hi, Ricky!"
> (Splash of white pail-wash, scuttling and laughter.)
> > > > (*"A"*-2 6)

The chain of associations moves from Agamemnon's womanizing to his ideal seamen to "the" sailors, a more contemporary bunch who appear to resemble the uniformed fetish objects of a gay phantasmatic. Images like the tiny buttocks framed by the portholes and the straining uniforms "laced blue over torus" are treated in a lighthearted, glancing manner. "Torus" is a typical example of the frisson Zukofsky gets from wordplay; an obscure Latinate noun meaning both "donut-shaped" and "a bulge," the lewd joke is the reward for etymological digging. For all of the frivolity, however, it is important to note that these images arise here and at other key moments in the long poem in close proximity to the idealized categories of objectification, and later, marriage; they admit difference—social and bodily materiality—into the moments where "A" would reach "clear music."

Indeed, as the poet's response to Kay's criticism continues, it shifts from a "low" discursive mode into a higher, more lyric one. Human, pleasure-seeking Greeks give way to Ovidian metamorphosis, but not without a residue of the prior set of images:

> Half-human, half-equestrian, clatter of waves,
> Fabulous sea-horses up blind alleys,
> Never appeased, desire to break thru the walls
> > of alleyways:
> Till the moon, one afternoon,
> Launches with sea-whorl,
> Opening leaf within leaf floats, green
> On waves: liveforever.
>
> . . .
>
> As in Johann Sebastian,
> Listen Kay . . .
> The music is in the flower.
>
> > ("A"-2 7)

In this highly compressed passage, horses merge with the sea as the site of magical transformation. In "A"-7 the seahorses will become "sawhorses," their atemporal stillness hardened into the language of labor, but here they are representatives of a quieter world in which natural objects already embody absolute perfection. The implication is that work is "accessory" to the music of the sea and the flower, which ultimately resolve into a single image of organic plenitude. But as in the definition of "an objective" in "A"-6, subjectivity in the particular form of desire is never completely purged from the poem. Following close upon the "lust and lust" of the sailor interlude and confined as it is to "blind alleys" and "alleyways," desire shadows the ethereal light of the rest of the passage. Moving into the passage I've already cited—"I have stepped with haired ankle . . . "—"A"-2 confuses the two registers even further, mingling "lust and lust" with floral perfection.

Just as the sexualized play with the sailors erupts out of and corrupts organic images, Zukofsky's self-conscious literariness gives the lie to the ideal of poetry as fluorescing natural object ("nature as creator"). The poet lays claim to transubstantiative power for his verse, but makes do instead with the more mundane faculty of "style." The deictic incantation to pure presence, "This is my face / This is my form," gives way to secondhand Whitmanism: "Faces and forms, I would write you down / In a style of leaves growing" ("A"-2 8). The jingly internal rhyme of "Till the moon, one afternoon" also strikes an odd note in a passage devoted to celebrating the sublime music of the spheres and Bach as its earthly representative. A remnant of popular culture not yet reborn through sea change, this sound bite finds its visual counterpart in the commercial heresy at the close of "A"-2: "A sign behind trees reads (blood red as intertwined / Rose of the Passion) / Wrigleys" (8).[11]

"Desire / for what is objectively perfect" is, it appears, a logically impossible premise for a poetics. In rhetorical terms, "objective perfection" invokes the logic of metaphor, which would capture identity essentially, atemporally. "Desire" resists this logic; as the principal embodiment of the relational, ever-shifting trope of metonymy, it stands in the same secondary and ultimately corrosive relation to "objective perfection," "clear music," and/or "projective immediacy" (to hearken beack to Olsonian ideals) that writing (in the tradition that Derrida has traced throughout Western metaphysics) does to speech.[12] And early "A's" particular embodiment of desire may in fact be material to its subversive effect. In "Homographesis," an essay that has become something of a classic in queer theory, Lee Edelman suggests that the historical formation of the category of "the homosexual" as "sexual difference internal to male identity . . . generate[d] the necessity of reading certain bodies as *visibly* homosexual." It thus generated the necessity of *reading* identity and "produce[d] [the homosexual] in a determining relation to inscription itself" (9). Edelman names this determining interrelation of sexuality and textuality "homographesis," and devotes his essay to the fruits of analogy. The homograph is, of course, a word that looks the same as another but means differently. "Homographesis," Edelman maintains, "exposes the metonymic slippage, the difference internal to the 'same' signifier, that metaphor would undertake to stabilize or disavow" (14). Similarly, "the historical positing of the category of 'the homosexual' textualizes male identity as such, subjecting it to the alienating requirement that it be 'read,' and threatening, in consequence, to strip 'masculinity' of its privileged status as the self-authenticating paradigm of the natural or the self-evident itself" (12). The gay body—historically inscribed as such to delineate, and thus regulate, its corrosive difference—"like writing, confounds the security of the distinction between difference and sameness"; it reveals the "fictional status of logic's foundational gesture" (14).

In summoning Edelman here, I'm suggesting that the particular figures which body forth the tension between "objective perfection" and "historic and contemporary particulars" in early "A"—figures of homoerotic desire—are not coincidental. They emerge out of the struggle in which Zukofsky would engage throughout his career: to render his life and his writing identical, simultaneously "durable as one thing from itself never-turning" (*Bottom* 13). In early "A," the presence of difference within sameness—for Zukofsky this would be felt primarily as the disjunctive experience of "having contemporaries," the narcissistic wounding of the literary field—is inscribed, named "Ricky," in fact, and mournfully purged. As Edelman suggests, however, the very act of inscription has complex and continuing effects: it forever undoes the possibility of self-evident identity.

But desire isn't entirely purged from the younger Zukofsky's "poem of a life," and the results are happier for it. Behind the trees in the *"Objectivists" Anthology* version of "A"-5—edited but not completely excised in the final—something incongruous appears to be going on:

> Hid (chest to chest; Horse)
> Field-weed,
>
> Lie down you, I'll marry you!
>
> (Said:)
>
> Do you think we are sailors?
> New are, the trees,
> Purple in the violets' swath,
> Birds—birds—birds.
> Against bark a child's forehead
>   plein de rouges tourmentes—
> Rimbaud (no glasses stopping from bark touch);
> Forehead to bark, face to bark:
> Under sky clarities
> Winds' intercourse with the fields,
> Breath, love hardly over, trembling.
>
> Walking out:
> The trees showing sunlight,
> Sunlight trees,
> Words ranging forms.
>   (*OA* 131–32)

In the final version, "intercourse" is replaced with "breathe," and "love hardly over, trembling" is removed entirely. Also removed, interestingly enough, is the

mention of Rimbaud—an excision that repersonalizes the passage even as it
negates whatever decadence might be associated with that name. Though it
includes a reference to sailors (linking it to Ricky), this passage's "spot of time"-
like intensity is tonally distinct from shipboard rambunctiousness. Here, the
poet achieves his most sustained encounter with nature thus far, and the experience is both harmonious (wind miming breath miming wind) and discordant
("forehead to bark"). Unlike many other moments in early "A," the two registers
coexist without devolving into self-conscious doggerel. "Words ranging forms"
reads as a relaxed acknowledgment of the poem's capacity to include diverse
content in its diversity.

The debate with Kay continues into "A"-6, where doggerel directly precedes
the already-cited definition of "an objective." Again, when it comes to deciding
between clear music and this particular set of "historic and contemporary particulars," the poet wants to have it both ways. For even as he invokes the organ-
icity of "the flower—leaf around leaf wrapped / around center leaf," he contends that this song doesn't omit but rather "includes Kay" and

> . . . Anybody.
> Ricky's romance
> Of twenty-three years, in
> Detail, continues
>
>> He—a—pyjamas off—
>> Invites ants upon his ankle
>> Up-up, ta-ta,
>>   minus, but quite there:
>>
>>> "I beg your pardon
>>> I've a—"h" begins the rhyme here,
>>> Shall we now?"
>>
>> . . .
>>   The sailors in the carousel
>>   looking for a place to
>>   bury—Ricky;
>>   Seaweed, fellow voters, and
>>   spewn civic sidewalks.
>>   ("A"-6 23–24)

Ahearn claims that the suggestiveness in this passage is "part of 'A''s fertility
theme" (Zukosfsky's "A" 59), a reading that seems too humorlessly literary for
the bawdy material. The references to sailors and homosocial roughhousing
are light; the pleasure here has more to do with the semicovert use of dirty

words than with the intimation of actual sexual activity. As I hope my discussion of "homographesis" has made clear, my purpose in citing this and the other passages in this section has not been to "out" the young Zukofsky, nor to suggest that early *"A"* is *in fact* an extended elegy for the young man who may have been his lover—as James E. Miller, Jr., argues of Eliot and Jean Verdenal in *T. S. Eliot's Personal Waste Land*—though there is content to support a less categorical version of these readings. My reading locates itself at a more elusive and combustible crossing of the poetic and the biographical. I've tried to reveal the broad range of desire admitted into the long poem's early movements, and I've tried to show its disruptive effects on Zukofsky's plan to live/write his poem/life as "one thing from itself never turning." In so doing, I want to establish the conditions for highlighting the personal and social, rather than purely experimentalist, motives behind such purgative processes as "objectification" and its institutional correlate, "marriage," as they become increasingly dominant in later *"A."* In the pursuit of the "totality of perfect rest," the early Zukofsky knows, a world of loved objects is lost.

Late *"A,"* *Bottom*, and the Logic of "Love"

"A"-24
Celia's
L. Z. Masque

the gift—
she hears
the work
in its recurrence.
L. Z.

Thanks to Paul Zukofsky for suggestions regarding typography and for the loan of his copy of Handel's *Pièces pour le Clavecin* as printed for The German Handel Society.

C. Z.
L. Z.
(*"A"*-24 806)

How do we read the lines signed by Zukofsky at the end of *"A"*-24? In *Disjunctive Poetics,* Peter Quartermain refers to this passage as the "Dedication to Celia," and suggests that it "enjoins . . . the reader to [hear] / the work in its recurrence" (65), a reading that seems to me interesting for its unexpressed doubleness. Why would a dedication appear at the end of a text rather than at the beginning? Which text is being dedicated, the last movement or the entire long poem? For a poet who organized his collected critical essays around prepositions, the absence of a "to" or "for" indicating the trajectory of these lines seems particularly notable. "The gift— / she hears / the work / in its recurrence" reads more like an explanatory footnote—not an address—for a reader other than Celia than a dedication to her. What we are privy to here is the poem's delimitation of its audience, the creation of a circle of reading so closed—at least between husband and wife—that gestures of address like "to" are unnecessary. These lines at once include the outside reader and foreclose him or her from their circuitry. Celia, in hearing "the work / in its recurrence," has already performed the ideal reading of "A": "A"-24. The very fact that we need her work explained to us in note form suggests that we are not the readers the poem intends. Paul, the other set of eyes for which these lines were written, has also played a role in the writing of the poem by loaning his copy of Handel to his parents. His positioning at the production end of the circuit thus compensates for his slight distance—indicated by the fact that the "thanks" has to be sent along the lines of the "to"—from the marital dyad.

The figure of the family thus functions as the means toward what becomes the main end of the end of "A": shaping reception. Zukofsky conducts his most extended meditation on the issue of reception in *Bottom: On Shakespeare,* a massive critical exercise dedicated to tracing the theme "Love sees" through Shakespeare's works with the help of Spinoza, Aristotle, and Wittgenstein. *Bottom* was written over a period of thirteen years, its composition falling mainly into the gap between "A"-12 (1950–51) and "A"-13 (1960). With its melange of lengthy quotes from the *Tractatus,* the *Ethics,* and all of Shakespeare's plays, *Bottom* is an extremely difficult text to read. Beyond cursory acknowledgments of its existence and basic theme, critics have generally kept their distance. Approaching it here, I want to suggest that *Bottom* is best understood as an exercise in what Zukofsky called "continuously present analysis" (*OA* 23). It is his blueprint for the reading of "A" and for the production of his legacy.

To read *Bottom* in this way is to take Zukofsky seriously when he says in an interview with L. S. Dembo that the book was "written to do away with all philosophy" (Terrell 265). Understood by these lights, the main end of *Bottom,* to which tracing and explicating the thematic loop "love:reason :: eyes:mind" is the means, is to read Shakespeare's (and ultimately Zukofsky's) canon as "one work . . . always regardless of the time in which it was composed . . . durable as one thing from 'itself never turning'" (*Bottom* 13). Zukofsky argues that the "drive of Shakespeare's writing is the art of furthering the same theme over and over . . . to make it literal" (23). As criticism, *Bottom* models itself along these same lines, struggling through incessant repetition to achieve for itself the "simplicity" that it would claim for Shakespeare's text.

The instability of authorship in Shakespeare's canon presents the major, perhaps even the motivating, obstacle to such a project. From the beginning, Zukofsky's Shakespeare is a poet plagued by the concern that his "writing with fleshly pencils will loosely be considered the issue of himself," a fact of life for any writer, but particularly problematic for one engaged in producing "a poem of a life" (*Bottom* 13). In "Definition," the longest section of *Bottom*, Zukofsky confronts the additional problem that "no one really knows the exact date of any particular detail, poem or play" in Shakespeare's oeuvre; authority becomes subject to centuries of editorial whimsy. Set up as a dialogue between "I" and a combative character called "Son" who challenges the book's methodology, this section plays out at the level of form the question of paternity that it contemplates as theme via the notion of "issue." Here and in the later movements of *"A,"* Zukofsky registers a sense of unease in his portrayal of the figure of the son, a portrayal that is notably different from that of the placid, idealized wife. Arguing that Zukofsky "could have stopped before writing 300 pages" and simply selected a single example of the "definition of love" from each of Shakespeare's works, "Son" claims that "*that* procedure might add up to forty-four short proofs of the canon" (267). Then follows an extended effort on the part of "I" at once to meet the challenge of "proving" the canon and to dislodge the question of authorship from the discourse of paternity in which it is traditionally cast. The debate becomes particularly heated over the status of *Pericles,* a late play not included in the First Folio of Shakespeare's collected works allegedly because of its collaborative writing. Prodded by "Son's" questioning of Zukofsky's use of portions of *Pericles* said not to be Shakespeare's, "as tho the definition of love sufficiently proved them his," "I" responds by shifting the terms: "Not *his* then, if you wish. Let the writer be the *definition*" (322).

In emphasizing "being" over possessing or engendering—and "definition" over even the most intransitive of verbs—this refiguring of authority in Shakespeare's canon finds its correlate in the discussion of love, sight, and language that makes up the earlier, philosophical sections of *Bottom*. There Zukofsky is concerned to trace the anti-epistemological implications of the statement "Love sees." Formulating the main theme of Shakespeare's works in terms of the logical proposition "love:reason :: eyes:mind," Zukofsky attempts to link the relationship that "seeing love" achieves with its object to the revelation of the *Tractatus:* "'That which expresses itself in language, we cannot express by language. The propositions show the logical form of reality'"(89). The "wholeness [the eye] sees in looking is its inexpressible ethics," Zukofsky argues, emphasizing "inexpressible" and, not incidentally, reiterating a proposition expressed earlier in slightly different terms: "Love needs no tongue of reason if love and the eyes are 1—an identity" (39). An "avatar" of the object as "an event or incident in print," the propositional sign tautologically says what it is and is what it says. Just as "Love sees" proposes an identity that transcends the subject/object dichotomy—a looking in which "certain physical eyes disappear; and, in place of eyes, reality shows up abstractly in . . . verbal symbolism as duration"—propositional logic proposes a language that transcends the disjunctions of reference by positing the reality to which it refers (79). The resemblance of these claims to Olson's contention that the glyph is an "act of the instant" rather than an "act of thought about the instant" should be apparent (*SW* 50). Olson traveled to the Yucatan to find his version of Pound's ideograph; Zukofsky delved into his library—a distinction that encapsulates their divergent senses of the poet's "job."

Not surprisingly, the main trope Zukofsky uses to figure the perfect set of relations between subject and object, language and world, and ultimately reader and text is marriage. Not surprising because it becomes such an obsession in his poetry, and because the act of marriage, the moment when a duly empowered individual says, "I now pronounce you man and wife," is the paradigmatic speech act, an instance of a language doing what it says. Zukofsky writes that the logical proposition displays the "unconscionable marriage of talk and physical sense," citing Achilles in *Troilus and Cressida* explaining to Ulysses that "speculation turns not to itself / Till it hath travel'd and is married there / Where it may see itself" (*Bottom* 72). The resemblance to the circularity of the "dedication to Celia" at the end of *"A"*-24 (as well as to Olson's *Maximus* dedication to Creeley) is suggestive: the beloved is less a person than a position, "there / where [speculation] may see itself." Celia's "L. Z. Masque," for all of its musical and poetic idiosyncrasy, is best loved as a mirror of the poet himself. Zukofsky calls such a loving marriage "unconscionable" both because it emerges out of his reading of the "theme of revealed physical incest in *Pericles*," and because it is the antithesis of the "metaphysics of cognition" hampering Western philosophy since Aristotle. Not thinking, but "surely seeing," married love is "simple": when "love sees" it is free from the errors of "passions." Though he ultimately abandons Spinoza in favor of Wittgenstein, Zukofsky retains the former's conception of "'excessive love for a thing that is liable to many variations, and of which we may never seize mastery'" as the chaos against which he defines his order (16). The polymorphous opening movements of his own long poem may function as another—unexpressed—foil.

In his extremely helpful essay on *Bottom*, David Melnick ventures the critical assessment that "Zukofsky's world has no room for people in it," that in Zukofsky's anti-epistemology only "one set" of eyes count, the "objectifying 'I' of pure sight" (64). *Bottom* goes one step further: in the marriage of the seeing "I/eye" and the beloved object, Zukofsky writes, "certain physical eyes disappear"— ideally the eyes of both parties. In the case of the objectified literary work, this corresponds to the disappearance of the biographical author, his ideal reader, and their presumably shared frame of reference into the speech act of the text. Zukofsky proposes to resolve the problem of authority in Shakespeare's work by "let[ting] the writer be the definition," thus dismissing three hundred years of biographical and source scholarship as "groundless comment . . . by sleuths." In order to protect the objectified artwork from the "singulars and the accidents" of time and change and to preserve it as "one thing from itself never turning," readers must eschew biography and consider instead the "only begetting of the living poet—the words in their context" (334). If the reading of Shakespeare that takes up the preceding three hundred pages of *Bottom* has taught us anything, it is that "context" here means first and foremost "text." "Historic and contemporary particulars" cede their ground to the tautological completeness that Zukofsky would claim for his language.

This schematic exegesis exaggerates the conservatism of the poetics and program of reading advocated in *Bottom*. The extended dialogue between "I" and "Son" suggests that Zukofsky is thoroughly aware of how problematic his methodology is, and the length of the book—470 pages including the index— reveals a certain uneasiness with the notion of completion so crucial to the system elaborated within it. It is even possible to imagine a reading of *Bottom* as a parody of literary exegesis. Such an argument might take as its starting point this passage from *"A"*-18 in which Zukofsky cites Samuel Johnson on what he learned from his own attempts at "definition":

> 'Who shall imagine that his dictionary can embalm his
> language, that it is in his power to
> change sublunary nature. Sounds are too volatile for
> legal restraints. To enchain syllables and to lash
> the wind are equally undertakings of pride unwilling
> to measure its desires by its strength. That
> signs might be permanent . . . like the things?'
>
> (*"A"*-18 395)

That Zukofsky introduces the skeptical Johnson by saying, "he has become as / talkative as Bottom a weaver" suggests that *Bottom* may be less monolithic with respect to issues of language and control than my reading has allowed.

It is worth noting, however, just how far *Bottom* goes toward overcoming the tension between "poem as object" and "poem of objects" that marked Zukofsky's 1931 essay "An Objective," the definitional passage in "*A*"-6, and much of the poetry of the first six movements of "*A*." Compare, for instance, these internally contradictory lines from the earlier essay:

> A poem. A poem as object—And yet certainly it arose in the veins and capillaries, if only in the intelligence—Experienced . . . as an object—Perfect rest—Or nature as creator, existing perfect, experience perfecting activity of existence, making it—theologically perhaps—like the Ineffable—
>
> A poem. Also the materials which are outside (?) the veins and capillaries—The context—The context necessarily dealing with a world outside of it—The desire for what is objectively perfect, inextricably the direction of historic and contemporary particulars. (*Prepositions* 15)

In *Bottom,* Zukofsky rejects the suggestion that Shakespeare's work "arose in the veins and capillaries" of an authorial intelligence or "outside (?)." Instead, he transfers the bodily materiality of this earlier imagery to the growth and duration of the "one work" itself. This transposition is not without a remainder. Part 2 of *Bottom*'s densely collaged argument concludes with an elegiac lingering on Shakespeare's body: "But like the hazel, gentle eye he was said to have— and with no *straying thoughts* wanting to rest forever—not to wish to draw an end to thinking but merely to show its limits" (94).

"As I love: / My poetics," Zukofsky proclaims near the beginning of "*A*"-12 (151). Given the definition of "love" worked out in *Bottom,* this statement proposes a much more complex mingling of sociality and language than we might first imagine. In theory, "love sees" entails the disappearance of "certain physical eyes"; in the poetry, images of Louis and Celia's loving marriage emerge in tandem with repeated stagings of the poet's death. "*A*"-11 and "*A*"-18 are both self-elegies in which the poet speaks to his family from beyond the grave, and both have an oddly ambivalent quality absent from the more decisive final lines of "*A*"-23 and "*A*"-24. The figure of direct address is crucial to both movements. "*A*"-11 opens with the tag "for Celia and Paul," but in it the poet addresses his song: "River that must turn full after I stop dying" (124). These lines literalize *Bottom*'s excision of the biographical author, suggesting that for the literary work to achieve completion, to "turn full," the poet himself must be dead. Comens has argued that "in the course of '*A*'s 'twist,' the authorial or authoritative 'I' of the poem becomes more and more displaced from its customary position of mastery" (153). What we've come to discover through *Bottom,* however, is that a certain kind of mastery (control over reception) is the end toward which the "death of the author" (or, in Olson's terms, "getting rid of the individual as ego") is the means.

"*A*"-11 does not achieve this end with ease. The gerundive form of the verb "dying" (the dominant verb form in the movement) suggests a drawn-out, continuous process—potentially painful and certainly uncontrollable. Feminine endings like "ing," "er," and "ed" carry the burden of rhyme in this movement, tethering its aural unity to unfinished, rising inflections. Quartermain discusses this typically Zukofskyan form of enjambment in terms of the Greek figure of *apo koinu* and argues that it works "virtually to remove the author's own voice entirely from the poem, so that in effect the poem is authorless" (215 n.17). Quartermain reads the difficulty of a poem like "*A*"-11 as formal achievement, a full-blown display of the "disjunctive poetics" that Zukofsky shares with the most innovative subset of modernists. To the extent that the song does seem to motor itself along, driven by the aural imperatives of the line endings, this assessment is accurate. I want to suggest, however, that the hermeticism of the verse may exceed Zukofsky's aesthetic goals, that the difficulty palpable in the poetry may be more personal in nature. In other words, "*A*"-11 demands the reader go beyond formalism. Consider the middle two stanzas:

> Honor, song, sang the blest is delight in knowing
> We overcome ills by love. Hurt, song, nourish
> Eyes, think most of whom you hurt. For the flowing
> River's poison where what rod blossoms. Flourish
> By love's sweet lights and sing *in them I flourish.*
> No, song, not any one power
> May recall or forget, our
> Love to see your love flows into
> Us. If Venus lights, your words spin, to
> Live our desires lead us to honor.

The poem continues, making its posthumous predicament more explicit:

> Graced, your heart in nothing less than in death, go—
> I, dust - raise the great hem of the extended
> World that nothing can leave; having had breath go
> Face my son, say: 'If your father offended
> You with his mute wisdom, my words have not ended
> His second paradise where

> They turn, quick for you two—sick
> Or gone cannot make music
> You set less than all. Honor.
>
> ("A"-11 124–25)

In these stanzas, the language of woundedness prevails. "Hurt," "ills," "poison," "offen[se]": the words that gather around this theme suggest that the song is meant not simply to "raise grief to music" but to redress a grievance, a strife ongoing between father and son. There is even the implication that, rather than salving these particular wounds, the song might cause more pain. "Hurt, song, nourish / Eyes, think most of whom you hurt. For the flowing / River's poison where what rod blossoms" are the richest, most problematic lines for this reading. Is the poet commanding his verse to inflict pain and then reflect on it, or is he describing a painful situation caused by "eyes" (read "I") and commanding the song to "nourish"—that is, to make amends? Perhaps "hurt" is a past participle, referring to the state of his family after the poet's death. "Eyes" would then refer to the tearful visages of Celia and Paul that the song is commanded to "nourish." And what are we to make of the fact that the poet uses his song as a go-between, and that resolution can come only after he "stop[s] dying"? The final stanza in the movement figures the poet and his son as "from the same root," leading us to read the difficult "where what rod blossoms" as a reference to Paul as scion.[13] Why would the song, or "flowing river," be poisonous to its intended listener/spawn? These questions are left open; the surface of "A"-11 is troubled by incompletely articulated "desires," perhaps the "deep need" out of which "A"-12 springs. If *Bottom* poses marriage as a vessel for containing excesses of subjectivity, desire, and mutability within the bounds of artistic mastery, the fitful motion of "A"-11 suggests that it may not be sound.

The uneasy combination of "valentine," self-elegy, and epithalamium in "A"-18 reveals Zukofsky experiencing similar difficulties while working with similar figures of control. The movement sets itself a typically Zukofskyan formal program: after the opening "valentine," yoke wayward content into "eight words a line for love." Starting with the 1956 collection *Some Time,* the valentine became one of Zukofsky's principal conceits for shorter poems. Occasional, intimate, and requiring no postage let alone publication, valentines to Celia and Paul take Paul Goodman's proposal for a personal advance-garde writing to its limit. "Songs of Degrees," a poem whose two sections are headed "With / a Valentine / (the 12 February)" and "With a Valentine / (the 14 February)," generates six variations on a single hermetic statement by shifting the line breaks. The result is a strange combination of proceduralism and lovers' code. As in "A"-11, the poet appears to be trying to make amends. Here are the first two stanzas:

> Hear her
> (Clear mirror)
> Care.
> His error.
> In her care—
> Is clear.
>
> Hear, her
> Clear
> Mirror,
> Care
> His error.
> In her,
> Care
> Is clear.
> (*CSP* 145)

Other valentines are less experimentally charged. "To My Valentines," apparently written to be read by a young Paul, mingles family message with nursery rhyme:

> From one to two
> is one step up
> and one and two
> spell three
> and we agree
> three is the sum
> a run
> of two and one.
> (*CSP* 133)

"A"-18 contains similar play with numbers: there's "e.e.c. as young man saw / an old man 3/3 dead. if one / third seems wandered for 2 left alone figure / 6/3?" and "My sweet 9/3 wonder if I'm not you're 3" ("A"-18 391, 401). These verses don't seem geared for children, however. Unlike the other valentines' playful yet contained formality, "A"-18 is replete with troubling literary, political, and personal references. Much of the movement is devoted to a retrospective of the poet's work, commanding the reader to "look back, an, a, the." The goal is to view Zukofsky's canon, like Shakespeare's, as "one thing from itself never turning." But from the necrophilic edge given the opening valentine by its first words, "an unearthing / my valentine / if I say it now will / it always be said. / I always know / it is I who have died," bodies insist their way into "A"-18 (389). More accurately, body parts become a primary focus of this movement; the detached fetish object refuses assimilation into the complete, objectified form. Thus "When I am dead in the empty ear" takes on a curiously literal quality, and the Vietnam commentary—some of the most political content to enter the poem since Zukofsky's early Marxism—figures colonialism in sexual terms: "Troops fired their automatic weapons into *their* pond / . . . Other continents encroach as / we can see by the belly-fanny dancing / of the tights over the buttocks of 'our' / women the slim erectile trousers of 'their' men" ("A"-18 392). But perhaps the strangest literalization of the poem's failure to objectify its diverse content comes right in the middle of the valentine, between the "unearthing" song and "I Sent Thee Late," a short poem offered as a belated "wedding rite" for Louis and Celia. The intervening passage, set off from the surrounding text, reads:

> I am here let the days live their
> lines two days bird's down blown on wire
> mesh fence jot down assures life a note(book).
> who won't sense upper case anymore: iyyob (jōb)
> swift would have known sobbing it every birthday
> *yovad yom* yahweh the surgeon a surge on
> tall as the mast a nipponese liner rising
> sun on the flag of a high mast
> sails after the week in port into a
> seeled fog of sunset east having come west
> going home. *typee* tattoo the water woven as
> the surgeon operated on another wound offhand saw
> the mentula tattooed SWAN remarked later with the
> sailor's recovery *how charming how apt* and the
> buoy confused exclaimed SWAN? *that was SASKATCHEWAN.*
> or found in the debris of the acropolis
> a long lost right leg (wisdom?) athene's parthenon
> pediment.
>   forgive: I don't recall names: rote.
>   ("A"-18 390)

The first thing to note about this passage is that, linguistically speaking, it is the polar opposite of an idealized "marriage of talk and physical sense" as defined in *Bottom*. Zukofsky may not "recall names," but the "impertinence" of "historic and contemporary particulars" is unavoidable. While it would be impossible to pursue every allusion contained in these lines, which reference the Bible, Swift, Melville, and what sounds like borscht belt humor, it is equally difficult to ignore the dominant motif: the figure of assertion itself, the phallus. Of course the issue with which these lines comically contend is the actual bodily organ's failure to assert; images of castration and impotence abound. The sailor—always a figure of vigorous male sexuality—returns, though in a severely limited capacity. Images of writing are also plentiful—from the poet's constant notebook jottings, to transliterated Hebrew, to a painfully placed tattoo—and seem linked in difficult ways to the theme of bodily decline. Writing, as "graphesis," signals the corrosion of organic identity. The opening, "I am here let the days live their / lines," takes the conceit of "a poem of a life" and inflects it differently. A tricky preposition in Zukofsky since *Bottom*'s rejection of authorship as possession or engenderment, "of" has come to suggest less a poem generated by a life than a life that has become a poem, or at least aspires to. Zukofsky strives for "a poem of a life" in which "the days live their / lines" and the poet "lives" forever.

"I Sent Thee Late," the first poem Celia Zukofsky lists in her "Year by Year Bibliography of Louis Zukofsky," was written in 1922 but went unpublished until its appearance here in *"A"*-18. Presciently engaged with Zukofsky's post-*Bottom* concerns, this poem offers a distinctly less bodily sense of time and im/mortality than the rest of the movement:

> Vast, tremulous;
> Grave on grave of water-grave:
>
> Past.
>
> Futurity no more than duration
> Of a wave's rise, fall, rebound
> Against the shingles, in ever repeated mutation
> Of emptied returning sound.
>
> (*"A"*-18 391)

Written four years before "Poem beginning 'The,'" this short lyric has none of the bluster of that work. Laced with elegiac rhetoric, but void of affect, it would seem to be an unlikely "wedding rite." But we've seen that love, in the later Zukofsky, is better understood as "duration" than Eros. In "Grave on grave of water-grave" we hear the epitaphic roots of "to grave": to dig, as in a burial site, and to carve or press deeply as in engraved writing. With its sober refusal to raise its dead from the watery depths, this poem echoes Eliot's sea dirge for

Phlebas the Phoenician, whose sunken body rises and falls indefinitely. But whereas both *The Waste Land* and "Poem Beginning 'The'" seek to recuperate their losses in their apocalyptic conclusions, "I Sent Thee Late" suggests an alternate possibility: an appeal to the endurance of writing as self-generating and presocial. The "materiality of language" subsumes the more troubling material of the mortal body, its productions and its reproduction.

"Now That I'm an 'Acquisition'": The Texas Archive and the Collected Subject

In the 1962 preface to a never-published volume of poetry called "Found Objects (1962–1926)" Zukofsky reflects on forty years of his poetic production with characteristic ambivalence. He writes:

> With the years the personal prescriptions for one's work recede, thankfully, before an interest that *nature as creator* had more of a hand in it than one was aware. The work then owns perhaps something of the look of *found objects* in late exhibits—which arrange themselves as it were, one object near another—roots that have become sculpture, wood that appears talisman, and so on: charms, amulets maybe, but never really such things since the struggles so to speak that made them do not seem to have been human trials and evils—they appear entirely *natural*. (*Prepositions* 168)

"Personal prescriptions" may be forgotten, but poems—once written—are endlessly regenerative. Zukofsky quotes himself in this passage, excerpting lines from their more vexed context in "*A*"-6: "Natura Naturans— / Nature as creator, / Natura Naturata— / Nature as created / He who creates / Is a mode of these inertial systems" (23). That those lines are themselves citation—from Spinoza's *Ethics*—furthers his point.[14] No longer considered "issue of" a biographical author, language hardens to time and copyright; it becomes an object to be touched and contemplated, borrowed but not communicatively exchanged.

While the tone of the passage is difficult to decipher—a kind of uncanny relief—I read in it the satisfaction of a goal achieved. I've been suggesting some of the poetic ways in which Zukofsky sought to transform his output (as he did Shakespeare's) into "one work . . . always regardless of time in which it was composed . . . durable as one thing from 'itself never turning'" (*Bottom* 13). He began the process of "objectification" early, disassociated himself from many of the "personal prescriptions" of his youth, and set himself the formal task of "hear[ing] the work in its recurrence." In "A"-12 he wrote, "To begin a song: / If you cannot recall, / Forget," a maxim that his work follows quite consciously (140). Nothing is lost entirely in Zukofsky's "poem of a life," but neither is it remembered in an active, narrative sense. Instead, it lives on in the amber of the lines—as in these last six of "A"-23:

> . . . never-
> Unfinished hairlike water of notes
> vital free as Itself—impossible's
> sort-of think-cramp work x: moonwort:
> music, thought, drama, story, poem
> parks' sunburst—animals, gracenotes—
> z-sited path are but us.
>
> ("A"-23 563)

Though this is the conclusion of "a living calendar, names inwreath'd," there are no names here, only resonances: there are strains of Shakespeare and numerous family emblems, including the aforementioned Arbutus Street and "A"-24, Celia's five-part score for "music, thought, drama, story, poem." In "vital free as Itself," we get a (conceptual) echo of Charles Reznikoff's paradigmatically "Objectivist" couplet: "Among the heaps of brick and plaster lies / A girder, itself among the rubbish." At its close, the life's work is figured as a self-contained, assertive singularity.

Repeated assertions of autonomy and organicism notwithstanding, Zukofsky's canon was obviously the product of "fleshly pencils," and in 1960 he discovered that handwriting—his own, but more often his illustrious friends'—had market value. He thus found an institutional arena in which to work out the processes of (self-)objectification that he'd been attempting in his poetry. Though the facts of their initial meeting aren't readily available, in 1959–60 Zukofsky became affiliated with Lew David Feldman, a New York agent and book dealer whose firm—the eponymous House of El Dieff (L. D. F.)—was one of the primary players in a burgeoning segment of the literary field: institutional collecting of twentieth-century manuscripts. Feldman's most powerful client was the University of Texas at Austin where since 1957 a provost named Harry Ransom had been using a portion of the state's vast oil wealth to build a collection of literary materials that he hoped would rival Harvard's and Yale's. Ransom, after whom the Harry Ransom Humanities Research Center (HRHRC) at Texas was soon named, was one of many institutional actors seeking out the work of contemporary writers, though he was likely the best funded and is now the best documented.[15] In curatorial circles, he is often credited with motivating a large-scale revaluation of literary materials. The "Ransom Revolution," as it has been dubbed, was to displace the bibliographic primacy of the first edition in favor of an entire archeology of textual production—from original notes, to manuscripts, to multiple revised copies, etc., culminating in the printed book. In fact, the widening of the rare book and manuscript net began much earlier: in 1935, Charles Abbott of the Lockwood Library at the University of Buffalo sought to develop that institution's collection by acquiring what he called "worksheets . . . all the tangible papers that a poet uses in making a poem" (11–12, 31–33). Poets donated their work to the library without payment; there was little funding, and the commodity was simply too new for a price tag. As Abbott put it in his introduction to the 1948 volume of essays based on the Lockwood Modern Poetry collection:

> By what yardstick could we measure values? By what balance could we judge the respective market-weights of a Kipling whose phrases are on every tongue and a Hopkins whose images delight only the initiate? By what alchemy of divination could we determine whose accomplishment merited this sum, whose promise that? (33)

By the time Zukofsky entered the arena with a collection of the letters that he had received over the years from Pound, Williams, Marianne Moore, and Harriet Monroe, among others, Ransom's aggressive acquisition practices—his targeting of modernist materials, his use of booksellers, his own vast resources—had helped to turn twentieth-century manuscripts into a relatively big business. One might surmise that the New Critics' assiduous promotion of modernist writers, the increasing numbers of graduate students in need of research topics, general postwar expansion of the university, the establishment of agencies such as the National Endowment for the Humanities, and favorable tax laws all played roles as well. By 1964, biographer Leon Edel was lamenting what he called "the age of the archive . . . the great, blaring age of public relations as distinct from private relations" (5). Zukofsky's initial participation in this Zeitgeist was on a significantly lower key: through Feldman's efforts, the University of Texas Press agreed to publish "Letters to Louis Zukofsky 1923–55" in exchange for HRHRC's receiving the rights to the originals.[16] This publication project was stalled and ultimately tabled owing to Zukofsky's inability to get permission from Dorothy Pound for Pound's letters until 1965. Presented with his entire collection of modernist-inflected materials, however, HRHRC agreed to a different deal: it would "buy" Zukofsky's archive for a certain sum; Zukofsky would "pay" the University of Texas a significant portion of that amount for its publication of *Bottom: On Shakespeare* and split the remainder with Feldman (Feldman to F. W. Roberts, 9/19/61). This arrangement would result in a first-edition printing of over one thousand copies, a significantly larger run than Zukofsky—who had planned to self-publish one hundred copies—had ever anticipated (Zukofsky to Corman, 4/25/61). The negotiations around this agreement were protracted: Texas wanted a more well known figure to write a preface; Zukofsky successfully argued against it. Feldman demanded that *Bottom* be dedicated "To Lew David Feldman who made it possible"; he prevailed—prompting Zukofsky to marvel to Corman that he had only once dedicated a book to a single person—*The "Objectivists" Anthology* to Pound—and that he'd conceived that dedication as part of the text itself (5/8/61). I've suggested that Zukofsky's dedications are sites of complex sociopoetic engagement—places where he works out relations of reception at the heart of his career-project. A dedication in the name of commerce, rather than art or love—particularly in a text devoted so exclusively to conjoining these latter concepts—bore ironies of which Zukofsky was distinctly aware.

The *Bottom* transaction—despite its protraction and sacrifice—was the beginning of a twenty-year relationship between the Zukofskys and HRHRC. Celia Zukofsky did much of the organizing of the various sales and gifts and continued the process of culling and cataloguing thousands of pages of letters, notes, manuscripts, printers' galleys, and first editions after Louis's death. The awkward compromise between art and commerce persisted throughout the relationship, infusing the incremental process of building the collection with characteristically Zukofskyan aesthetic intentions and inflecting Zukofsky's poetic practice with a—new and unique for him—sense of "commercial" possibility. In the heat of the first sale to Texas, he wrote to Corman that he was now aware of the market every time he put pen to paper (3/1/61) His packaging of archivable material was certainly an exercise in marketing. The first submission to the archive includes a blurb page compiled and typed by Celia. The sheet contains excerpts from favorable notices on Zukofsky, ranging from a review of *Some Time* in *Poetry* magazine, to a (curt but positive) letter from Pound, to what appears to be a letter in praise of Zukofsky from Corman to Williams. Also submitted with the manuscripts for sale was a 154-item bibliography of Zukofsky's printed work, a list of his public readings—including lists of poetry read—and an extraordinary 201-item list of references to Zukofsky, with asterisks marking especially favorable notices. The resemblance of this process of selection and organization to Zukofsky's poetic compulsion to excerpt and serialize is striking. The Zukofskys divided the material for sale mostly by chronology—organizing periodic packages of the new work—but they were also careful not to make the material too readily available, as Zukofsky suggested in a letter to Corman (12/11/63), and they appear to have withheld certain materials related to early "A" until later installments.

In *Reading Zukofsky's 80 Flowers*—the most sustained scholarly work based on the Zukofsky archive material yet published—Michelle Leggott speculates on the poet's motives for producing such a collection. She proposes a mixture of generosity toward readers struggling with the late work, and the classic desire for literary immortality. On the incongruity of a poet's insisting that "the work says all there needs to be said" and then meticulously culling and cataloguing his draft material, Leggott writes, "the condescension of explanations was as distasteful as ever to Zukofsky, just the same there was a real risk of losing his audience altogether" due to the difficulty of "A"-22 and 23. "The solution . . . was to legitimize use of the draft material by housing it in a public collection" (32). She goes on to claim that "the notebooks now at Texas are part of Louis Zukofsky's intention to go on living forever" (33).

I agree in part. I hope, however, that this chapter's examination of the variety of practices through which Zukofsky sought to "collect himself" might suggest that his relationship to the Texas archive was more complexly constitutive of his identity than Leggott's explanation allows. The practice of building the collection—in its tangential relation to market dynamics, its closed system of exchange, and its intent to produce a synchronic "system of objects" out of the noisy diachrony of a life—takes place at an intersection of public and private that seems to me peculiarly Zukofskyan. The *Bottom* transaction approximates the kind of barter that Olson and Creeley idealized in their own models of exchange; though in Zukofsky's case, intimacy is mediated by multiple participants, one of which is a large-scale institution. While the financial motive for selling his materials is impossible to discount, I'd argue that the incremental rhythm of a letting-go which is at the same time a building-up—the mournful process of "making [the object] absent and then recalling it from out of that absence" (Baudrillard 17)—is more consistent with Zukofsky's career strategy and psychosocial patterns than simple economics. As in his poetic efforts at objectification, the attempt to consolidate an identity via the collection founders on the tension between the "desire for what is objectively perfect" and the resistant reality of "historical and contemporary particulars." Baudrillard has argued that the collection allows the subject to "assert himself as an autonomous totality outside the world" by means of a "colossal tautology": the "absolute singularity" of a collected object "depends entirely upon the fact that it is

I who possess it—which, in turn, allows me to recognize myself in it as an absolutely singular being" (8). Housed in Texas, strewn with the markings of "fleshly pencils," and available for consumption by any number of "physical eyes," however, Zukofsky's collection—like his poetry—reveals its subject irremediably immersed in the world.

4

"Worrying about Making It"

Ted Berrigan's Social Poetics

From its position of relative obscurity in the hazy canon of 1960s experimental poetry, Ted Berrigan's *The Sonnets* mounts an assault on its scholarly future.

> *"The academy*
> *of the future*
> *is opening its doors"*
> —*John Ashbery*

The academy of the future is opening its doors
my dream a crumpled horn
Under the blue sky the big earth is floating into "The
     Poems."
"A fruitful vista, this, our South," laughs Andrew to his Pa.
But his rough woe slithers o'er the land.
Ford Madox Ford is not a dream. The farm
was the family farm. On the real farm
I understood "The Poems."
          Red-faced and romping in the wind, I, too,
am reading the technical journals. The only travelled sea
that I still dream of
is a cold black pond, where once

on a fragrant evening fraught with sadness
I launched a boat frail as a butterfly.

(62)

Sonnet 74, above, appeals simultaneously to two distinct audiences: to the dis-interested reader, the poem offers itself as a "readymade," ideal for consumption within the terms of postmodernism, but undisciplined and probably not very good. Within the first few lines one can say something about citation, repeti-tion, and pastiche, quite efficiently characterize *The Sonnets'* approach to both literary history and poetic form, and move on. From the avant-garde insider, however, the poem demands a closer reading. If one knows Berrigan's biogra-phy, or knew Berrigan, the apparently nonsensical splicings are narratable in personal terms; tracking down the poem's many references is a worthwhile exercise in nostalgia, or at least sociology.[1] But one needn't have been there to get the jokes. The poem produces its own insiders by adhering to the first principle of comedy, repetition-with-a-difference. Re-citing the epigraph, the first line takes it literally, inflecting the Ashberian middle voice with an ob-viously inappropriate declamatory tone. Lines 6–8 function similarly: "The farm / was the family farm. On the real farm / I understood 'The Poems'" begins with a bad imitation of confessionalism and then retrospectively takes itself seriously; the words remain stolidly the same while the poem works through a series of shifts in tonal context. Sonnet 74 becomes a kind of user's guide to literary parody.

Hailing a variety of professionally invested readerships, Berrigan's work makes visible the contours of the literary field in its contemporary moment and, presciently, in ours. Reading it is an experience in reflexivity, as revealing of the critic as it is of the poet. But does cultural savvy translate into cultural value? Does positing an audience actually produce one? Can a poet do as Frank O'Hara says in "Personism: A Manifesto" and make it on "nerve" alone? (O'Hara, *Selected* xiii).

"My Name a Household Name": Making Reputation

"I came to New York to become this wonderful poet, and I was to be very serious. Not to become but to be. That took about a year and a half, then I wrote this major work and there I was" (Waldman, *Nice* 20). In the scores of interviews and talks he gave between the 1967 publication of his debut book, *The Sonnets,* and his death in 1983, Ted Berrigan recounts the beginnings of his poetic career in this way; he compresses the bildungsroman's developmental narrative until it yields the immediacy of the "star-is-born" story. Berrigan's working-class high artist is a pop persona: part ingenu, part impresario. This chapter traces this model of the poetic career through *The Sonnets* and Berrigan's little magazine *"C,"* and into the avant-garde art worlds where he sought to be both an innovator and an institutional force—a producer not only of poetic collages but of poetic coteries. The double positioning readable in these two works emblematizes the predicament of a postwar avant-garde ambitiously laying the institutional groundwork for its own posterity. As with many of the poets in his cohort, Berrigan's formal experiments are best understood through their social aims and effects. In what follows, I analyze the sonnet sequence and the little magazine as "position-takings" on the cultural field. But I depart from Bourdieu in focusing my analysis of the way cultural value is created and contested on an individual actor—a largely unknown poet playing the field in an attempt to produce a self-legitimating career. Gauging the pressures of the role he lived on the works he made, and showing how the works contributed to fashioning that role, I articulate the intersection of individual ambition and collective production, a space where the chiasmic formulations of literary biography have living, human consequence.

Berrigan claimed that he "used the sonnet sequence to be my big jump into poetry and stardom, as it were" (Ratcliffe and Scalapino 160). For most readers, the closing qualification rings truer than the initial bravado. Perhaps no other contemporary poet better illustrates the relativity of stardom, the multiple constellations in which poets rise to prominence. Official indicators of reputation—from commercial success to notice by major institutions of consecration—suggest that even at the height of his career, Berrigan's was decidedly minor.[2] Through introductory anthologies like Paul Carroll's *The Young American Poets* (1968), Ron Schreiber's *31 New American Poets* (1969), and a 1969 *Newsweek* article entitled "The Young Poets," Berrigan achieved a modicum of mainstream renown in his lifetime, but always and only as a member of a generation, a school, or a scene. "Among O'Hara's followers," preceding his name more often than not, what canonical security Berrigan continues to enjoy is largely appositional; he's famous by association. As editor of *"C"* magazine and publisher of *"C"* press, he brought O'Hara, Ashbery, and James Schuyler together with Ron Padgett, Richard Gallup, and himself and, he claimed, founded the New York School of poets (Ratcliffe and Scalapino 90–91). Along with Anne Waldman, he launched the St. Mark's Poetry Project, still an organizing force in the New York poetry community.[3] A chronicler, publicist, and tireless talker, Berrigan lives on as an agent of literary history, rather than a fixture within it.

And yet among the more consecrated avant-garde poets of his generation and prior, Berrigan made an early and lasting impression. He was one of five "young" poets invited to read at the Berkeley Poetry Conference of 1965. Virtually unknown, he made his entrance at age thirty-one as, in his words, "rookie of the year" and, with *The Sonnets,* achieved a kind of instant majority. He even spawned parodies: Robert Duncan wrote a poem at the conference entitled "At the Poetry Conference: Berkeley after the New York Style" which he described as "a Black Mountain / Berrigan imitation North Carolina / Lovely needed poem for O'Hara" (Waldman, *Nice* 12). The timing was perfect for Berrigan's combination of individual bravura and imitative reverence. With its poetic of citation and collage, *The Sonnets* enacted on the level of rhetoric the self-canonizing maneuvers that were taking place at the conference's readings, panel discussions, and, most of all, cocktail parties. Berrigan wrote himself into the institution of the avant-garde by anticipating the moment when the institutions around poetry fold back into poetry itself.[4]

In the literary field, the degree to which any individual agent can calculate the terms of her own success is limited, extremely limited in Bourdieu's view. He argues that sociopoetic acts, or "position-takings," arise "quasi-mechanistically . . . from the relationship between positions . . . and being determined relationally, negatively, they may remain virtually empty, little more than a parti pris of refusal, difference, rupture" (*Field* 59). In Bourdieu's analysis, the history of the field of restricted production emerges from the necessary struggle between artistic generations, the old guard and the new. The shape of the struggle, that is, its aesthetic manifestation, is mediated but not fully determined by the socio-economic and cultural "dispositions" of the various actors involved. This is a vision of transhistoric artistic community as Newtonian battlefield; skirmishes are continuous and inevitable, but they are motored more by the "logic of action and reaction" than by individual desire or will (58).

Against this strange amalgam of economic determinism and avant-gardist revolutionism, Berrigan's communal model of influence appears benignly stagnant. The crown of "second generation" sat easily on Berrigan's head. Indeed, his poetry is so roomy, so full of other poets' names and lines, that it emerges as a kind of free-love alternative to traditional figurations of literary family as necessarily nuclear, claustrophobic, and oedipal. But Berrigan is also an ambitious poet in the line of Keats, whose wranglings with tradition and his own poethood tended more toward solipsism. In *Keats' Life of Allegory*, Marjorie Levinson calls Keats's poetic "masturbatory"—both passive and active, open and reflexive, somehow perpetually adolescent—and argues that it is a stylistic response to a largely class-based alienation from authority. Though Keats enjoys a secure canonicity in the twentieth century, Levinson reminds us of the harsh and personal criticism he suffered in his own time. Fellow poets found repugnant Keats' fetishistic relation to the props of poethood; Byron, for instance, reviled him for "frigging his Imagination"(Levinson 18). That Keats anticipated such criticism in the sonnets "On Fame" confirms the self-reflexiveness of which he is accused. Sonnet 14, for instance, purports to sermonize about the dangers of self-promotion, but the baroque, sexually charged imagery with which the octet presents the problem of ambitious self-fashioning ("As if a Naiad, like a meddling elf, / Should darken her pure grot with muddy gloom") overshadows the prim lesson of the sestet. The poem ends inconclusively on a question: "Why then should man, teasing the world for grace, / Spoil his salvation for a fierce miscreed?" (469). For Keats, who began working with the then-unpopular Shakespearean sonnet in a "Spirit of Outlawry" against first-generation romantics, the answer lies in the form itself. The challenge of fully inhabiting the Shakespearean mold—not only rhyme scheme, but also metrical variation, cadence, and even rhetorical device—teases the poet into visions of bardic greatness. Indeed, Keats's experiments with the sonnet led directly to the development of his ode stanza and to a period of heightened productivity unparalleled in his brief career.

In seeking to launch himself into posterity via the sonnet sequence, Berrigan tries on not so much a model of poetic form signed by Shakespeare as a model of poetic career signed—at least for the purposes of twentieth-century poets—by Keats.[5] In typical collagist fashion, however, he cuts out the middleman. In a 1980 interview, Berrigan recalled *The Sonnets'* original impetus: "I thought something like, 'What do you do if you're a poet and you're just starting out and you want to be big? And I mean, who was bigger than Shakespeare? . . . And I decided you wrote a sonnet sequence. So I wrote a sonnet sequence" (Ratcliffe and Scalapino 160). Here, Keats's labor of formal imitation and innovation disappears, leaving only the self-conscious ambition with which it was conducted. Setting out to make his name a "household name" (*Sonnets* 69) as only a high lyric poet writing in the age of television advertising could, Berrigan stirs up the "pure grot" of tradition with the provocative brittleness of his claims for inclusion. Without making too much of a canonical mismatch, it seems fruitful to suggest that in his ambition, his fraught relation to poethood, the poetic he crafted, and the ambivalence with which he is received, Berrigan resembles Keats, whom he names "the baiter of bears who died of lust" in sonnet 77 (65). As with the earlier sonneteer, Berrigan's vocational self-fashioning often takes the form of an excessive sexuality; his poems engage the fantasy of both being and having the object of desire, in this case, a fully authorized poetic and social identity. The fact that Berrigan was aware of the Keats analogy and worked it—comedically—into his poetry is itself a Keatsian gesture. Like so many of his poetic identifications, Berrigan's approximation to his model is always only partial, and his failures—often quite conscientious—are as instructive as his successes. In the strong glare of Keats's career, Berrigan's is easily dwarfed. Aligning them throws the local vocational challenges of the 1960s New York scene into historical relief even as it makes the case for the poetic career as an overdetermined, reflexively literary phenomenon.

The Sonnets and the Sonneteer

In a much-cited interview, William Carlos Williams remarked, "Forcing twentieth century America into a sonnet—gosh how I hate sonnets—is like putting a crab into a square box. You've got to cut his legs off to make him fit. When you get through, you don't have a crab anymore" (*Interviews* 30). Berrigan began work on *The Sonnets* with Williams' moratorium on the form ringing in his ears. By the late fifties, Williams' influence was widespread, and his stance toward traditional form—as promoted by poets from Olson to Lowell—was becoming a kind of dogma. But the Doctor didn't so much pull the plug on the sonnet as pronounce it dead on arrival. In the first half of the century, committed practitioners of the form were limited to such marginalized modernists as e. e. cummings, Edna St. Vincent Millay, Elinor Wylie, and Edward Arlington Robinson. After the war, only Edwin Denby, known more as a dance critic than as a poet, and John Berryman, who withheld his sequence from publication until after *77 Dream Songs* won the Pulitzer Prize, took their places on the field as serious sonneteers. *Notebook*, Robert Lowell's sequence of what he called "fourteen-line blank verse sections," came out several years after *The Sonnets*. Once considered de rigueur for poets with epic ambitions—indeed Williams himself wrote a number of imitation Keats sonnets early in his career—the sonnet had become a somewhat embarrassing place to stake one's poetic claim, more congenial for the already established poet than the initiate.

Williams died on March 4, 1963. Berrigan wrote the majority of his sequence in the three months that followed. Elegiac notes sound throughout the
work. Paying tribute to the paterfamilias of one's prospective tradition in the
form he most famously disdained would seem like a rebellious, even disre-
spectful way to enter the literary arena, but Berrigan's animus was not negative.
Despite the obvious flouting of all but the most rudimentary of the sonnet's
conventions—the numbered, boxed, usually fourteem-lined poems *look* like
sonnets, but they don't rhyme; they aren't continuous; they don't conform to
traditional argumentative structure—the primary impulse of the sequence is
consolidation, not revolution. Number 15, for instance, can be unscrambled
by reading the lines in the following order: 1–14, 2–13, 3–12, etc.:[6]

> In Joe Brainard's collage its white arrow
> He's not in it, the hungry dead doctor
> Of Marilyn Monroe, her white teeth white-
> I am truly horribly upset because Marilyn
> and ate King Korn popcorn," he wrote in his
> of glass in Joe Brainard's collage
> Doctor, but they say "I LOVE YOU"
> and the sonnet is not dead.
> takes the eyes away from the gray words,
> *Diary.* The black heart beside the fifteen pieces
> Monroe died, so I went to a matinee B-movie
> washed by Joe's throbbing hands. "Today
> What is in it is sixteen ripped pictures
> does not point to William Carlos Williams.
>
> (20)

The poem creates a kind of cocoon around the battle cry, "and the sonnet is
not dead," muffling it a little. For a work that claims not only to resurrect a
dying poetic form by approximating a radical visual one, but also to immortal-
ize such diverse cultural figures as Williams, Monroe, Brainard, and, implicitly,
Berrigan, sonnet 15 is a halting, careful poem. Its workmanlike quality is the
source of its affective success. The poet has constructed his shrine with an
earnestness that runs counter to the kitschy pop imagery and the mechanistic
form. In sonnet 15, experimentalist virtuosity is mostly show, easily deciphered
and forgotten; the poem works because in it, the "throbbing hands" of the poet
seem almost palpable. Written within a year of the New York debut of Andy
Warhol's *Marilyn* series, sonnet 15 gestures at pop elegy but resists its reveling
in mechanical reproduction. Berrigan's poetic collage reproduces Brainard's vis-

ual one with an aching imprecision. Apostrophizing Williams and compelling the reader to repeat the mournful process of assembling a whole from fragments, it is closer to the elegiac tradition than might first appear.

This tension between *pathos* and *procedure* characterizes the poetic incongruities of the sequence as a whole. Despite the myriad commentaries on form that Berrigan supplied in interviews after *The Sonnets'* publication, it is not primarily an experimentalist work. The compositional process combines elements of proceduralism and seriality; beginning with several imitations of Ashbery, Berrigan automatically excerpted lines into two sestets, and then allowed the newly formed poem to generate the final couplet via semantic and acoustic association. Working in this way enabled him to develop *The Sonnets'* characteristic rhythm; repetition of words and lines within individual poems and across the book as a whole produces a kind of "reverb"—a synthetic echo that interrupts the lyric voice whenever it threatens to extend into song. But Berrigan also maintained that "there's a deliberate parade into it—of the first twelve or so—and there's a deliberate parade out of about the last six or seven," suggesting at least the underlying armature of a linear order (Ratcliffe and Scalapino 51). Elsewhere, he claimed that the sequence was determined chronologically, a collaged diary of the three months in 1963 when it was composed (Ratcliffe and Scalapino 160). Pressed by admirers and students to theorize his debut work, Berrigan adduced a wide variety of metaphors for form—from "block" to "room" to "still life" to "field" to "voice" to "story." These figures stand in for a host of poetic agendas, a representative history of conceptions of form more reflective of the professionalized context of interpretation than the compositional process itself. The poems' rhetorical ruse is to already encompass this context, to deploy its formal experiments with the retrospective confidence of the literary interview.[7] The few critical accounts we have of the book take the bait; at least among avant-gardes, Berrigan registers as a formal innovator, a process poet. But in spite of its internal incoherences, the book is at great pains to present itself as a singular aesthetic statement, and to present its poet as a force to be reckoned with.

Assembling Vocation

Just how carefully wrought Berrigan's debut work is becomes apparent when we compare it to *"C"* magazine, which Berrigan conceived as a periodical workshop for the development of group poetics. Sonnets 1–6 were originally published in the first number of "*C*," alongside several other Berrigan poems, including an imitation of Ashbery's "Two Scenes" and a homage to Mayakofsky. Unlike *The Sonnets,* which rarely cites its sources, sonnet 1 here emerges as the culmination of an extended process of imitation and combination; virtually all of its lines appear in three of the five poems (including ones by other hands) that directly precede it in the magazine. The reader is encouraged to retrace the compositional steps from the Ashbery poem, to Berrigan's imitation of that poem, to the collaged sonnet. Ashbery's "Two Scenes" is not included, suggesting that it would (or should) be fresh in the minds of Berrigan's intended audience. Since I cannot assume such familiarity, and since "*C*" magazine is not readily available, I will reproduce the poems here. Ashbery's first stanza reads:

> We see us as we truly behave:
> From every corner comes a distinctive offering.
> The train comes bearing joy;
> The sparks it strikes illuminate the table.
> Destiny guides the water-pilot, and it is destiny.
> For long we hadn't heard so much news, such noise.
> The day was warm and pleasant.
> "We see you in your hair,
> Air resting around the tips of mountains."

Berrigan's version proceeds:

> I see myself upon the steps at night:
> From every corner comes my motivation.
> My book is architecture:
> I cultivate it on the colonnade.
> Hands point to a dim frieze in the dark night.
> Such a sight has not been mine in many months.
> Winds from the sky are piercing, and they pierce me.
> I bend to my gaze,
> Wind on the strictures like stars.

Ashbery's second stanza:

> A fine rain anoints the canal machinery.
> This is perhaps a day of general honesty
> Without example in the world's history
> Though the fumes are not of a singular authority
> And indeed are dry as poverty.

> Terrific units are on an old man
> In the blue shadow of some paint cans
> As laughing cadets say, "In the evening
> Everything has a schedule, if you can find out what it is."
>
>   (3)

And Berrigan's:

> A fragmentary music clears the room.
> This is a night not without precedent
> Recorded in journals whose sentiments
> Weave among incidents
> Colorless, tactile and frequent.
> Structure becomes a picture of poet and daughter
> In sudden decline to frontiers
> While the orchestra plays for its encore,
> "Boris Alone On His Trail."

In his "Two Scenes," Berrigan retains the syntax, punctuation, lineation, off-rhyme, and some of the language of Ashbery's poem, particularly the language of seeing and revealing around which the "scenes" are organized. But Berrigan replaces Ashbery's elusive "we" with his more aggressive "I." In line 2, the disembodied "offering" becomes "my motivation"; Berrigan turns Ashbery's exteriorized world inward, claims it for his own. As the opening poem in *Some Trees*, Ashbery's "Two Scenes" was daringly unmoored from reference, gesturing to various urban and industrial landscapes but rooted in none of them, and wafting instead on "hair" and "air," "fine rain" and "fumes." Berrigan gives his settings a sculptural solidity; "architecture" and "stricture" lend aural and imaginative structure to the winds that would vanish in Ashbery's evanescent universe. Taking up the theatrical register of "Two Scenes," Berrigan sets his version of the poem with set pieces, aesthetic readymades, not the least of which is Ashbery's poem itself.

The next two poems in "*C*," "Homage to Mayakofsky" and "It Is a Big Red House," derive most of their language from (Berrigan's) "Two Scenes." They thus extend the mechanism through which the source poem is altered and refined—processed—into the final poetic product. Ashbery's "Two Scenes" recedes, passes through imitation Mayakofsky, and finally reemerges in sonnet 1 in the much diminished form of a tonal echo. "From every corner comes my motivation. / My book is architecture" and "A fragmentary music clears the room" combine to become "In the book of his music the corners have straightened." The two final lines of sonnet 1, "Wind giving presence to fragments" and "We are the sleeping fragments of his sky," emerge when "fragmentary music" is added to "Winds from the sky are piercing, and they pierce me" and "This is a night not without precedent." A charged lyric word like "presence," repeated and revamped numerous times throughout *The Sonnets,* here originates as a derivation of "precedent"—a term closer to the quasi-bureaucratic diction of Ashbery's poem. Berrigan thus mobilizes Ashbery's techniques of verbal transformation—generating words metonymically out of shared sound-values—in the service of returning Ashbery's rigorously antipoetic language to its lyrical "roots." In the final product, a few letters suggest an entirely different stance toward poetic subjectivity.

When sonnet 1 is republished as the opening poem of the sequence, however, it appears without this sourcing machinery. Disjunctive and haunted by a sense of their previous poetic environments, the individual words and lines nevertheless compose the opening poem of a sonnet sequence, and demand to be read in that saturated literary context:

> His piercing pince-nez. Some dim frieze
> Hands point to a dim frieze, in the dark night.
> In the book of his music the corners have straightened:
> Which owe their presence to our sleeping hands.
> The ox-blood from the hands which play
> For fire for warmth for hands for growth
> Is there room in the room that you room in?
> Upon his structured tomb:
> Still they mean something. For the dance
> And the architecture.
> Weave among incidents
> May be portentous to him
> We are sleeping fragments of his sky,
> Wind giving presence to fragments.

(7)

Though the opening line appears to refer more to the generative possibilities of the letters *i* and *e* and *z* than to a particular subject or scene, the poem's repetitions quickly create a sense of internal consistency; self-reference takes the place of reference. We don't need to know that line 3 first appeared in "Homage to Mayakofsky" to deduce that "he" is a poet (if not the Poet), perhaps a dead poet, and certainly a figure of some creative power. The third person here opens the sequence under the sign of intertextuality, suggesting that the work depends on some other poet, that it is, primarily, "his." It thus sets forth the central tension of the sequence in classically literary terms; the problem of individuation, which emerges as a social problem later in *The Sonnets* and in the works that follow it, appears here as an invocation of tradition.

While Berrigan doesn't try with any degree of seriousness to build a future exegetical industry into his work, there is, in this first portentous poem in particular, an invitation to interpret; we can't simply let "sleeping fragments" lie. Heroic monumentality, shadowy indecision, and collage come together in the first line; the "dim frieze" is a vaguely Eliotic image of the literary tradition that may not, its dimness and indeterminacy suggest, be accessible to a poet whose individual talent is so easily obscured by his collaging of other poets' materials. "His piercing pince-nez" points suggestively to Charles Olson's claim that in the *Cantos*, Pound drove through his material "by the beak of his ego" (*SW* 82), though here the phallic figure is a nose whose potency is undermined by its "pinced" condition. Throughout *The Sonnets*, Berrigan presents his inclusion in this illustrious brotherhood as a claim, a question, a joke, and, more aggressively, a challenge. In this first poem, it's also a kind of plea. "Is there room in the room that you room in" reads like an example from a handbook of English usage, showing the different meanings of the word *room;* it's an anxious demonstration of virtuosity, and an earnest request for inclusion. The insistent hands—inspired by Ashbery and Mayakofsky—point as well to Keats's "living hand," held toward and gladly accepted by the poet embarking on his career-making book. Sonnet 1 figures tradition doubly: it is stony and sepulchral, but also "warm and capable," even playful. "Piercing" gives way to a collaborative caress.

Berrigan claimed that the first eight lines of each sonnet concerned the notation of sensory data while the last six were more interior and metaphysical, and while this pattern doesn't hold for all of the poems in the sequence, it does provide one account of sonnet 1's relatively tight organization (Lewis 150). Whereas the octave inundates the reader with a variety of semantically unrelated but sonically overlapping images, the sestet adopts a prophetic, universalizing tone. And though "Still they mean something. For the dance / And the architecture. / Weave among incidents" opens more questions than it resolves, it does gesture at the ordering potential of aesthetic activity, the capacity of art to shape fragments into structure. In this context, the final line reads as an invocation of inspiration, the wind that will awaken the "sleeping fragments" of the next eighty-seven poems. In it, we hear a hollowed, somewhat mechanical echo of the "pure serene" that Keats breathes in "On First Looking into Chapman's Homer," or the breath with which Wordsworth opens *The Prelude*.

"Writing a Name for a Day": Poetic Occasion, Poetic Artifact

The last sonnet in the sequence retrospectively reinforces the portentousness of the opening. Though it reverses the order of the octave and the sestet, sonnet 88 follows a similar pattern; the opening six lines cull a series of disjunct images from the rest of the sequence, while the last eight appear to comment on and, in effect, to transcend them. Not surprisingly, "A Final Sonnet" meditates on the question of poetic immortality:

> How strange to be gone in a minute!   A man
> Signs a shovel and so he digs   Everything
> Turns into writing a name for a day
>
>   Someone
> is having a birthday and someone is getting
> married and someone is telling a joke   my dream
> a white tree   I dream of the code of the west
> But this rough magic I here abjure   and
> When I have required some heavenly music   which even
>   now
> I do   to work mine end upon *their* senses
> That this aery charm is for   I'll break
> My staff   bury it certain fathoms in the earth
> And deeper than did ever plummet sound
> I'll drown my book.
> It is 5:15 a.m.   Dear Chris, hello.
>
>   (72)

Berrigan composed the first eighty-seven poems during a two-month period, and then spent another month casting about for the "door out of the sequence" (Ratcliffe and Scalapino 160). The kernel of sonnet 88 occurred to him in rereading *The Tempest* on a bus ride from New York City to Providence, Rhode Island. Unlike the other readymade texts, which—like the reference to Duchamp's *In Advance of a Broken Arm* in this poem—find their way into *The Sonnets* in much-fragmented or transmuted forms, the final lines of Prospero's penultimate speech are imported whole-cloth into this poem. Most of the sonnets in the final third of the sequence are composed of recycled content from the first two-thirds of the book, creating a structure of anticipation. The citation from *The Tempest,* the only "new" material in "A Final Sonnet," punctures this relatively hermetic environment, opening the sequence out into a broader realm of poetic possibility even as it signals—with one of the most famous swan songs in the language—its conclusion.

Prospero's speech marks the end of a poetic career; his own, and, indirectly, Shakespeare's. Why, then, does Berrigan give it such a prominent place in the volume intended to *launch* his career? In interviews and talks on the subject, Berrigan insisted that *The Sonnets* was "the finish of something, not the beginning" (Waldman, *Nice* 22); he said that it was his "first and last adolescent book," and that, completing it, he "gave up that way of writing" (Ratcliffe and Scalapino 161). A quick perusal of *So Going around Cities,* the collected poems assembled five years before his death, suggests that this assessment is in many ways accurate. Excepting, most notably, the collaborations with Ron Padgett, Anselm Hollo, and Anne Waldman, the vast majority of the poetry that followed *The Sonnets* eschewed proceduralism and collage for more narrative, epistolary, or diaristic modes.

"A Final Sonnet" can be read as anticipating this development and commenting on it. Like many of the sonnets, and much of the work that would follow, "A Final Sonnet" is dedicated; though, atypically for Berrigan, the name of the intended recipient—simply "Chris"—is not a recognizably literary one. Dedication had been a signature convention of the New York School for several years before O'Hara's "Personism: A Manifesto" half mockingly founded a movement on the practice of "put[ting] the poem squarely between the poet and the person, Lucky Pierre style" (O'Hara, *Selected* xiv). For Berrigan, it was one of many ways of "writing a name for a day," freighting a poem with human as well as verbal material in an effort, it seems, to rescue temporarily poem, recipient, and by association, poet, from oblivion. *The Sonnets* and later work employ different strategies to accomplish this aim: epigraphs by O'Hara and Ashbery, or tag lines that position a poem "after" or in "homage to" a relatively well known poet reveal just how public, impersonal, and frankly strategic "personism" could be. Borrowing strategies from first-generation New York poets, Berrigan explodes the fiction of their naiveté. He recognizes that a poet of experience in the O'Hara mold is first and foremost a Poet; the publicity of that role pervades even the most intimately intersubjective poetic scenarios. Dedicating "A Final Sonnet" to the unknown "Chris" is a less reflexive, more ingenuous gesture. Here, naming names keeps the poet immersed in the comedy of the quotidian. "Someone / is having a birthday and someone is getting / married and someone is telling a joke" condenses the subject range of this occasional poetic into its most basic elements.

What's missing from this list, most obviously, in a poem otherwise so elegiac, is "someone is dead." As the poet Alice Notley, his second wife, suggests in her introduction to his posthumously published *Selected Poems,* "death as a theme, death and new birth and the loomingness of his own death" became increasingly central to Berrigan's poetry from the mid-seventies on (*Selected* iv). It is central to *The Sonnets* as well, though often leavened with slapstick humor or patent falsehood: "Bearden is dead Gallup is dead Margie is dead." In the 1969 poem "People Who Died," Berrigan would make a sonnet of sorts out of a list of fourteen such "name[s] for a day," only in this poem, the deaths are real and they are delivered straight: "Frank . . . Frank O'Hara . . . hit by a car on Fire Island, 1966. / Woody Guthrie . . . dead of Huntington's Chorea in 1968" (*So Going* 230). *The Sonnets* is notable, however, for the fact that the poet's death, conceived specifically in terms of a literary posterity, is already a concern. Dead poets populate the sequence. From Williams, "the hungry dead doctor," to Keats, the "baiter of bears who died / of lust!" to Guillaume Apollinaire, who is, simply, dead, poets in *The Sonnets* are best known for their mortality. And Berrigan is no exception. As early as sonnet 2, his own epitaph emerges out of the collage: "Dear Margie, hello. It is 5:15 a.m. / dear Berrigan. He died / Back to books. I read."

The Sonnets thus anticipates a personal as well as a poetic end, and in so doing make a bid for the ultimate endurance. Saying good-bye not only to the form that enabled him to embark on his first major project, but also to the crowded, chaotic world of the living, Berrigan strives for majority in Eliot's sense; he produces his sequence as already a synecdoche for his entire oeuvre and thus proleptically "implies a significant unity in his whole work" ("What Is Minor Poetry?" 47). This is the doubleness of *The Sonnets*: full of dailiness, it is zeitgeist poetry that nevertheless attempts to evade the contemporary by pressing time until only the essential elements of the poetic career remain. It's "strange to be gone in a minute," but also preferable to a life of anonymous poverty, however congenial the company. For the poet impatient to be great, bohemia quickly loses its romance. The air is dank with aspiration:

> There is only off-white mescalin to be had
> Anne is writing poems to me and worrying about "making it"
> and Ron is writing poems and worrying about "making it"
> and Pat is worrying but not working on anything
> and Gude is worrying about his sex life
> It is 1959 and I am waiting for the mail

(40)

There's a persistent sense in *The Sonnets* that writing poetry of communal experience is something to do while waiting, for the mail, or—more ominously—

for posterity to distinguish the "I" from Anne and Ron and Pat and Gude. It seems worth noting that the experience Berrigan records in these poems is often falsified, or at least pureed by the cut-up procedure until it is no longer organically autobiographical. Treating even his own life as a "readymade," the poet anticipates an afterlife in the archives and syllabi of secure canonicity.

Sonnet 88 thus pits the occasional against the artifactual in a test of endurance. Prospero drowns his book but Shakespeare lives on, and so, he hopes, would Berrigan. The last line of the poem, "It is 5:15 a.m. Dear Chris, hello," suggests that this kind of survival comes at the cost of immediacy. Telling the time, an O'Haraism that Berrigan often used to kick-start a poem in the urgency of a moment, here concludes the sequence on a somewhat uneasy note. Recycled throughout *The Sonnets,* "it is 5:15 a.m." comes paradoxically to designate timelessness even as it gestures toward a new day and another occasion for poetry. Time, written and reiterated in *The Sonnets,* proves itself to be something that it is not in two very different senses: it becomes a fragment in the spatialized collage system, and an allegorical sign—a marker of its own passing. In the former, Berrigan takes a kind of experimentalist glee; he has developed a sonnet machine which, if he keeps the gears oiled, will pump out infinite poetic product. But the mournful note that sounds in each obsessive iteration of the time undercuts triumphant proceduralism. Geoff Ward has suggested that in O'Hara, accumulated names and times form a kind of group symbol, a "humanist refuge against temporality, seeking by the mutual support of its members to stave off the negative impact of time on each individual subject." O'Hara's struggle to beat time at its own game "by ingesting and acknowledging certain of its powers" in his occasional poetic is ironic but also earnest; his playfulness is underwritten by "the will to believe, in friendship, in art" (62).

In *The Sonnets,* "writing a name for a day" and then shuffling it through the already heavily populated poetic deck represents one response to this problematic. The mechanistic form generates poems against mutability, but its success has the mildly sour taste of a kind of Faustian bargain—submitting to procedure, the poet simply preempts time's mortifying effects. He gets to define the terms in which, inevitably, "a hard core is 'formed'" (*Sonnets* 66). The irony of this situation is not lost on the poet of *The Sonnets,* but, in the flush of inspiration, it is temporarily ignored. In Berrigan's first work, the fact that "The poem upon the page / will not kneel for everything comes to it" fascinates and excites the poet, who is confident in the capacities of his form to shape and contain, comfortable with the balance of power between his art and his life. "The cooling wind keeps blow- / ing and my poems are coming," Berrigan writes in sonnet 75, one of the several poems he composed prior to the conception of the sequence. *The Sonnets* is motivated by the fiction that the poet *chooses* to become, as he put it, "the instrument of the technique"; formal mastery and a certain relinquishing of agency are not mutually exclusive (Ratcliffe and Scalapino 77). *The Sonnets* entrusts the poet's fate to the fate of his words with great good cheer. Monumental, self-elegizing gestures are often coupled with comedic ones, as in sonnet 87, in which "these sonnets are a homage to King Ubu" preemptively undercuts "these sonnets are a homage to myself."

Sonnet 36, one of the more narrative poems from the middle of the sequence, brings the conflict between personal, communal, and aesthetic endurance into sharp thematic focus. Berrigan republished this poem as "Personal Poem #9" in his 1969 collection *Many Happy Returns;* within *The Sonnets* it prefigures his later mode. When the poem first appeared in the second number of *"C,"* the dedication read "homage to Frank O'Hara." In "Personal Poem #9," the tag line disappears entirely. Here, "after Frank O'Hara" reflects *The Sonnets'* abiding concern with literary-historical positioning, the effort to imitate and thus rightfully succeed not only one's master but also, as the poem suggests, oneself:

> It's 8:54 a.m. in Brooklyn it's the 28th of July and
> it's probably 8:54 in Manhattan but I'm
> in Brooklyn I'm eating English muffins and drinking
> pepsi and I'm thinking of how Brooklyn is New
> York city too how odd I usually think of it as
> something all its own like Bellows Falls like Little
> Chute like Uijongbu
>   I never thought on the Williams-
> burg bridge I'd come so much to Brooklyn
> just to see lawyers and cops who don't even carry
> guns taking my wife away and bringing her back
>   No
> and I never thought Dick would be back at Gude's
> beard shaved off long hair cut and Carol reading
> his books when we were playing cribbage and
> watching the sun come up over the Navy Yard
> across the river
>   I think I was thinking when I was
> ahead I'd be somewhere like Perry street erudite
> dazzling slim and badly loved
> contemplating my new book of poems

> to be printed in simple type on old brown paper
> feminine marvelous and tough

A study in verb tense, this poem begins with the present, "I do this I do that" mode, but—like "A Final Sonnet"—quickly leaves it behind for a more contemplative, less immanent verbal register that forms an implicit commentary on the fiction of immediacy. Indeed, "thinking" is the central action of the poem; changes in the form of that verb mark time. This "sonnet" (at twenty-two lines it is one of the longest in the sequence) turns on the fact that poems, like poets, exist in time as well as space; the distance from Brooklyn to Manhattan, like the distance from the first line to the second, is the difference between 8:54 and 8:55, between now and then.

It's also the difference between I and "I." Sonnet 36 takes as its theme the double positioning of the poetic self in time that, I've been arguing, characterizes the rhetorical strategy of the sequence (and of ambitious avant-garde "careerists") as a whole. Despite the fact that in Berrigan's personal mythology the West Village replaces Parnassus as the idealized final resting place, fame, in the more intimate sense of being "badly loved," is still the ultimate goal. Or was. This poem figures literary stardom as the fantasy of a somewhat naive earlier self, a self ironized, even playfully disavowed, by the speaker of the poem who, despite the fact that he's across the river, is implicitly "ahead." The tone is bemused, speculative, not rueful; the humor lies in the realization that Brooklyn, an unglamorous land of professionals, low crime rates, and reformed bohemians, is a strangely comfortable place to be.

The joke, of course, is that the poet is not yet "ahead." Unpublished, he's contemplating his breakfast, not his book of poems, and in composing this one in homage to Frank O'Hara, he's trying to write himself into a modified image of greatness. The humor of sonnet 36 masks the gravity with which Berrigan approaches this project of self-making. Within the sequence, poems trip lightly across time zones and poetic postures; the poet of English muffins and sensuous experience can become a textual artifact—a type, a name—and then happily resume his fleshly identity. He has this flexibility because he presides over the process of premature aging that in turn produces him as a legend in his own time. Whether he is instructing a prospective publisher that his "new book" is "to be printed . . . on old brown paper,"[8] or republishing his own poems and thus conferring the prestigious aura of a "selected" on his second book, Berrigan is his own best promoter. He doesn't attempt to cheat time so much as to put it to work in his public relations campaign. In this early poem at least, the fiction of control is powerful. When majority is a matter of paper selection, the

Dorian Gray–like poet can have his greatness and remain "dazzling slim" too; the sense of disassociation that the poem manifests seems a small price to pay.

O'Hara's own time travels are far less directed; his flirtations with self-difference border more closely on dissolution. Berrigan's optimism results in part from his belatedness; with O'Hara's career as a map, he is free to deviate at will. "How to Get There," first published in the winter 1962 number of *Locus Solus,* appears to have been one of the O'Hara poems that guided sonnet 36's composition. A meditation on the lies that poems tell about time, "How to Get There" figures the self's temporal progress as spatial displacement, a series of positionings across the New York cityscape. But unlike the sonnet 36 speaker, the subject of this poem isn't contemplating his future from the comfortable domesticity of a Brooklyn breakfast; when the poem begins, he's out in the streets and it's not clear what time it is:

> White the October air, no snow, easy to breathe
> beneath the sky, lies, lies everywhere writhing and gasping
> clutching and tangling, it is not easy to breathe . . .
> . . . I see the fog lunge in
> and hide it
>   where are you?
>   here I am on the sidewalk
>   (O'Hara, *Collected Poems* 369)

The city is covered in fog and "soft white lies" and so, we soon see, is the poem. Line 3 gives the lie to the opening line's breathy confidence; the speaking voice shifts from first to second person and back; at the beginning, there's "no snow," but midway through the weather turns several times in the course of two lines: "it is snowing now, it is already too late / the snow will go away, but nobody will be there." Whereas Berrigan's poem seems to thrill in poetic language's capacity to shift time zones and city boroughs, particularly when it enables the poet to indulge the fantasy of being present for his own posterity, "How to Get There" seems caught between times, not even fully present to the present. The poem's concluding confusion brings the point home:

>   never to be alone again
>   never to be loved
>   sailing through space: didn't I have you once for my self?
>   West Side?
>   for a couple of hours, but I am not that person.

"Never to be alone again / never to be loved"—hell, for the famous coterie poet, is not only other people, but the other person whom the poetic self inevitably becomes. In the spectral light of these lines, sonnet 36's vision of being "badly loved" takes on a slightly sickly hue. It is tempting to read these poems as presaging the tragic fall that, in myths of celebrity, always seems to doom the star too quickly risen. As we've seen in *The Sonnets,* Berrigan works by mobilizing such narratives on his own behalf, pushing self-consciousness to the point where it folds back into naiveté, the pleasant illusion that he has it all under control. O'Hara's poetry is itself full of intimations of mortality consciously linked to the strain of living a public persona. "Getting Up Ahead of Someone (Sun)," a poem set on Fire Island and often cited as a foreshadowing of his death there several years later, concludes:

> and the house wakes up and goes
> to get the dog in Sag Harbor I make
> myself a bourbon and commence
> to write one of my "I do this I do that"
> poems in a sketch pad
>
>   it is tomorrow
> though only six hours have gone by
> each day's light has more significance these days.
>   (O'Hara, *Collected Poems* 341)

Written in 1959, five years before the City Lights Books' publication of *Lunch Poems* brought together a critical mass of so-called "I do this I do that" poems in one volume, "Getting Up" performs the literary-historical task of genre definition on itself. The tone is only slightly jaded; there's an unexpected sincerity in the last line's meditation on mutability. But the poem sets up an abyssal structure into which it must fall: writing poetry of experience about writing poetry of experience takes its toll; experience dries up, demanding poetry or bourbon for lubrication. For O'Hara, the "I do this I do that" poem *is* the day, and once it's written, "it is tomorrow."

In sonnet 36, "feminine marvelous and tough" gestures to a future in which a poet is words, and not even necessarily his own. Contemplating his new book of poetry, Berrigan composes his own jacket blurb and, presciently, writes his own epitaph. Berrigan had a special talent for recognizing durability: "Grace to be born and live as variously as possible," the line from "In Memory of My Feelings" used as both the epigraph and opening of sonnet 55, is in fact etched on O'Hara's grave. "Feminine marvelous and tough," while not literally etched in stone, comes to have a similar posthumous value as it is repeated, mantra-like, throughout so many of the homages and elegies written for Berrigan. The poet of *The Sonnets* anticipates the irony of this fate, lost on most of his mourning friends. The line seems representative, so very "Ted," because—as Berrigan writes in an elegy for O'Hara—it "will never be less than perfectly frank" (Berkson and LeSueur 11). "Marvelous," in particular, ventriloquizes O'Hara in his campier moments and seems markedly out of place in Berrigan's rigorously macho lexicon. Indeed, it appears three times in "In Favor of One's Time," which O'Hara first published in the May 1960 issue of *Poetry* magazine. Spelled "marvellous," the word puns on Andrew Marvell, with whose "The Garden" the poem mischievously plays. The true subject of "In Favor of One's Time" is the compression of poets into words, how—for the historically conscious poet— all words encrypt the names of the poets who once used them. "When I think of Ted, I think of the fact that one of my favorite putative lines of O'Hara was written by him ('feminine marvelous and tough') in an extraordinary homage," writes David Shapiro in his contribution to Berrigan's funereal volume (Waldman, *Nice* 226). *The Sonnets* is itself an extraordinary homage, not least because it founds a career on the tenuous ground of a mistaken identity.

"Alone and Crowded, Unhappy Fate": Editorship and/as Authorship

In *From Outlaw to Classic: Canons in American Poetry,* Alan Golding elaborates two competing models of canon formation, the "aesthetic" and the "institutional." Narrowly construed, the aesthetic model maintains that poets produce canons by admiring, imitating, and transforming the work of their precursors—all within the bounds of their poems. Golding cites Helen Vendler as a representative proponent of this school of thought: "It is because Virgil admired Homer, and Milton Virgil, and Keats Milton, and Stevens Keats, that those writers turn up in classrooms and anthologies," she argues (Golding 46). Conversely, the institutional model holds that the value of poets, poems, indeed the "literary" itself is determined within institutions and by their functionaries. In the twentieth century, most institutional theorists agree, the academy, with its team of teacher-critics, is the only game in town. Golding takes issue with both of these models: he argues that advocates of the aesthetic model don't acknowledge their own institutional positioning and its shaping effect on the canons they discuss, and that the institutional model has no place for individual agency, robbing poets and critics alike of any hand in their own destinies. In their stead, Golding proposes a synthetic theory of canon formation. Discussing the canonizing efforts of poet-produced little magazines like Cid Corman's *Origin,* he suggests that while poets (especially those in the avant-garde) do engage in such efforts—either in their poems or in other institutions—the academy remains the site where they "get preserved, perpetuated, and disseminated (or, alternatively, suppressed) by nonpoets" (51). However, while the academy may determine poetry's reception amongst scholars and students, "it does not therefore define the terms of poetry's practice or its relevance for other poets, its power to generate further production" (141).

I have been arguing that Ted Berrigan works at the intersection of the institutional and the aesthetic, and I've been tracing the effects of his double positioning in poetic, social, and biographical terms. My subject, career building, differs from canon formation mostly in terms of temporal scope, but the two are also importantly related. In *The Sonnets,* in his professional relations with such institutional figures as Lita Hornick of *Kulchur,* as well as in *"C,"* Berrigan launched his career—that is, created the conditions for his own persistence as a working poet—by admiring, imitating, and transforming, as well as "preserving, perpetuating, and disseminating" the works of other poets. Berrigan was quite literally a "poet's poet"; deriving his poetic material (even his identity) from that of his friends and colleagues, he had a personal stake in facilitating their success. Invoking posterity and positing canonicity were means of generating further production—his own as well as others'—in the hopes that someday, someone might do the same for him. This dialectical strategy emblematizes the historical situation of an avant-garde so complex and internally evolved that, as Bourdieu puts it, "the very structure of field [is] present in every act of production," and the "irreducibility of the work of the cultural production to the artist's own labor" appears more clearly than ever before (*Field* 108–9). Berrigan played both tradition and the individual talent, as it were. In this last section, I will look briefly at *"C"* and suggest how the little magazine worked as a stage for this acrobatic performance.

In May 1964, one year and eight issues into its publication, Berrigan sold the editorial materials surrounding *"C"* magazine to a local bookseller, who then sold them to the Syracuse University library. For a fee of one dollar per page, he also wrote a ten-page journalistic account ("It's 6:15 a. m. May 22nd, 1964") of a year in the life of the magazine and its editor, to be included in the archive along with dummy issues, correspondence, financial records, and original authors' manuscripts. It was a prescient gesture. The magazine ran for another five issues and became, by the time it phased out in 1966, one of the dominant organs of the second-generation New York School and a spur to the organizing impulses of the St. Mark's Poetry Project. Establishing *"C"* in the wake of the by-then-defunct first-generation journal *Locus Solus,* Berrigan positioned himself on the cusp of a literary period; he and his peers were to be the heirs to Ashbery, O'Hara, Schuyler, and Koch, and the execution of the estate would take place in the pages of the little magazine.

In an interview a decade later, Berrigan described the combination of chance and design by which he founded *"C"* and became the unofficial historian, ringleader, and bursar of the New York School:

> There were these four people, and when I first came to New York . . . from Oklahoma . . . I was very interested in these four people . . . There weren't many people that were interested in those four people . . . so I got very interested in them. They seemed to me to open up a lot of possibilities. Then someone asked me if I wanted to edit a magazine. So I said, "Sure!" My plan for that magazine was to publish these four people in conjunction with four or five younger people, myself and people that I knew . . . And I put them in too. And then I realized that there was such a thing as New York School because there was a second generation. So in essence, *we* were the New York School because these guys, although they were the real New York School, weren't doing anything about it and we were. And that struck me as very funny . . . I used to tell people they could join for five dollars. (Ratcliffe and Scalapino 90–91)

At least in this telling, Berrigan's attraction to Ashbery, Schuyler, Koch, and O'Hara is directly tied to their relative marginality to the publishing and critical industries. Despite the promise of the Allen anthology, these poets had limited critical recognition and only four books in print between them. The "possibilities" they opened for Berrigan were varied. They not only offered Berrigan-the-poet models and materials for his experiments in verse, but also made possible the emergence of Berrigan-the-editor and avant-garde canon maker, which in turn paved the way for his own canonization (in a limited sense) as a poet.

Berrigan figures his editorial activity as a chance alchemy. Composing his little magazine, he "put in" a selection of poets and the brew produced literary-historical gold. Editing thus represents one variation on the "collaborative" ethos that Berrigan developed throughout his career: making "works"—poetic or otherwise—is a matter of "changing one thing in someone else's work and making it be your work," "putting in" or "slapping on" found material and "making the changes demanded by that" (Ratcliffe and Scalapino 121). In conceiving of collaboration as an encounter between any number of different writings, set in motion but not controlled by a single writer, and in exploring this practice through the medium of the little magazine, Berrigan followed the lead of Ashbery and Koch, who edited a special issue of *Locus Solus* devoted to collaboration. That issue includes selections from such varied collaborative works as the ancient Chinese "A Garland of Roses," Coleridge and Southey's "Joan of Arc," Breton and Eluard's "Immaculate Conception," and troubadour, Metaphysical, and Cavalier works, along with more expected contributions from Ashbery and Schuyler's "A Nest of Ninnies" and Koch and Jane Freilicher's "The Car." Koch's brief essay on collaboration and a section of notes and commentary on the individual authors and texts combine to make the case for the historical and scholarly significance of the practice. The second in *Locus Solus*' five-number run, the collaboration issue followed a debut issue containing extended selections from members of the journal's editorial board and their immediate circle. The second issue makes an appeal to a broader public; didacticism prevails over performance. Having posited a new (collective) agent in the field, the editors take a step back to trace the lineage of their dominant poetic.

The first issue of "*C*" contains no such theorization of its poetic or its positioning. The brief note on the contents page states simply that "*C*" "will print anything the Editor likes, and will appear monthly." In "Some Notes about '*C*,'" Berrigan claims that "the first issue of '*C*' was deliberately put together by me to reflect the SIMILARITY of the poetry, since I felt the differences to be obvious, and the NEWNESS of such a point of view as we (I) had." Toward that end, he left out page numbers and names of individual authors from the body of the issue, and limited the information in the table of contents to the number of poems included by each of the four contributors—an even more radical departure from conventional modes of authorial attribution than Corman's play with *Origin*'s table of contents. While it is possible to distinguish amongst the works of Berrigan, Dick Gallup, and Ron Padgett, the formating choices conspire against it. All of the poems (with the exception of the Joe Brainard's "diary" and "play") fill approximately the same amount of space on the legal-sized pages; both Padgett and Berrigan include poems titled "Sonnet" in their selections; lines echo across contributors. Berrigan's "A fragmentary music clears the room" responds as much to Gallup's "endless resoundings fill the room" as it does to the source line from Ashbery's "Two Scenes." Like *The Sonnets,* the magazine stands as one work in conversation with itself.

But if "baffling combustions are everywhere," in '*C*' as in *The Sonnets,* they are nonetheless subject to the editor's control and harnessed toward his ends. Berrigan makes this clear in "Some Notes": "I was and am '*C*' magazine . . . And I intended and intend for '*C*' to exist as a personal aesthetic statement by me." Claims like these are always at least partially ironized in Berrigan's self-mythology. As I've been arguing throughout this book, however, poetic careers consist of more than their rhetorical performances. In the retrospective light of literary biography, the ends justify the means and demand to be examined empirically as well as read rhetorically. Berrigan sent copies of "*C*" to "names" like Barbara Guest, Jasper Johns, Edwin Denby, all culled from the New York City phone book. Kenneth Koch, whom he already knew, gave him other "names"—John Ashbery, Joe Ceravolo, and Jane Freilicher. Such assiduous marketing efforts resulted in personal notes, financial contributions, and promises of poetry; names became material realities. Johns sent ten dollars and a request that the painter Frank Stella be included on the "*C*" mailing list. O'Hara, with whom Berrigan had been corresponding at his Museum of Modern Art office, invited him to a cocktail party welcoming Ashbery back from Paris. Of this event, at which he secured Ashbery's permission to publish several poems in issue no. 5, Berrigan writes: "For me this made '*C*' more real than anything that happened so far" ("Some Notes" 8).

As much as the sonnet sequence, then, Berrigan "used [the little magazine] to be [his] big jump into poetry and stardom, as it were." And as in many of Berrigan's longer poetic works, the relatively fixed procedure on which the little magazine was founded quickly begins to generate itself; the collaborative circle widens, guest editors take over, the budget increases, and an institution is born. Berrigan was characteristically ambivalent about the ripple effects of "*C*'s" success—thrilled by the society it enabled him to enter, but wary of the challenges to his creative control. In the fourth issue, as in issue 2 of *Locus Solus,* the hermetic organization of the first three issues gives way to a more public, even academic mode. Devoted to Denby's sonnets, this issue contains an essay on his work by O'Hara (originally printed in *Poetry* magazine), as well as an introduction by John Wieners and a notes section at the end. The front and back covers, designed by Andy Warhol, feature photographs of Denby and Gerard Malanga—elderly and distinguished and darkly handsome, respectively—in various stages of embrace. On the "question of taste" raised by the image of the two men kissing, Berrigan cites O'Hara's cocktail party quip as the "final word": "if poetry can't survive a little faggotism, then I don't know what can!" ("Some Notes" 10).

The homoerotics of the fourth issue function on a number of levels: depicting the sexualized spectacle of elder and ephebe, the cover photos help to enact the transmission of cultural capital from one poetic generation to the next, at least on the cocktail circuit. Urbane gayness, however veiled, was a signature of the *Locus Solus* group; in "*C*" it works as a citation, a positioning act, but one with multiple repercussions. If New York wasn't the "high-powered homosexual scene in the arts" that Amiri Baraka claims it was in *The Autobiography of LeRoi Jones* (187), the City Poet's casting couch did hold a certain power. And "C" did in fact gain Berrigan access to O'Hara's bedroom, where he rummaged through unpublished manuscripts and discovered several gems. In her recent book *Andy Warhol, Poetry, and Gossip in the 1960s,* Reva Wolf argues that Warhol placed these pictures in "C" in an effort to anger O'Hara, with whom the artist had an ongoing rivalry (19–25). Denby was perceived as an untouchable deity in the O'Hara circle, whereas Malanga was a young arrival (working as Warhol's assistant) of questionable sexual reputation (21). Wolf contends that by coupling them on the covers of "C"—a journal she places within O'Hara's domain—Warhol aimed to insult O'Hara on his home turf. While this reading is laudable for its interpretation of artistic practice as social strategy, it founders on a number of issues. It gives short shrift to Berrigan's editorial control: he mobilized "C," at least its early issues, very much in the service of his own interests, and he would have no interest in helping Warhol snub O'Hara. Moreover, O'Hara did not appear to mind the cover, as the light-hearted response cited above suggests.[9]

But Wolf's analysis of the Denby/Malanga cover as a site of Warholian social maneuver does open to question the motivations and anxieties behind this particular positioning act *for Berrigan*. He and his immediate cohort were as insistently straight as O'Hara's circle was gay, a fact that produced a certain insecurity on the part of the would-be heir, which in turn produced such moments of apparently compensatory comedic excess as these lines from "Tambourine Life": "I have many men friends / I would like to fuck / However, I am unable to do so / because I am not a homosexual / fortunately / this makes my life complex / rather than simple" (*So Going* 111). The question, of course, is how to read the "fortunately," for Berrigan's straightness did make intimacy with O'Hara—and thereby access to his authority—"complex," both psychosexually and in more frankly institutional terms. Read from Berrigan's perspective, Malanga and Denby might function as wishful substitutes for himself and O'Hara, respectively.

But the dynamic appears to be even more "complex": bisexual and equally committed to the poetic and the visual arts, Malanga moved freely in and out of Berrigan's cohort, transcending generic and sexual boundaries and thereby rendering them open in a way that would have been both enviable and discomfiting. Rather than a clean substitution for Berrigan, Malanga more likely functioned, in the language of "Personism," as a "Lucky Pierre." Capable of both giving and receiving pleasure and intimacy, he could achieve the kind of immediate connections that Berrigan could enjoy only vicariously. Gregory Bredbeck has used O'Hara's notion of the poem as "Lucky Pierre" to help figure the workings of a gay discursive strategy that he calls the "trick." Bredbeck defines the

"trick" as "the material site energized by the full symbolic potentiality of homosexual eroticism . . characterized by a doubleness that the (heterosexual)
phallus/penis represses" (274). In its association of gay-identified bodies with
deconstructive potentialities in language, Bredbeck's "trick" resembles Edelman's notion of "homographesis," which I discussed with respect to the poly-
morphously desirous poetry of early "A" in the previous chapter. Both discursive phenomena are said to supplement, and thereby reveal, the fundamental
conditionality of a phallic linguistic order in which signs would have a self-
evident and unidirectional relation to truth. Bredbeck's and Edelman's models
help to connect poetic and more fully psychosocial planes, and they resonate
with the specific kind of anxiety that three of the four poets in this study ex-
hibit. For Berrigan, Zukofsky, and Olson as well, certain figures of sexual ambiguity appear to undermine the precise version of self-legitimating authorial
identity whose value they worked to institutionalize; these figures give the lie
to projective self-fashioning, as it were. As I suggested with regard to Olson at
Berkeley, homosexuality gets registered as threat at moments when the boundaries of poetic authority are particularly vulnerable. Panic and the instinct to
repudiate appear a function less of sexual insecurity and phobia than of the
tenuous social and institutional structures grounding poetic identities that
would be organic and self-legitimating. Malanga's compromising position on
the cover of Berrigan's position-taking publication allowed Berrigan to make
headway in the gay world of his poetic heroes, but it also compromised whatever sense of self-sufficiency he still maintained. Indeed the privileges of editorship came at the cost of authorship. Padgett edited issue no. 7, and filled it
with selections from Kenward Elmslie, Schuyler, Koch, Guest, O'Hara, and
Ashbery. With issue no. 8, Berrigan regained control, resuming his policy of
presenting himself and a few largely unknown poets.

And five issues later, he ceased publication. Little magazines have been described as kamikazes on the literary battlefield; death is part of their function.
Avant-gardes fertilize the soil, and the culture at large grows. I've been arguing,
however, that from the perspective of the struggling poet, the rhythms of literary history are not nearly so inevitable. Anticipating and even performing his
own demise is one of the ways in which the ambitious poet attempts to assert
control over his career. For a coterie poet like Berrigan, death was a seductive
means of individuation.

But the institutional strategy leaves traces which survive, and potentially
overshadow, the aesthetic vicissitudes of the individual agent. For Berrigan,
whose work so assiduously advanced and internalized the social structures that
conditioned its reception, collaboration—increasingly with his own alienated

self—was addictive. Starting with "Tambourine Life," the long "open form" poem that Berrigan added to daily, the poetry of experience and the poetry of citation and collage begin to merge in less productive ways. The conceptual aggressiveness and personal investment of *The Sonnets* give way to what Berrigan called his "machine ability." Having produced himself as "this wonderful poet," "Ted" begins to live as the subject of his own gossip column—a condition not conducive to either life or writing. The post-*Sonnets* list poems— "Things to Do in New York City," "Things to Do in Ann Arbor," "Things to Do on Speed"—manifest the difficulty of living a public persona. In them, the present imperative transforms the private, diaristic mode into a bohemian guide to daily life:

> Wake up high up
>   frame bent & turned on
> Moving slowly
>   & by the numbers
> light cigarette
> Dress in basic black.
>   (*So Going* 134)

The implied audience of the list poems is doubled. Written for a public, they make a tourist attraction of the poet's home and an example of his life. Written for Berrigan himself, they stand as, in Charles Bernstein's words, "not . . . a document of a life in writing, but, inversely, an appropriation of a life by writing" (Waldman, *Nice* 154). Posterity aside, making lists is necessary for survival; writing compels living:

> Now I'm going to do it
>   deliberately
>
>   . . .
>
>   get into the bed
>   be alone
>   suffocate
>   don't die
>   & it's that easy.
>   (*So Going* 196–97)

Berrigan died of liver failure in 1983 at the age of forty-eight.

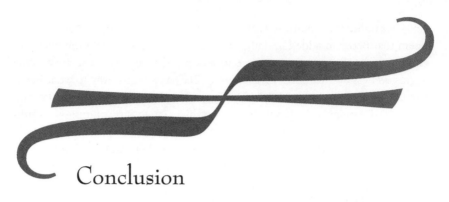

Conclusion

Unnatural Acts and the Next Acts

"I know how to work the machines!" Anne Waldman declares near the beginning of "Fast Speaking Woman" (*Helping* 42). An incantatory rush of first-
person declaratives, "Fast Speaking Woman" begins in the ether: "Because I am
air / let me try you with my magic power" (36). But with "I know how to work
the machines!" Waldman celebrates a more mundane and yet world-changing
kind of power. In 1965–66, downtown poetry readings began moving from
cafés like Le Metro and the Deux Magots to the vestibule of a community
church called St. Mark's on the Bowery. The Office of Economic Opportunity
delivered a grant to develop an arts program there for local youth, Joel Oppen-
heimer—a relative outsider to the café scene—was selected to direct it, and
Waldman was hired on as his assistant. In the next two years, the St. Mark's
Poetry Project emerged as a powerful locus of workshops, readings, and publication ventures, the gal Friday became the boss, and the postwar avant-garde
had its first major woman-run institution.[1]

   While its official history has yet to be written, from its inception the St.
Mark's Poetry Project left a paper trail in a range of genres. Part of its initial
grant included a publication, and after a single issue of a glossy journal called
The Genre of Silence, a new mimeo magazine called the *World* became the primary focus, coming out every month in its initial phase and more sporadically
after that. Edited at the outset by Waldman, along with Lewis Warsh, Joel Slo-

man, and various guest editors, the *World* reflected the particular flavor of St. Mark's writing, and in the early days its production—especially the collating parties held at Waldman's apartment—helped to consolidate the community. The *World* is still in publication, as is the *Poetry Project Newsletter,* which began in 1972 under Ron Padgett's editorship (he was then director of the Project) and continues to come out monthly.

Poet and organizer Bob Holman drafted an oral history of the Poetry Project in 1979, but like most such documents, its factual reliability remains uncertain. The challenge, for now, is to read the social dynamics of the institution in its literary productions. One key question that I hope the foregoing study might prompt is whether the Poetry Project's deviations from its "projective" forebears—the institutions I've been discussing—are a product of the gender of its early leadership or, rather, conditioned it. Heterogeneous and subject on occasion to factionalism, like all of the alternative poetic institutions I've analyzed, St. Mark's in its first decade was not a monolith. What makes it significantly different from those other institutions, however, is that it didn't strive to be. Full of strong personalities, the Poetry Project struggled to institute mechanisms of accountability and inclusion: among them, regular community meetings, the election of an advisory board, and open readings on Monday nights.[2] Waldman herself appears to have been a boundlessly energetic leader, willing to take charge and thus taking charge of many of the Project's projects. The persona in "Fast Speaking Woman" reflects this encompassing energy. Waldman borrowed the chant form from a Mazatec Indian shamaness named Maria Sabina; in making the form her own, the poem both decenters the self and, especially in performance, gives it space for indefinite expansion.[3] Waldman's mode thus takes its cues from Olsonian projective size; indeed in the volume *Fast Speaking Woman,* she recounts her attendance at the Berkeley Poetry Conference and grounds her emergence as a poet in her experience of his performance there (145–46).

Bernadette Mayer, a central participant in the early Poetry Project and the leader of several of its workshops, was tending, in the early 1970s, toward very different poetic modes, in general favoring experiments in collaboration, fracture, and linguistic immersion over the visionary expressivism in which Waldman was then beginning to work. *Unnatural Acts,* the magazine that emerged in three issues from Mayer's 1971–75 workshop, manifests something of her aesthetic sensibility, and suggests the social structure of her workshop as it contributed to the variegated nature of the St. Mark's scene as a whole. In its treatment of authorship and issues of literary property, *Unnatural Acts* might be situated on a continuum with Corman's *Origin* and Berrigan's "*C,*" but it positions itself so far down that line that it ends up constituting a major departure. In its first issues, *Origin's* table of contents listed contributors and their poems, but no page numbers. When Berrigan started *"C,"* he left out page numbers and names of individual authors from the body of the issue, and limited the information in the table of contents to the number of poems included by each of the contributors. In its first issue, *Unnatural Acts* came out entirely without attribution or editorial information. Issue no. 1 consists of fifty-seven numbered sections, which include such varied poetic interventions as the diaristic "radio plays nothing but news why don't you tickle me"; the definitional "homeostasis is the process by which living beings resist the general stream of corruption and decay . . . "; the satirically political "In resistance, the policy of (necessarily) limited involvement or cooperation is the only possible answer that has any hope of toppling the enormous cupcake dilemma now plaguing us"; the orgiastic/erotic "Hurrah for armpits and eyes / Ears / toes and toenails / And now its hair / Hair in the pubic crotch / Hair on the head / Who knows or cares what will come next / So long as it excites / and I get some of it"; and finally, in number fifty-seven, the plaintive/comic "Does everyone here know what / an ashram is except me?"

The product of a group of people gathering at Mayer's loft, writing for eight hours, and then publishing the results, this first issue of *Unnatural Acts* exhibits all of the unevenness that might be expected from such a process.[4] As was the case with later issues of *"C,"* the second issue offers a more explicit account of editorial policy and aesthetic agenda. A sidebar that continues from the front to the back cover declares that "each issue of unnatural acts magazine will be a collaborative writing experiment," going on to name the eleven contributors, indicate the date (November 11, 1972) on which the issue was written, and describe the process: Each writer brought a page of writing which was traded, rewritten, and discarded. Participants then selected one of the rewritten documents and used it as the basis for a new piece of writing. They noted the time at which their new work was completed, returned it to a common pile, and then chose another page to begin the process again. The front and back covers contain a scattering of quotes—obviously without attribution—commenting on this process and theorizing collaboration more generally. Some of these pieces come together in a kind of disembodied discussion:

> do we say problem or
> experiment

the first time we said experiment . this
time we would be more accurate if we said

> problem because there were more concrete
> expectations . their influence . these
> expectations

Unnatural Acts no. 5 also elaborates its process, which directed writers and visual artists through four stages of collaborative engagement and exchange. After that issue, which was in fact only the third *Unnatural Acts* to be produced, the project terminated, a fact attributable, at least in part, to the rigorous, protracted nature of its various experiments.[5]

"Our poems aren't our appearances," one excerpt from the issue no. 2 cover maintains, "when you take out the I's / everybody is matched." It is tempting to imagine a community as well as a poetics founded on "taking out the I's," and it seems that Mayer's workshop and the extended group of writers and artists surrounding it began to approximate such a space. In its desire to take on the "unnatural"—the corrupt, the stolen, the disembodied—as its primary model for producing artworks, the workshop deviates radically from the fantasies of self-legitimation and organicism manifest in Olson, Creeley, Zukofsky, and even Berrigan's poetic and institutional productions. The "necessity . . to be as wood is," declared by Olson in "Projective Verse," is nowhere felt in *Unnatural Acts*, and Berrigan's half-ironic claim, cited in the last chapter, that "I was and am '*C*' magazine . . . And I intended and intend for '*C*' to exist as a personal aesthetic statement by me," finds no correlative in Mayer's near-invisible self-positioning. In place of individual ambition, process itself appears to reign. For better or for worse, this presages innovative poetry's governing ethos for the next decade. "Experiments," Mayer's contribution to *The L=A=N=G=U=A=G=E Book*—a signature volume for that decade—closes with the command "work yr ass off to change the language & dont ever get famous" (83). That such a proscription never became dogma at the St. Mark's Poetry Project is itself indicative of that institution's openness to difference, an openness Mayer helped to instill.

Language Writing Institutions

I have traced the development of the postwar avant-garde's "social evaluation" back from the concentrated moment at Berkeley in 1965 to Olson and Creeley's first letter exchanges in 1950, and then on through the vortex of Zukofsky's epoch-spanning career to Berrigan who, though he was just a rookie at the

Berkeley conference, is nevertheless contemporaneous with the cultural moment that was reaching fruition then and there.[6] Chronology is not secure in
avant-garde careers; each of the poets tampers with it, inventing forms to contain, reverse, spatialize, mechanize, or render its immediacy or duration. I have
obviously adjusted it as well, in order to convey something of their experience
of the perpetually emergent cultural formation in and through which they constructed their careers. Creeley's ongoing career has been given the shortest
shrift; Zukofsky's "Objectivist" years and Berrigan's later work vie for a close
second. Dying in 1970, and helping to get things started in the late 1940s and
early 1950s, Olson gets the fullest treatment here. By dint of accident, scholarly
expedience, and his own intention, his career brackets the moment, giving a
particular shape to the "permanent revolution" in which individual and collective identities got made and remade.

That the poets associated with language writing—along with *their* younger
contemporaries—have been engaged for more than twenty years in a process
of emergence as internally fractious as that of their New American forebears is
a credit to the avant-garde's revolutionary permanence. The "politics of intention"[7] don't guarantee univocality or consensus; rather, they often entail contention, aggression, and wounded narcissism staged more publicly than the
etiquette of large-scale cultural institutions would allow. In this regard, Olson's
on-air crisis at Berkeley—performed on the grounds of the University while
shattering much of its decorum—finds a contemporary correlate in an event
staged in response to Bob Perelman's book *The Marginalization of Poetry: Language Writing and Literary History* (1996). This event—held at an East Village
performance space on March 22, 1997, and published two months later as an
installment in *The Impercipient Lecture Series*—reproduces aspects of Olson's
talk in both theme and social context.[8] At issue is the collective identity and
revolutionary status of a literary movement well into its second decade of existence; under scrutiny is a text attempting to vocalize and historically position
that movement's internal "antinomies" from "the stance of being both inside
and outside" (Perelman, "Counter-Response" 43). Perelman's "double per-
sonnage" status as both avant-garde participant and academic professional
grounds both his book's and the evening's partisan struggle.

The *Marginalization* event reproduces the crisis at Berkeley in its outward
display of internal dissention: Perelman's text and Perelman himself face the
harshest criticism from San Francisco language peer Ron Silliman, who accuses
both of complicity with an academic regime he perceives to be constitutively
hostile to the polysemous presence of radical poetry. But the deviations from
Olson's performance at Berkeley are even more notable; they bring into relief

the peculiar problems of the avant-garde social formation that was reaching its peak in 1965, and they suggest some of the ways the next generation sought to solve those problems. The event of March 22, 1997, was organized as a group of "readings and responses," judiciously regulated in length, and distributed evenly among established and emergent members of the community—Silliman and Ann Lauterbach, and Julianna Spahr and Steve Evans, respectively. Reproduced in the *Impercipient* in edited and footnoted form, the performances never attempted extemporaneity, and whatever stammers and digressions may have occurred orally have been excised from the printed version. What has disappeared, in other words, is the vatic singularity valorized in Olson's performance and in its subsequent transcription and publication. As I've suggested, the emphasis on the present-tense "talk" of the hero-poet was itself a species of institutional strategy, and the tense coexistence of the two modes put Olson's performance under special pressure. In the current avant-garde formation, no single poet would take on the burden of articulating the collective.

Nor would mechanisms of publication and distribution support such an endeavor. In this regard, it is worth looking at the *Impercipient* as one example of the forms of reproduction current poets and editors are choosing. In place of the rough- and ready-transcriptions of the talk at Berkeley, which attempted to take literally Olson's declaration that "writing is publishing I am now publishing tonight . . . because I'm talking writing," the *Impercipient* editors offer clever packaging and design: from font, to footnotes, to the knowing subheadings placed in the margins, the material text campily suggests the format of the nineteenth-century philosophical treatise as an alternative to *PMLA* professional antistyle. Produced monthly and distributed to a mailing list, it optimizes a certain neat predictability over "projective" values such as speed, energy, etc. Though the *Impercipient* calls itself a lecture series, the majority of issues offer texts that have never been publicly performed, and those that have—as I suggested above—are reproduced in such a way as to foreground their status as writing. Whereas Olson's performance worked to collapse the realms of individual impulse and institutional codification into a singular revolutionary event, the *Impercipient* event and publication suggest that at least one branch of the current avant-garde is rearticulating production and reproduction, and replacing the hero-poet with a more diversified cadre of players.[9]

A Contemporary Career

Alice Notley's new collection of poetry, the latest in a career spanning over twenty published volumes, is unabashedly autobiographical. The central elements of *Mysteries of Small Houses* are time, its passage, and the self in it. But the book is not so much narrative as fiercely chronological; the poems are relatively brief, self-contained, and beginning with early childhood they proceed through the life—looking back, of course, but marching pretty much straight ahead. Time—being "trapped in time" or being "unlocated, untimed" (114)—is Notley's subject, but she doesn't take great liberties with it, nor does she seek to invent forms that might contain, reverse, spatialize, mechanize, or render it immediacy or duration. *Mysteries of Small Houses* is full of other people, especially the named and unnamed members of the poetry crowd that crammed itself into the apartment Notley shared with Berrigan and their two sons at 101 St. Mark's Place. In a poem called "101" she writes of that place, "This apartment wasn't really me it was everyone else it was the outer world" (113). The book as a whole hews to this distinction. Though it is unavoidably social, in this volume the poetic career, which coincides, for Notley, with the life, is finally the self's; mutability and solitude are given and then lived into. "The shape of a life is impoverishment," she writes in the final poem, going on to ask, "what / can that mean / except that loss is both beauty and knowledge" (138).

Over the course of her career, Notley has "had the task of creating the taste by which [s]he is to be enjoyed"; as an active, early participant in the St. Mark's Poetry Project, and in her work up through the present, she has also helped to create the conditions of possibility for ongoing innovations in poetry and poetic institutions, especially, though not exclusively, among women poets. More recently, Penguin has published two of her books—*Mysteries* is the second—and she has received numerous prestigious grants, but her position in the large-scale literary field is not completely secure. Like her late husband, she runs the risk of entering the canon for her association value: i.e., "like her late husband." It's an ironic predicament, given that she has helped to secure his posthumous reception; among other things, she stewarded into publication and wrote the introduction to his Penguin *Selected Poems,* the only volume of his poetry in print and accessible at the present moment.

In her current volume, Notley writes poetry so fully aware of her situation in the field that it begins to float loose. In a poem entitled "If I Didn't Shiver I Wouldn't Be Cold," she figures the vicissitudes of the literary world in these terms:

skating
down the white river, now a
breakup of ice god that's pleasurable
or dangerous a melting, coming apart in floes
people on other floes . . . poets I was younger with
separate and floating too.

(115)

But she is also engaged with the proposition of the poetic career in a complete, one wants to say *inescapable,* way. Positioned close to the middle of *Mysteries,* "Flowers" reflects this engagement; it gives human heat and social texture to the icy world imagined above. Loosely a recollection of the last years of her ménage with Berrigan, their joint immersion in the life of poetry, and finally her emergence—survival—as a poet, this poem concludes with lived conviction I offer it here as incitement:

I was there because of the poetry
I thought it only grew in really dirty dirt
And there was so much of it everywhere
Ugly-beautiful red rag petals, folksongs of agitation elation
Waving streaming or floating in or through bad air

I lived in a lovely redpetal slowly burning house
On fire because
I lived in a situation which would end
With someone who would die because
Ill-health, excess, poverty, neglect
Are a common sight along roadsides
Orange to scarlet then deep blue as I always say

And so some of it we did and some was done to us
Of the so-called negative characteristics and happenstance
Some of flowers were ugly and leathery
Swamp-stink brown-spotted fights
I'm not being clear, we had inappropriate emotions
The American poetry vacant lot's small and overgrown

So you squabble with everyone
That can be healthy or vicious
When someone's dying for years

He does and doesn't say so: We sip at our sweet poisons
Jewel-colored legendary chemicals
At our emotions splenetic and ecstatic
We are used for various purposes in return for subsistence
But it's always hoped that one
Will contain oneself . . .
Will you not overflow into the lot
As anything beyond your dirt as
Prophecy cry-for-help cry-of-rage cry-of-too-much-
Love cry-of-knowledge, not overflow?

I feel that others don't want to know.
Speaking even now as a later presence.
But in order to be honest
I must change my poem
Drastically, can't get there this way—
I am now the poet in this story

I have a headache in a burning house for years
Hardly know that it's burning
Then after the death-event itself
There's threat of flood and drowning
Scatter marijuana on the waters
To quieten them—is Atlantis sinking?
Nothing so grand as that dream in our lot
Where I'm still choked in dense clusters
I must leave the lot of flowers
To find a purple female cunt-lipped tree
"Drink of the spring inside me"
Water in a tree . . .
This water's really dark and purple
Deathlike and dangerous and free
And drink of it if you can; she says, "I'm
The laurel tree"
But if I drink of her who knows it
If I've drunk from the actual tree
Who can tell except her and me?
Laurel's not for the public head it's a
Secret intoxication

I wonder if this is an obnoxious poem
I wonder if it's really understood that
Poetry and I are its subject, not
The death of a husband in neglect
It's my neglect I'm entranced by
And my garland of the everlasting laurel leaves
Evergreen darkgreen elliptical thick and bunched
(80–81)

Notes
Works Cited

NOTES

Works frequently cited have been identified by the following abbreviations.

CC   *Charles Olson and Robert Creeley: The Complete Correspondence,* ed. George Butterick. Santa Barbara, Calif.: Black Sparrow Press, 1980.

CPCO   Charles Olson, *The Collected Poems of Charles Olson,* ed. George Butterick. Berkeley: University of California Press, 1987.

CPRC   Robert Creeley, *The Collected Poems of Robert Creeley.* Berkeley: University of California Press, 1982.

CSP   Louis Zukofsky, *The Complete Short Poetry.* Baltimore: Johns Hopkins University Press, 1991.

OA   *An "Objectivists" Anthology,* ed. Louis Zukofsky. New York: To Publications, 1932.

SW   *Selected Writings of Charles Olson,* ed. Robert Creeley. New York: New Directions, 1966.

Introduction: Reading the Poetic Career

1. James Butler and Karen Green discuss Coleridge's role in the text's publication in their introduction to Wordsworth's *Lyrical Ballads and Other Poems, 1797–1800* (21–24).

2. For a highly specific exception to this latter claim, see Jauss's "Lyric in 1857" in *Towards an Aesthetic of Reception.*

3. In *Marginal Forces/Cultural Centers,* Michael Bérubé proposes the notion of "authorization" to capture the various processes by which an author is "put into discourse," namely, "the . . . complex interactions with readers, agents, publishers, reviewers, award committees and other institutions" (57). Authorization is a kind of protocanonization; analyzing it helps to demystify the latter dynamic, and intervening in it can be a subversive political act. This is a hopeful prospect for progressive teachers and critics, but— premised on the idea that "academic reception is both the determinant and measure of canonicity and the single most salient characteristic of the literary climate"—it leaves living poets little agency.

4. John Guillory's *Cultural Capital: The Problem of the Literary Canon* (1993), where the use of the term "school" is critical for the sweep of the argument, is the most recent and relevant study in this tradition, which flourished in the 1980s with such landmark

institutional/intellectual histories of literary studies as Gerald Graff's *Professing Litera-ture: An Institutional History* (1987); Jonathan Arac's avowedly Marxist *Critical Genealo-gies: Historical Situations for Postmodern Literary Studies* (1987), which attempts to inte-grate the history of criticism and literary practice; and Frank Lentricchia's *After the New Criticism* (1980), which also proposes to rectify what it sees as contemporary theory's "denial of history" by historicizing contemporary theory (xxiii). These texts, I would argue, place too singular an emphasis on interpretation and judgment as practiced within the university, by its credentialed employees. Written from the perspective of an avant-garde poetry partisan, Jed Rasula's history of canon formation as cooptation in *The American Poetry Wax Museum: Reality Effects, 1940–1990* (1996) nevertheless repre-sents the university in more monolithic terms than did the poets themselves.

5. The most important contributions to this discussion include Rachel Blau du Plessis' critique of Olson's manifesto "Projective Verse," in "Manifests"; Michael David-son's discussion of women's absence as "a structural necessity for the liberation of a new, male subject" in "Compulsory Homosociality: Charles Olson, Jack Spicer, and the Gender of Poetics" (198); and Alan Golding's recent analysis of the cultural politics (including gender biases) of Donald Allen's groundbreaking anthology *The New Ameri-can Poetry* in "*The New American Poetry* Revisited, Again."

6. Sedgwick's concern with the ways in which male/male relationships along the homosocial continuum position women, and her analysis of the importance—for women, or at least for herself as a woman scholar—of studying such relationships, were also useful for me as I positioned myself in relation to the (male) poets and poetic communities in this book. Since postwar avant-garde institutions are still so little stud-ied, I see this work's analysis of their structures of exclusion as a provisional step toward understanding not only the disappearance of women poets from positions of institu-tional power from the end of modernism through, approximately, 1965, but also the particular ways in which they would come to occupy such positions in the period just following this book's primary focus.

1. Charles Olson's "Queer University"

1. The "anthology wars" of the 1960s and beyond have been extensively docu-mented, most effectively by Alan Golding in *From Outlaw to Classic* (3–41) and more recently in "*The New American Poetry* Revisited, Again," and Jed Rasula in *The American Poetry Wax Museum,* where extended appendices cross-reference poets by number and location of anthology appearances, birthdate, prizes received, etc. (485–547). The con-sensus of much ongoing discussion of this issue seems to be that oppositions between "raw" and "cooked," academic and anti-academic, etc., have been overstated, and that the exclusion of women and poets of color from both camps has been underrecognized.

2. Bourdieu describes the sphere of restricted production as a space of "permanent revolution" (*Rules* 239–42). I will be discussing this formulation later in the chapter.

For more on the poetic avant-garde's evolving relation to the academy and popular media from 1945 to 1960, see Jed Rasula's *The American Poetry Wax Museum: Reality Effects,* and James Breslin's *From Modern to Contemporary;* see Robert Von Hallberg's *American Poetry and Culture, 1945–1980* for a discussion of the "centering" of avant-garde poetry in the 1960s, and Walter Kalaidjian's *Languages of Liberation* for a critical reading of that process as the consciousness industry's inevitable incorporation of oppositional projects. I will be resisting the fall topos that structures many of these accounts.

3. For different accounts of the event, see Tom Clark's biography, *Charles Olson: The Allegory of a Poet's Life* (223–25); George Butterick's introduction to Charles Olson, *Muthologos: The Collected Lectures and Interviews;* Ralph Maud's *Charles Olson's Reading: A Biography* (170–72); Michael Davidson's *The San Francisco Poetry Renaissance* (203–4); and Kevin Killian's extended account in his biography of Jack Spicer, *Poet, Be Like God* (344–46). The conference was Spicer's last major public appearance.

4. Recent avant-garde–oriented work is beginning to take up institutional questions while generally maintaining an emphasis on aesthetics. See, for instance, Aldon Lynn Nielsen's *Black Chant: Languages of African-American Postmodernism* (1997), Rasula (1996), and Golding (1995). Nielsen's work is a long overdue genealogy, rooting postmodern poetic innovation (primarily but not exclusively African American) in the tangle of modernist experiment and traditions of black orality and musical improvisation. He discusses the work of African American experimentalists associated with such pre– and post– "Black Arts" circles as the "Dasein" and "Umbra" groups, but he seems more interested in presenting an array of poetries than in tracing the connections between the shape of particular social formations and the kinds of poetry that emerged from them. His long chapter, "A New York State of Mind," approaches the kind of sociopoetic mapping that I attempt here. Golding's book comes the closest to an institutional history of postwar avant-garde formations with its excellent chapter on *Origin* magazine. Despite the promise of "culture" in its title, Daniel Belgrad's *The Culture of Spontaneity: Improvisation and the Arts in Postwar America* (1998), which ranges over painting, sculpture, dance, bee-bop, as well as poetry, presents more of an intellectual than an institutional history of the period.

5. I briefly discuss Jauss's evolutionary model in the introduction and elaborate it further in chapter 2. Iser develops his notion of the "implied reader" in two major theoretical works: *The Implied Reader: Patterns of Communication from Bunyan to Beckett* (1974), and *The Act of Reading: A Theory of Aesthetic Response* (1978). Iser distinguishes himself from Jauss by narrowing the latter's "horizon of expectation" to the notion that texts demand particular readerly contributions in order to "concretize" their meanings.

6. For instance, Svetlana Boym analyzes the very different stakes of aesthetic autonomy for Russian avant-gardes facing state sanction in *Death in Quotation Marks: Cultural Myths of the Modern Poet.* I will be discussing her politically and culturally informed critique of "death of the author" motifs in chapter 3.

7. This is Ron Silliman's formulation, used to describe language writers' efforts to generate their own networks of publication, reviewing, and reading (*Politics of Poetic*

Form 149–74). I contend that this strategy was already operative among the "New American" poets.

8. For more on poets' travels and their relationship to postwar U.S. economic imperialism and "custodianship" of European cultural traditions, see von Hallberg, *American Poetry* (70–72, 252–53). Von Hallberg argues that after the war, modernist expatriatism gave way to tourism as America consolidated a "vital artistic center" (71).

9. These terms come from "Causal Mythology," the lecture that Olson had delivered three days earlier (*Muthologus* 1:94).

10. Olson's exploration of Mayan culture in the Yucatan is often cited as an example of the poet putting himself "in the open" in a directly social, as opposed to purely textual, sense. The texts from this period, *The Mayan Letters* and "Human Universe" (which I will be discussing in the next chapter), avoid the hysteria of the Berkeley talk because Olson doesn't register the subjectivity of the Mayan people as fully as he does his avant-garde peers'. Celebrating the fleshly world of the "common" that he attributes to the Mayans, Olson is able to ignore the differences of language, culture, and discipline that divide him from both the Mayans and the professional archeologists and anthropologists with whom he shares the "field." At Berkeley, I've been arguing, the complexities of the social moment were impossible to avoid.

11. O'Hara wrote in a letter to Jane Freilicher, "I read Paul Goodman's current manifesto in *Kenyon Review* and if you haven't devoured its delicious message, rush to your nearest newstand! . . . its so heartening to know that someone else thinks these things" (Gooch 187). See Golding's account of the article's role in the conception of *Origin* magazine in *From Outlaw to Classic* (122–23).

2. "The Company of Love"

1. *Sagetrieb: A Journal in the Pound-Williams-H.D. Tradition* and the *Man and Poet* series are the National Poetry Foundation's primary publications.

2. In a similarly ventriloquizing mode, Bob Perelman voices some of the more polemical generalizations about mainstream poetry and poetic institutions made by language writers in the early stages of their formation: "the mainstream poet guarded a highly distinct individuality; while craft and literary knowledge contributed to poetry, sensibility and intuition reigned supreme. The mainstream poet was not an intellectual and especially not a theoretician. Hostility to analysis and, later, to theory, were constitutive of such a poetic stance" (*Marginalization* 12).

3. Olson had befriended Metcalf while researching Melville for the book that would become *Call Me Ishmael* (Clark 24–29, 207).

4. Mary Novick, Creeley's bibliographer, reports that by 1971 *For Love* had gone through several printings, for a total of 39,000 copies (7).

5. See George Butterick's account of searching the poet's Gloucester home after his

death for archivable material. Butterick reports finding poetry and poetic fragments on the lid of a coffee container, restaurant napkins, placemats, menus, and sorting through "perhaps ten thousand pages" of the poet's notes ("Modern Literary Manuscripts" 81–104). Some of the materials found there are now included in Butterick's edition of *The Collected Poems*, others have appeared in OLSON: *A Journal of the Charles Olson Archive*.

6. Thomas Strychacz, in *Modernism, Mass Culture, and Professionalism*, and Bruce Robins, in *Secular Vocations: Intellectuals, Professionalism, Culture*, both offer concise renderings of this argument.

7. Bob Perelman suggests that Pound's subject in this passage is "professionalism" (*Trouble* 54–55.) It seems worth noting, however, that this word isn't used here. Expertise is instead associated with both "technique" and the more blue collar-sounding "job." In his preface to An *"Objectivists" Anthology*, Zukofsky inflects the word "job" a bit differently: "a poet-critic-analyst is interested in growing degrees of intelligence. He has an economic bias. He has been doing a job . . . Guillaume de Poitiers had several jobs. He was a poet. He went to war. Obviously he divided his energy, perhaps, perhaps not, to the hindrance of his poetry. At any rate—poetry defined as a job, a piece of work" (14).

8. See Butterick, *Guide*; Sherman Paul, *Olson's Push*; and von Hallberg, *Charles Olson*.

9. Compare the opening of *Paterson* I: "Paterson lies in the valley under the Passaic Falls / its spent waters forming the outline of his back. He / lies on his right side, head near the thunder of the waters filling his dreams!" (Williams, *Paterson* 6). To my ear, Williams's prosiness renders the equation of body and geography less compressed, less literal, than Olson's exhortation.

10. The first of the three volumes is composed mainly of "letters," an appropriate form for a poet who was the son of a lifelong postal worker. In the later, more private volumes, the letter gives way to something more like a journal entry.

11. Gender is always a vexed issue in mythopoetic accounts of Olson's work. Mythopoetics offers an acceptably masculine alternative to the "neuter" constraints of formalism, while giving the scholar access to the female-coded primitive. Take, for instance, *Olson's Push: Origin, Black Mountain, and Recent American Poetry*, in which Sherman Paul focuses on the birthing imagery of the opening stanzas, suggesting that Maximus is born "out of the unconscious, out of the inseparable waters, the sea-blood of self-and-world"(120–21). If the sea is a mythopoetic figure for the "unselectedness" that Olson in "Human Universe" claims is "man's original condition," then "I . . . tell you" enacts a rhetorical process of "selection," positing a subject distinct enough from its object to address it directly (*SW* 59).

12. See the introduction for a fuller discussion of Sedgwick's work and its relevance to the postwar avant-garde more generally.

13. Butterick died in 1988, just after completing the introductory essay for volume 9. Richard Blevins edited that volume and dedicated it to Butterick. This publication history seems worth noting for the way it follows the example of Olson and Creeley's own legacy making in print. As can be told from his regular presence in these notes,

Butterick was the most important of a series of editor figures, including Vincent Ferrini, Cid Corman, and Ralph Maud, who facilitated the poets' publication and set the stage for the miniature exegetical industry that surrounds Olson's work.

14. Clark discusses Olson's complicated relationship with Bolderoff in great depth. See especially 153–76.

15. See Christopher Beach's more involved account of the two poems in *The ABC of Influence* (122–24).

16. *This* magazine, founded by Barrett Watten and Robert Grenier in 1971, also marks its late-stage entry into this tradition (in which Olson and Creeley were by then masters) with the deictic gesture. See Perelman's account of Grenier's remarkably compressed encounters with both literary history and phenomenology, and their formative role in early language writing (*Marginalization* 38–57).

17. See Butterick, *Guide* (262–64), for a careful accounting of Olson's borrowings from Whitehead's *Adventures of Ideas*.

18. In a June 22, 1950, letter responding to Creeley's request that he write a piece on Pound for a little magazine called *Mood,* Olson suggests that Creeley write it for him: "You got my letters. I ain't. Also, I trust bro CREEL" (*CC* 139).

19. Golding discusses this ironic situation (*Outlaw* 125). Corman wrote to Olson: "Must you be forever publishing in PNY's where the entire context militates against and negates your argument?" (G. Evans 1:56).

20. Lisa Steinman discusses modernists' fascination with the new physics—Einstein, Heisenberg, etc.—in *Made in America: Science, Technology and American Modernist Poets.* See especially her discussion of Williams' "force field" poetics in the context of Albert Einstein and Alfred North Whitehead (97–112).

21. Rachel Blau du Plessis' "Manifests" (1996), is the first extended critique of the "exclusionary gender subtext" of Olson's formative essay, a fascinating attempt by a woman experimental poet to determine whether there is in fact "any use" in "Projective Verse" *for her.* Although it is critical, du Plessis' feminist reading of the manifesto nevertheless confines itself to such tentative observations as: "it is interesting that to constitute oneself as a poet with its attendant vulnerabilities and doubts, one reaches for a homosocial and exclusionary gender context." She also notes that "no female poet is mentioned" in Olson's essay, and that, more damningly, the poetics of "rapidity of movement" and "high energy transfer" may have their origin in the work of Marianne Moore. She cites Williams' own 1925 essay on Moore in support of this claim. "If in one genealogical history, Williams (and thus Olson) are born from the rib . . . of the Moore of the teens and early 1920s," she writes, "in another Williams is being born from the head of Olson," and Moore is forgotten entirely (45).

"Projective Verse" is clearly driven by the figure of poetic creation as ejaculation, though I've been suggesting that such an organic "high energy-discharge" requires a good deal of fine-tuning. If Olson's aim is to "mak[e] poetry a serious discourse of assertive, exploratory, and sometimes aggressive manhood," as du Plessis suggests, he also covets the professionalized though somewhat "neuter" authority of the technical expert.

Note as well the modernist, and especially Poundian, origins of ejaculatory poetics. See Koestenbaum's discussion of Pound's claim that "the mind is an upspurt of sperm," and of Pound as midwife of *The Waste Land,* in *Double Talk* (114–29).

22. Alan Golding's chapter on *Origin* in *From Outlaw to Classic* is a model for any analysis of the little magazine—as an independent literary work, and as a player in the politics of canon formation. Golding focuses primarily on *Origin*'s formative role in the "alternative canon" of "New American" poets, as well as the ways in which the little magazine mediated between mainstream and margin. I'm more interested in the internal politics of the little magazine as an institution, the role of boundaries and their trespass *within* the avant-garde community.

23. See Creeley, "On *Black Mountain Review*," in Anderson and Kinzie (248–61) for more on the magazine's founding.

24. Creeley describes Olson and Levertov's responses to Duncan's piece in "On *Black Mountain Review*" (258). Creeley himself liked the poem, saying, "it remains for me an extraordinary summary and exemplar of the possibilities in poetry" (258).

25. See Martin Duberman, *Black Mountain: An Exploration in Community,* especially the final chapter, for the best account of the college's last days.

26. Note the echo of Pound's Gaudier-Brzeska, "who was accustomed to looking at the real shape of things [and] could read a certain amount of Chinese writing without ANY STUDY. He said, 'of course you can *see* it's a horse!'" (Pound, *ABC* 21).

27. In letters to Creeley and Corman, Olson cites archeologist Leo Frobenius and anthropologists Alfred Tozzer and Bronislaw Malinowski as forerunners in the field of culture morphology. Frobenius, the founder of the Research Institute for the Morphology of Civilization in Frankfurt, had achieved notoriety in the United States for the "cave" exhibition he organized at the Museum of Modern Art in 1937 (*CC* 5:204 n. 105).

28. Olson cites Benedict twice in the correspondence with Creeley, each time quoting the following passage, "a people is provided with a technique of cultural change which is limited only by the unimaginativeness of the human mind" (*CC* 1:27, 5:86). Olson takes this pronouncement to confirm the central role of the artist, who has a sense of "the reach of man's imagination."

29. James Clifford discusses Malinowski's project in terms of "ethnographic self-fashioning," the construction of an "authoritative persona" out of the disparate traces of his experience in an alien culture. In the case of Malinowski, this highly complicated, idiosyncratic persona became the model for an entire profession. Clifford suggests that in creating a professional category out of the experience of "participant observation," the "condition of off-centeredness in a world of distinct meaning systems, a state of being in culture while looking at culture," anthropology "transformed a widespread predicament into a scientific method" (Clifford 92–115). Olson's continuing effort to construct the "stance" of the projective poet "in the open" can be seen as a similar "professionalization" of "predicament."

30. The cultural cross-pollination went the other direction as well: a boom in ama-

teur anthropology followed the popularity of figures like Mead and Benedict (whose study of Japanese culture, *The Chrysanthemum and the Sword*, was conducted for American intelligence).

31. In "Charles Olson and the American Thing: The Ideology of Literary Revolution," Philip Kuberski argues that Olson's return to the Mayans is a typically American, typically modernist form of cultural imperialism, in which radical poetics (and nationalist ideologies) must produce a primitive other as ground (175–93). While this binary dynamic is clearly operative in Olson's Mayan works, I've been more interested in the ways in which it gets refracted through his local struggles in the literary and anthropological fields.

3. The Legacy of Louis Zukofsky

1. Carroll F. Terrell speaks for this group when he declares Zukofsky "the greatest poet born in this century" in his introduction to *Louis Zukofsky: Man and Poet* (1979), the festschrift that he edited (15).

2. The primary proponents of this reading are Bruce Comens, in *Apocalypse and After: Modern Strategy and Postmodern Tactics in Pound, Williams, and Zukofsky;* Ron Silliman in *The New Sentence;* Burton Hatlen in "From Modernism to Postmodernism: Zukofsky's 'A'-12"; and in less hagiographic terms, Peter Quartermain in *Disjunctive Poetics: From Gertrude Stein and Louis Zukofsky to Susan Howe.*

3. For more on the poetic and personal connections between the two poets, see Neil Baldwin, "Zukofsky, Williams, and *The Wedge:* Toward a Dynamic Convergence" (129–42).

4. My understanding of this transaction comes from letters to Zukofsky from Levertov (5/6/64, 7/10/64 Harry Ransom Humanities Research Center [HRHRC]). Excepting those from *Pound/Zukofsky: Selected Letters of Ezra Pound and Louis Zukofsky,* all other letters come from the Zukofsky collection at the HRHRC. I have paraphrased the letters from the collection. Where sender and recipient are apparent from context, letters will be cited in the text by date.

5. This is Raymond Williams' term for the power-inflected movement of an agent from "emergent" to "dominant" to "residual" status within a given cultural system (121). I owe my understanding of Williams' concept to Steve Evans' encyclopedic digest of theories of history relevant to twentieth-century avant-garde experience: "The Dynamics of Literary Change: Four Excursuses in Lieu of a Lecture."

6. Bob Perelman's excellent chapter on Zukofsky, "The Allegory of Louis Zukofsky," in *The Trouble with Genius,* is the major exception to my criticism of Zukofsky scholarship. I am deeply indebted to his reading of "A." This chapter aims to extend Perelman's contention that Zukofsky's long poem is "an allegory of what it means to be a poet" (174) more deeply into the poet's biography and reception history.

7. Michelle Leggott reports that in one of the spiral notebooks at HRHRC, Zukofsky

plotted "A"-22 and 23 along two datelines, spanning from pre-3000 B.C. to the twentieth century (55).

8. See Eric Mottram, "1924–1951: Politics and Form in Zukofsky" (76–103), and Silliman (*New Sentence* 150–54) for more on Zukofsky's ambivalent relationship to organized political activity.

9. "An Objective," dated 1950 and published in *Prepositions*, is a composite of the *Anthology* preface and "Sincerity and Objectification: With Special Reference to the Work of Charles Reznikoff," initially published in the "Objectivist" issue of *Poetry*. Zukofsky's commitment to revision clearly extended to prose as well; the *Prepositions* piece has been emptied of many of the early essays' specific references to other poets.

10. Leggott's *Reading Zukofsky's 80 Flowers* provides an exhaustive account of the production of this work, based on her study of the notebooks and drafts collected at the University of Texas Humanities Research Center. She cites this "schema" for the book from Zukofsky's notes: "8-line songs of 5-word lines: 40 words to each poem, growing out of and *condensing* my previous books, '*A*', *All, Arise, arise, Bottom: On Shakespeare, Catullus, Little,* etc." (12). Leggott's persistence with the raw material is admirable, and her readings of "A"-22 and 23 are illuminating, but her account verges on the fetishistic: "On 30 September 1974, Zukofsky took an unlined piece of paper without punch holes (did it reside in the back pocket of the binder?) and headed it '80 Flowers.' Then he wrote . . . " (121). I'm arguing that this kind of fetishism has its roots in Zukofsky's own object system.

11. Perelman's reading of this passage suggests that Wrigley's sign "wavers between an ironic literariness and a non-ironic Marxist teleological acceptance of the here and now" (*Trouble* 41).

12. See, for instance, Derrida's discussion of writing as iteration, and of the sign as "the non-self-identity which regularly refers to the same" (297). Lee Edelman cites this particular passage (245).

13. In "A"-18, Zukofsky asks, "Has scion so much sheet music scores books / to which I have added . . . ?" "A"-12, the elegy for Zukofsky's father, pursues a host of associations around roots, branches, and inheritance, especially the artistic sort.

14. Ahearn discusses Zukofsky's borrowings from Spinoza in some detail (*Zukofsky's "A"-12* 202–3).

15. Studies of Ransom and the development of twentieth century manuscript collections include Thomas Staley, "Literary Canons, Literary Studies, and Library Collections: A Retrospective on Collecting Twentieth Century Writers"; Nicholas Basbanes, *A Gentle Madness: Bibliophiles, Bibliomanes, and the Eternal Passion for Books;* William Matheson, "Institutional Collecting of Twentieth Century Literature"; Anthony Rota, "The Collecting of Twentieth Century Literary Manuscripts"; Descherd Turner, "A Collection Not So Easily Explained"; and Timothy Murray, "The Origins of Institutional Collecting of Contemporary Literary Manuscripts."

16. My understanding of Zukofsky's relationship with HRHRC comes from a file of letters documenting transactions between Zukofsky, F. W. Roberts, then assistant direc-

tor of HRHRC, and Feldman. The facts of the initial "Letters to Louis Zukofsky" agreement are laid out in a letter to Zukofsky from Roberts (10/17/60).

4. "Worrying about Making It"

1. The vast majority of writing on Berrigan takes the form of memoir/homage, and all of it appears in small press publications. More critical engagements include Joel Lewis' "'Everything Turns into Writing': The Sonnets of Ted Berrigan," Barrett Watten's "After Ted," and Charles Bernstein's "Writing against the Body," all of which frame textual reading in terms of a personal knowledge of the poet.

2. Except for Penguin's posthumous publication of the *Selected Poems,* Grove was the largest press to publish his poetry, and—despite his imprecations—they never took him on as a house poet. The MLA bibliography indexes only six scholarly articles devoted to Berrigan, and he is certainly not a regular presence on syllabi of postwar American poetry courses. *The Sonnets* received brief, favorable mention by Hayden Carruth and Kenneth Koch in omnibus "new poetry" reviews for Hudson Review and New York Times Book Review, respectively. Nor is his work widely anthologized: despite his collegiality with Robert Creeley, Frank O'Hara, and the other core poets in Donald Allen's *New American Poetry* (1961) anthology, Berrigan wasn't included in Allen and George Butterick's revised edition, *The Postmoderns* (1982), nor in M. L. Rosenthal and Sally M. Gall's *The Modern Poetic Sequence* (1983). *The Norton Anthology of Modern Poetry* (1973) contains three of Berrigan's sonnets, along with a disparaging headnote.

3. St. Mark's, an East Village church with a long cultural history, became a focal institution for poets and other downtown artists in 1966 when Harry Silverstein, a sociologist from the New School of Social Research, got a grant from the Office of Economic Opportunity to administer an arts project for local youth. Anne Waldman was hired to assist in the development of the poetry component of the program, which came to include reading series and several important publications (Waldman, *Out* 1–6).

4. See chapter 1 for a critical discussion of Peter Bürger's claim, in *The Theory of the Avant-Garde,* that the historical avant-garde exposed the ideal of aesthetic autonomy as an institution with historical and material determinants, but failed in its mission to reintegrate art and life (46). At the Berkeley Poetry Conference of 1965, representatives of the avant-garde poetic communities that had been developing throughout the 1950s witnessed themselves as an institution with internal power structures, systems of communication and reproduction, protections from the market, etc. I'm suggesting that by virtue of his relative belatedness and his poetic of collaged citation, Berrigan was uniquely positioned to "reintegrate art and life" by making the historical predicament of the avant-garde his poetic subject.

5. Lawrence Lipking begins *The Life of the Poet: Beginnings and Endings of Poetic Careers* with Keats's sonnet "On Looking into Chapman's Homer" and suggests that Keats up-

dated the Virgilian model of genre/career development—from bucolic, to didactic, to epic—for the modern poet (3–11, 76–93).

6. I'm indebted to Bob Perelman's discussion of this poem in *Marginalization* (65–66).

7. Berrigan was fascinated by the interview form and exploited it throughout his career. This interest led, most notoriously, to the fabricated interview with John Cage that won $1,000 and inclusion in the *National Literary Anthology*. Berrigan made up both sides of the dialogue, parodying the interviewer's treatment of his subject as "an object to be used." He also collaged in material from recently published interviews with Bob Dylan and Andy Warhol (Ratcliffe and Scalapino 100–101).

8. In 1964, three years before Grove brought the book out, Berrigan published *The Sonnets* himself, under the aegis of "C" press. Ron Padgett edited and oversaw the printing of the mimeographed book, and Berrigan sent copies to, as he put it, "all the poets"—apparently referring to those who would be in attendance at the Berkeley conference (Ratcliffe and Scalapino 126).

9. Wolf's is one of the only books published by an academic press to give sustained consideration to the lively arts scene in which Berrigan (and, of course, Warhol) moved. In its interdisciplinary approach alone, the book goes a long way toward decentering, and thus clearing a space to analyze, the cult of personality with which the name of Warhol is virtually synonymous. But its packaging—from the cover photo to the narrowly biographical way in which its (in fact much richer) argument is framed—ends up elevating the 1960s Warhol to superstardom and reducing the poets to supporting players. Wolf summons Warhol's connection to more marginal figures such as Malanga and Berrigan as a way of giving the architect of our still-current model of fame a kind of "street cred"—not just as an avant-garde, but as an *artist*. In *Andy Warhol, Poetry, and Gossip in the 1960s*, poetry comes to stand in for all that is artistically genuine, in the most traditional, humanist sense. It's ironic that urbane, postmodern poets should be mobilized in this fashion, and their hipness suffers a bit as a result.

Conclusion: *Unnatural Acts* and the Next Acts

1. Waldman makes the connection between this line and her administrative triumph at St. Mark's in Foster, 67. For more on the prehistory of the Poetry Project, see Waldman, *Out* 1–6.

2. Ed Friedman, the current director of the Project and an early participant, discussed these features of the institution in a telephone interview (January 19, 1999). Friedman emphasized that the sheer number of public events held at St. Mark's was itself a mechanism of accountability. The aesthetic and social direction of the Poetry Project depended very much on audiences, who "voted with their feet," according to Friedman.

3. In a note to the poem, Waldman describes the work as "indebted" to Sabina (*Helping* 58).

4. According to Friedman, the immersive nature of the process was designed to open questions about poetic value, and, implicitly, its relationship to the idea of owning a given poem (interview, January 19, 1999).

5. With issue nos. 2 and 5, the magazine extended its borders to include contributors from outside the workshop. According to Friedman, the logistics of production became unsustainable for the core members of the group, all of whom were working on other projects. The members had applied for a grant from the Coordinating Council of Little Magazines (CCLM) between issue nos. 1 and 2 and did not receive it. Lack of funding clearly contributed to *Unnatural Acts'* early demise.

6. See the introduction for a fuller framing of the Bakhtinian notion of the "social evaluation."

7. This phrase, cited in chapter 1, comes from one of the few documents that might qualify as a manifesto for language writing, the collectively written essay, "Aesthetic Tendency and the Politics of Poetry" (see Silliman et al.).

8. Edited by Steve Evans and Jennifer Moxley, the pamphlet series emerges from the nexus of younger poets and writers sometimes known as the New Coast poets and more recently collected in a volume edited by Lisa Jarnot, Leonard Schwartz, and Chris Stroffolino entitled *An Anthology of New (American) Poetry.* The *Impercipient Lecture Series* was originally published in Providence, R.I., and has since followed its editors to Paris. Committed to innovative criticism and theory, with the exception of the *Marginalization* issue, each *Impercipient* is devoted to a single-author monograph.

9. The explosion of Web 'zines and poetry listserves, such as the one linked to the Electronic Poetry Center at Buffalo, instances another mode of reproduction obviously popular among innovative poets. Interesting work is still to be done on the analogues and differences between electronic immediacy and the projective immediacy that Olson hoped the typewriter would revolutionize.

WORKS CITED

Abbott, Charles. Introduction. *Poets at Work,* ed. Abbott. New York: Harcourt, Brace, 1948.

Ahearn, Barry, ed. *Pound/Zukofsky: Selected Letters of Ezra Pound and Louis Zukofsky.* New York: New Directions Press, 1987.

Ahearn, Barry. *Zukofsky's "A": An Introduction.* Berkeley: University of California Press, 1982.

Allen, Donald, ed. *The New American Poetry, 1945–1960.* New York: Grove Press, 1960.

Allen, Donald, and George Butterick. *The Postmoderns:* The New American Poetry Revised. New York: Grove Press, 1982.

Anderson, Elliot, and Mary Kinzie, eds. *The Little Magazine in America: A Modern Documentary History.* Yonkers, N.Y.: Pushcart Press, 1978.

Andrews, Bruce, and Charles Bernstein, eds. *The L=A=N=G=U=A=G=E Book.* Carbondale: Southern Illinois University Press, 1984.

Arac, Jonathan. *Critical Genealogies: Historical Situations for Postmodern Literary Studies.* New York: Columbia University Press, 1987.

Ashbery, John. "Two Scenes." *Selected Poems.* New York: Penguin Books, 1986.

Bakhtin, M. M. *The Formal Method in Literary Scholarship: A Critical Introduction to Sociological Poetics.* Trans. Albert J. Wehrle. Baltimore: Johns Hopkins University Press, 1978.

Baldwin, Neil. "Zukofsky, Williams, and *The Wedge:* Toward a Dynamic Convergence." In *Louis Zukofsky: Man and Poet,* ed. Carroll F. Terrell. Orono, Me.: National Poetry Foundation, 1979. 129.

Baraka, Amiri. *The Autobiography of LeRoi Jones.* New York: Freundlich Books, 1987.

Barthes, Roland. *The Rustle of Language.* Trans. Richard Howard. New York: Hill and Wang, 1986.

Basbanes, Nicholas. *A Gentle Madness: Bibliophiles, Bibliomanes, and the Eternal Passion for Books.* New York: Holt, 1995.

Baudrillard, Jean. "The System of Collecting." In *The Cultures of Collecting,* ed. John Elsner and Roger Cardinal. London: Reaktion Books, 1994. 7.

Beach, Christopher. *The ABC of Influence: Ezra Pound and the Remaking of American Poetic Tradition.* Berkeley: University of California Press, 1992.

Belgrad, Daniel. *The Culture of Spontaneity: Improvisation and the Arts in Postwar America.* Chicago: University of Chicago Press, 1998.

Benjamin, Walter. *Reflections: Essays, Aphorisms, Autobiographical Writings.* Trans. Edmund Jephcott. New York: Harcourt, Brace & Jovanovich, 1978.

Berkson, Bill, and Joe LeSueur, eds. *Homage to Frank O'Hara.* Bolinas, Calif.: Big Sky, 1988.

Bernstein, Charles. "Writing against the Body." In *Nice to See You: Homage to Ted Berrigan,* ed. Anne Waldman. Minneapolis: Coffee House Press, 1991. 154.

Berrigan, Ted. *Many Happy Returns.* New York: Corinth Books, 1969.

Berrigan, Ted. "Some Notes About 'C.'" Ted Berrigan Papers. Syracuse University Library, Department of Special Collections.

Berrigan, Ted. *The Sonnets.* New York: Grove Press, 1967.

Berrigan, Ted. *So Going around Cities: New and Selected Poems, 1958–1979.* Berkeley, Calif.: Blue Wind Press, 1980.

Bérubé, Michael. *Marginal Forces/Cultural Centers: Tolson, Pynchon, and the Politics of the Canon.* Ithaca, N.Y.: Cornell University Press, 1992.

Bourdieu, Pierre. *The Field of Cultural Production: Essays on Art and Literature.* Ed. Randal Johnson. New York: Columbia University Press, 1993.

Bourdieu, Pierre. *The Rules of Art: Genesis and Structure of the Literary Field.* Trans. Susan Emanuel. Stanford, Calif.: Stanford University Press, 1996.

Boym, Svetlana. *Death in Quotation Marks: Cultural Myths of the Modern Poet.* Cambridge, Mass.: Harvard University Press, 1991.

Bredbeck, Gregory. "B/O: Barthes' Text, O'Hara's Trick." *PMLA* 108.2 (March 1993): 268–81.

Breslin, James. *From Modern to Contemporary: American Poetry, 1945–1965.* Chicago: University of Chicago Press, 1985.

Breton, André. "The Second Surrealist Manifesto." Trans. Richard Seaver. In *Manifestos of Surrealism,* ed. Helen R. Lane. Ann Arbor: University of Michigan Press, 1972.

Bürger, Peter. "The Problem of Aesthetic Value." In *Literary Theory Today,* ed. Peter Collier. Ithaca: Cornell University Press, 1990. 23.

Bürger, Peter. *The Theory of the Avant-Garde.* Trans. Michael Shaw. Minneapolis: University of Minnesota Press, 1984.

Butterick, George, ed. *Charles Olson and Robert Creeley: The Complete Correspondence.* 10 vols. Santa Barbara, Calif.: Black Sparrow Press, 1980–90.

Butterick, George. *Guide to the Maximus Poems of Charles Olson.* Berkeley: University of California Press, 1978.

Butterick, George. "Modern Literary Manuscripts and Archives: A Field Report." *Credences* 1.1 (1981): 81.

Calinescu, Matei. *Faces of Modernity: Avant-garde, Decadence, Kitsch.* Bloomington: Indiana University Press, 1977.

Carroll, Paul, ed. *The Young American Poets.* Chicago: Big Table, 1968.

Carruth, Hayden. "Making It New." *Hudson Review* 21 (1968): 399.

Chambers, Whittaker. "October 21st, 1926." *Poetry* 37 (1931): 258.

Chambers, Whittaker. *Witness.* New York: Random House, 1952.

Clark, Tom. *Charles Olson: The Allegory of a Poet's Life.* New York: Norton, 1991.

Clifford, James. *The Predicament of Culture: Twentieth Century Ethnography, Literature, and Art.* Cambridge, Mass.: Harvard University Press, 1988.

Comens, Bruce. *Apocalypse and After: Modern Strategy and Postmodern Tactics in Pound, Williams, and Zukofsky.* Tuscaloosa: University of Alabama Press, 1995.

Crane, Hart. *The Complete Poems and Selected Letters and Prose.* Ed. Brom Weber. New York: Liveright, 1966.

Creeley, Robert. *The Collected Poems of Robert Creeley.* Berkeley: University of California Press, 1982.

Creeley, Robert. *Contexts of Poetry: Interviews, 1961–1971.* Bolinas, Calif.: Four Seasons Foundation, 1973.

Creeley, Robert. "Notes for a New Prose." *Origin* 2 (1951):95.

Creeley, Robert. "On *Black Mountain Review.*" In *The Little Magazine in America: A Modern Documentary History,* ed. Elliott Anderson and Mary Kinzie. Yonkers, N.Y.: Pushcart Press, 1978.

Creeley, Robert. *A Quick Graph: Collected Notes and Essays.* Ed. Donald Allen. San Francisco: Four Seasons Foundation, 1970.

Culler, Jonathan. *Framing the Sign: Criticism and Its Institutions.* Oxford: Blackwell, 1988.

Davidson, Michael. "Compulsory Homosociality: Charles Olson, Jack Spicer, and the Gender of Poetics." In *Cruising the Performative: Interventions into the Representation of Ethnicity, Nationality, and Sexuality,* ed. Sue-Ellen Case, Philip Brett, and Susan Leigh Foster. Bloomington: Indiana University Press, 1995.

Davidson, Michael. *The San Francisco Poetry Renaissance: Poetics and Community at Mid-Century.* Cambridge: Cambridge University Press, 1989.

Dembo, L. S. "Louis Zukofsky: Objectivist Poetics and the Quest for Form." In *Louis Zukofsky: Man and Poet,* ed. Carroll F. Terrell. Orono, Me.: National Poetry Foundation, 1979. 265.

Derrida, Jacques. *Writing and Difference.* Trans. Alan Bass. Chicago: University of Chicago Press, 1978.

Duberman, Martin. *Black Mountain: An Exploration in Community.* New York: Dutton, 1972.

Duncan, Robert. "Letters for Denise Levertov: An A Muse Ment." *Black Mountain Review* 1.3 (1955): 19.

du Plessis, Rachel Blau. "Manifests." *Diacritics* (fall-winter 1996): 31–53.

Edel, Leon. "The Age of the Archive." Princeton Center for Advanced Studies: Monday Evening Papers. 7 (1965): 1.

Edelman, Lee. *Homographesis: Essays in Gay Literary and Cultural Theory.* New York and London: Routledge, 1994.

Eliot, T. S. *Collected Poems, 1909–1962.* New York: Harcourt Brace Jovanovich, 1991.

Eliot, T. S. *Selected Essays, 1917–1932.* New York: Harcourt, Brace, 1950.

Eliot, T. S. "The Social Function of Poetry." In *On Poetry and Poets.* New York: Farrar, Straus and Cudahy, 1957.

Eliot, T. S. "What Is Minor Poetry?" *On Poetry and Poets.* New York: Farrar, Straus and Cudahy, 1967.

Enzensberger, Hans-Magnus. "The Aporias of the Avant-Garde." *The Consciousness Industry: On Literature, Politics, and the Media.* New York: Seabury Press, 1974.

Evans, George, ed. *Charles Olson and Cid Corman: Complete Correspondence, 1950–1964.* 2 vols. Orono, Me.: National Poetry Foundation, 1987.

Evans, Steve. "The Dynamics of Literary Change: Four Excursuses in Lieu of a Lecture." Providence, R.I.: Impercipient Lecture Series, 1997.

Foster, Ed. "An Interview with Anne Waldman." *Talisman* 13 (fall 1994/winter 1995): 62–78.

Foucault, Michel. *The Archeology of Knowledge and The Discourse on Language.* Trans. A. M. Sheridan Smith. New York: Pantheon Books, 1972.

Golding, Alan. *From Outlaw to Classic: Canons in American Poetry.* Madison: University of Wisconsin Press, 1995.

Golding, Alan. "*The New American Poetry* Revisited, Again." *Contemporary Literature* 39.2 (summer 1998): 180–211.

Gooch, Brad. *City Poet: The Life of Frank O'Hara.* New York: Knopf, 1993.

Goodman, Paul. "Advance-Guard Writing, 1900–1950." *Kenyon Review* 13.3 (1951): 357–80.

Graff, Gerald. *Professing Literature: An Institutional History.* Chicago: University of Chicago Press, 1987.

Guillory, John. *Cultural Capital: The Problem of the Literary Canon.* Chicago: University of Chicago Press, 1993.

Hatlen, Burton. "From Modernism to Postmodernism: Zukofsky's 'A'-12." In *Upper Limit Music: The Writing of Louis Zukofsky,* ed. Mark Scroggins. Berkeley: University of California Press, 1997.

Herrnstein-Smith, Barbara. *Contingencies of Value: Alternative Perspectives for Critical Theory.* Cambridge, Mass.: Harvard University Press, 1988.

Hohendahl, Peter Uwe. *Building a National Literature.* Trans. Renate Baron Franciscono. Ithaca, N.Y.: Cornell University Press, 1989.

Howe, Irving. *The Decline of the New.* New York: Harcourt, Brace & World, 1970.

Iser, Wolfgang. *The Act of Reading: A Theory of Aesthetic Response.* Baltimore: Johns Hopkins University Press, 1978.

Iser, Wolfgang. *The Implied Reader: Patterns of Communication from Bunyan to Beckett.* Baltimore: Johns Hopkins University Press, 1974.

Jarnot, Lisa, Leonard Schwartz, and Chris Stroffolino, eds. *An Anthology of New (American) Poets.* Hoboken, N.J.: Talisman Press, 1998.

Jauss, Hans Robert. *Towards an Aesthetic of Reception.* Trans. Timothy Bahti. Minneapolis: University of Minnesota Press, 1982.

Junker, Howard. "The Young Poets." *Newsweek,* 3 March 1969, 83.

Kalaidjian, Walter. *Languages of Liberation: The Social Text in Contemporary American Poetry.* New York: Columbia University Press, 1989.

Keats, John. *Poetical Works*. Ed. Paul D. Sheats. Boston: Houghton Mifflin, 1975.

Kemp, Lysander. "Eliot and the Sense of History." Black Mountain Review 3 (1955): 38–42.

Killian, Kevin. *Poet, Be Like God: Jack Spicer and the San Francisco Renaissance*. Hanover, N.H.: Wesleyan University Press published by University Press of New England, 1998.

Koch, Kenneth. "Poetry in Paperback." *New York Times Book Review*, 28 April 1968, 7.

Koestenbaum, Wayne. *Double Talk: The Erotics of Male Literary Collaboration*. New York: Routledge, 1989.

Kuberski, Philip. "Charles Olson and the American Thing: The Ideology of Literary Revolution." *Criticism* 27.2 (1985): 175–95.

Leggott, Michelle. *Reading Zukofsky's 80 Flowers*. Baltimore: Johns Hopkins University Press, 1989.

Lentricchia, Frank. *After the New Criticism*. Chicago: University of Chicago Press, 1980.

Levinson, Marjorie. *Keats' Life of Allegory: The Origins of a Style*. Oxford: Blackwell, 1988.

Lewis, Joel. "'Everything Turns into Writing': The Sonnets of Ted Berrigan." *Transfer* 2 (1988/89): 128–55.

Lipking, Lawrence. *The Life of the Poet: Beginnings and Endings of Poetic Careers*. Chicago: University of Chicago Press, 1981.

Malinowski, Bronislaw. *Argonauts of the Western Pacific*. New York: E. P. Dutton, 1950.

Mann, Paul. *The Theory-Death of the Avant-Garde*. Bloomington: Indiana University Press, 1991.

Matheson, William. "Institutional Collecting of Twentieth Century Literature." *Rare Books and Manuscripts Librarianship* 4 (1989): 7.

Maud, Ralph. *Charles Olson's Reading: A Biography*. Carbondale: Southern Illinois University Press, 1996.

Melnick, David. "The 'Ought' of Seeing: Zukofsky's Bottom." *Maps* 5 (1973): 55.

Miller, James E., Jr. *T. S. Eliot's Personal Waste Land: Exorcism of the Demons*. University Park: Pennsylvania State University Press, 1977.

Mottram, Eric. "1924–1951: Politics and Form in Zukofsky." *Maps* 5 (1973): 76.

Murray, Timothy. "The Origins of Institutional Collecting of Contemporary Literary Manuscripts." Unpublished Talk. 1994.

Nielsen, Aldon Lynn. *Black Chant: Languages of African-American Postmodernism*. New York: Cambridge University Press, 1997.

The Norton Anthology of Modern Poetry, Ed. Richard Ellman. New York: Norton, 1973.

Notley, Alice. Introduction. *The Selected Poems of Ted Berrigan*. New York: Penguin Books, 1994. i–ix.

Notley, Alice. *Mysteries of Small Houses*. New York: Penguin Books, 1998.

Novick, Mary. *Robert Creeley: An Inventory, 1945–1970*. Kent, Ohio: Kent State University Press, 1973.

O'Hara, Frank. *The Collected Poems of Frank O'Hara*. Ed. Donald Allen. Berkeley: University of California Press, 1995.

O'Hara, Frank. *Selected Poems of Frank O'Hara.* Ed. Donald Allen. New York: Vintage Books, 1974.

Olson, Charles. *The Berkeley Reading: A Triptite Edition.* Ed. Ralph Maud. Burnaby, B.C.: Simon Fraser University, 1970.

Olson, Charles. *The Collected Poems of Charles Olson.* Ed. George Butterick. Berkeley: University of California Press, 1987.

Olson, Charles. *The Maximus Poems.* 1978. Berkeley: University of California Press, 1983.

Olson, Charles. *The Mayan Letters.* Ed. Robert Creeley. Palma de Majorca, Spain: Divers Press, 1954.

Olson, Charles. *Muthologos: The Collected Lectures amd Interviews.* Vol. 1 of 2 vols. Bolinas, Calif.: Four Seasons Foundation, 1979.

Olson, Charles. *Selected Writings of Charles Olson.* Ed. Robert Creeley. New York: New Directions, 1966.

Paul, Sherman. *Olson's Push: Origin, Black Mountain, and Recent American Poetry.* Baton Rouge: Louisiana State University Press, 1978.

Pearson, Ted. "A Form of Assumption." *Poetics Journal* 7 (1989): 159.

Perelman, Bob. "A Counter-Response." Providence, R.I.: Impercipient Lecture Series, 1997.

Perelman, Bob. *The Marginalization of Poetry: Language Writing and Literary History.* Princeton, N.J.: Princeton University Press, 1996

Perelman, Bob. *The Trouble with Genius.* Berkeley: University of California Press, 1994.

Perloff, Marjorie. "Charles Olson and the Inferior Predecessors: Projective Verse Revisited." *ELH* 40 (1973): 285.

Poggioli, Renato. *The Theory of the Avant-Garde.* Trans. Gerald Fitzgerald. New York: Harper & Row, 1971.

Polizotti, Mark. *Revolution of the Mind: The Life of André Breton.* New York: Farrar, Straus & Giroux, 1995.

Pound, Ezra. *The ABC of Reading.* Norfolk, Conn.: New Directions Press, 1951.

Pound, Ezra. *Personae.* New York: New Directions Press, 1990.

Pound, Ezra. *Selected Prose.* Ed. William Cookson. New York: New Directions Books, 1973.

Pound, Ezra, ed. *Active Anthology.* London: Faber & Faber, 1933.

Quartermain, Peter. *Disjunctive Poetics: From Gertrude Stein and Louis Zukofsky to Susan Howe.* Cambridge: Cambridge University Press, 1992.

Rasula, Jed. *The American Poetry Wax Museum: Reality Effects, 1940–1990.* Urbana, Ill.: National Council of Teachers of English, 1996.

Ratcliffe, Stephen, and Leslie Scalapino, eds. *Talking in Tranquility: Interviews with Ted Berrigan.* Bolinas and Oakland, Calif.: Avenue B/O Books, 1991.

Reznikoff, Charles. "A Group of Verse." *Poetry* 37.5 (1931): 252.

Robins, Bruce. *Secular Vocations: Intellectuals, Professionalism, Culture.* London: Verso, 1993.

Rosenthal, M. L., and Sally M. Gall, eds. *The Modern Poetic Sequence: The Genius of Modern Poetry.* New York: Oxford University Press, 1983.

Rota, Anthony. "The Collecting of Twentieth Century Literary Manuscripts." *Rare Books and Manuscripts Librarianship* 1.1 (1986): 39.

Schreiber, Ron, ed. *31 New American Poets.* New York: Hill and Wang, 1969.

Sedgwick, Eve Kosofsky. *Between Men: English Literature and Male Homosocial Desire.* New York: Columbia University Press, 1985.

Sedgwick, Eve Kosofsky. *Epistemology of the Closet.* Berkeley: University of California Press, 1990.

Shapiro, David. "On a Poet." In *Nice to See You: Homage to Ted Berrigan,* ed. Anne Waldman. Minneapolis: Coffee House Press, 1991. 226.

Silliman, Ron. "Canons and Institutions: New Hope for the Disappeared." In *The Politics of Poetic Form,* ed. Charles Bernstein. New York: ROOF, 1993.

Silliman, Ron. *The New Sentence.* New York: Roof Press, 1987.

Silliman, Ron. "Poets and Intellectuals." *Temblor* 9 (1989): 122–24.

Silliman, Ron, et al. "Aesthetic Tendency and the Politics of Poetry." *Social Text* 7.19/20 (1988): 271.

Simpson, David. *The Academic Postmodern and the Rule of Literature: A Report on Half-Knowledge.* Chicago: University of Chicago Press, 1995.

Staley, Thomas. "Literary Canons, Literary Studies, and Library Collections: A Retrospective on Collecting Twentieth Century Writers." *Rare Books and Manuscripts Librarianship* 5.1 (1990): 9.

Stein, Gertrude. "Composition as Explanation." In *The Selected Writings of Gertrude Stein,* ed. Carl Van Vechten. New York: Vintage Books, 1990.

Steinman, Lisa M. *Made in America: Science, Technology, and American Modernist Poets.* New Haven, Conn.: Yale University Press, 1987.

Strychacz, Thomas. *Modernism, Mass Culture, and Professionalism.* Cambridge: Cambridge University Press, 1993.

Terrell, Carroll F., ed. *Louis Zukofsky: Man and Poet.* Orono, Me.: National Poetry Foundation, 1979.

Tompkins, Jane, ed. *Reader-Response Criticism: From Formalism to Postructuralism.* Baltimore: Johns Hopkins University Press, 1980.

Turner, Descherd. "A Collection Not So Easily Explained." *Gazette of the Grolier Club* 38 (1986): 30.

von Hallberg, Robert. *American Poetry and Culture, 1945–1980.* Cambridge, Mass.: Harvard University Press, 1985.

von Hallberg, Robert. *Charles Olson: The Scholar's Art.* Cambridge, Mass.: Harvard University Press, 1978.

Waldman, Anne. *Fast Speaking Woman.* San Francisco: City Lights Books, 1996.

Waldman, Anne. *Helping the Dreamer: New and Selected Poems, 1966–1988.* Minneapolis: Coffee House Press, 1989.

Waldman, Anne, ed. *Nice to See You: Homage to Ted Berrigan.* Minneapolis: Coffee House Press, 1991.

Waldman, Anne, ed. *Out of This World: An Anthology of the St. Mark's Poetry Project.* New York: Crown, 1991.

Ward, Geoff. *Statutes of Liberty: The New York School of Poets*. New York: St. Martin's Press, 1988.

Watten, Barrett. "After Ted." In *Ariel* 8, ed. Rod Smith. Washington, D.C.: Edge Books, 1995.

Watten, Barrett. "The Secret History of the Equals Sign: L=A=N=G=U=A=G=E between Discourse and Text." Unpublished paper.

Watten, Barrett. *Total Syntax*. Carbondale: Southern Illinois University Press, 1984.

Williams, Raymond. *Marxism and Literature*. Oxford: Oxford University Press, 1977.

Williams, William Carlos. *Interviews with William Carlos Williams: Speaking Straight Ahead*. Ed. Linda Welshiner Wagner. New York: New Directions Books, 1976. 30.

Williams, William Carlos. *Paterson*. New York: New Directions Press, 1992.

Wolf, Reva. *Andy Warhol, Poetry, and Gossip in the 1960s*. Chicago: University of Chicago Press, 1997.

Wordsworth, William. *Lyrical Ballads and Other Poems, 1797–1800*. Ed. James Butler and Karen Green. Ithaca, N.Y.: Cornell University Press, 1992.

Wordsworth, William. *William Wordsworth. The Oxford Authors*. London: Oxford University Press, 1992.

Zukofsky, Louis. *"A."* Baltimore: Johns Hopkins University Press, 1993.

Zukofsky, Louis. *Autobiography*. New York: Grossman, 1970.

Zukofsky, Louis. *Bottom: On Shakespeare*. Berkeley: University of California Press, 1987.

Zukofsky, Louis. *The Complete Short Poetry*. Baltimore: Johns Hopkins University Press, 1991.

Zukofsky, Louis. *Prepositions: The Collected Essays of Louis Zukofsky*. Berkeley: University of California Press, 1981.

Zukofsky, Louis. "Sincerity and Objectification: With Special Reference to the Work of Charles Reznikoff." *Poetry* 37 (1931): 272.

Zukofsky, Louis, ed. *An "Objectivists" Anthology*. New York: To Publications, 1932.

INDEX

Abbott, Charles, 104
Apollinaire, Guillaume, 122
Ashberry, John, 19, 108, 110, 116–19, 130–32, 134
Aristotle, 92, 94

Bach, J. S., 83
Bakhtin, M. M., 6, 21
Baraka, Amiri, 132. *See also* Jones, LeRoi
Barlow, Robert, 61
Barthes, Roland, 77
Baudrillard, Jean, 76, 81, 106–7
Benjamin, Walter, 28
Berrigan, Ted, 4, 7–11, 18–19, 74, 108–35, 142
Berrigan, Ted (works): "Homage to Mayakofsky," 117–8; "It Is a Big Red House," 117; *Many Happy Returns,* 124; "Personal Poem #9," 124; *So Going around Cities,* 121; "The Sonnets," 108–25 *passim,* 127–29, 131, 135; "Tambourine Life," 135; "Things to Do in New York City," 135; "Things to Do in Ann Arbor," 135; "Things to Do on Speed," 135; "Two Scenes," 117
Berryman, John, 13
Bernstein, Charles, 135
Bérubé, Michael, 5–6
Blackburn, Paul, 74
Black Mountain College, 7, 24, 32–35, 45, 56–58, 66, 74, 111
Black Mountain Review, 9, 24, 54, 56–58, 74
Blazer, Robin, 18, 36
Bourdieu, Pierre, 9–10, 16–18, 30–31, 111
Bourdieu, Pierre (works): *Field of Cultural Production,* 9; *Rules of Art,* 9–10, 17, 30–31
Boym, Svetlana, 77
Brainard, Joe, 114–15, 131

Bredbeck, Gregory, 133–34
Bronk, William, 56
Bunting, Basil, 4
Bürger, Peter, 14–15
Butterick, George, 36, 38, 40, 43–44, 48

"C," 74, 110, 115–17, 129–33, 138–39
Ceravolo, Joe, 132
Chambers, Richard "Ricky," 80–81, 90
Chambers, Whittaker, 80
Clark, Tom, 23, 25
Coleridge, Samuel Taylor, 3, 131
Corman, Cid, 21, 38, 55, 60–62, 74, 105, 128–29, 137
Crane, Hart, 69
Creeley, Robert, 4, 7, 10–11, 21, 35–36, 39, 41–52, 54–59, 61, 63, 66–67, 71–78 *passim,* 94, 106, 139–40
Creeley, Robert (works): "The Business," 67–68; *For Love,* 35–36, 44, 47, 67, 69–70; *Gold Diggers,* 44; "The Invoice," 67–68; *Pieces,* 69–70; "Unsuccessful Husband," 49
cummings, e. e., 113
Curriculum of the Soul, 36–37

Dahlberg, Edward, 74
Davidson, Michael, 18–19
Dembo, L. S., 92
Denby, Edwin, 113, 132–33
Derrida, Jacques, 88
Donald, Allen, 21
Doolittle, Hilda. *See* H. D.
Dorn, Ed, 32–34
Duchamp, Marcel, 120
Duberman, Martin, 7

169